Landscapes of Betrayal, Landscapes of Joy

SUNY series in Environmental and Architectural Phenomenology

David Seamon, editor

The SUNY series in Environmental and Architectural Phenomenology presents authored and edited volumes that emphasize a qualitative, descriptive approach to architectural and environmental experience and behavior. A key concern is scholarship, education, planning, and design that support and enhance natural and built environments that are beautiful, alive, and humane. A clear conceptural stance is integral to informed research and design, and the series gives first priority to phenomenological and hermeneutical approaches to the environment but also sponsors other styles of qualitative, interpretive reseach.

Volumes in the series include:

- David Seamon, editor, *Dwelling, Seeing, and Designing: Toward a Phenomenological Ecology* (1993).
- Robert Mugerauer, *Interpretations on Behalf of Place: Environmental Displacements and Alternative Responses* (1994).
- Louise Chawla, *In the First Country of Places: Nature, Poetry, and Childhood Memory* (1994).
- David Seamon and Arthur Zajonc, editors. *Goethe's Way of Science: A Phenomenology of Nature* (1998).
- Ingrid Leman Stefanovic, *Safeguarding Our Common Future: Rethinking Sustainability* (2000).

Landscapes of Betrayal, Landscapes of Joy

Curtisville in the Lives of its Teenagers

Herb Childress

State University of New York Press

Published by
State University of New York Press, Albany

For information, address State University of New York Press, State
University Plaza, Albany, N.Y., 12246

Cover art: *Youth Center* © 1994 Herb Childress

Production by Diane Ganeles
Marketing by Anne Valentine

Library of Congress Cataloging-in-Publication Data
Childress, Herb, 1958–
    Landscapes of betrayal, landscapes of joy: Curtisville in the lives of its
    teenagers/Herb Childress.
        p. cm.—(SUNY series in environmental and architectural
    phenomenology) Includes bibliographical references and index.
    ISBN 0-7914-4577-1 (HC : alk. paper)—ISBN 0-7914-4578-X (PB : alk.
paper)
    1. Teenagers—California—Social conditions—Case studies. 2. Adolescent
psychology—California—Case studies. 3. Spatial behavior—California—
Case studies. 4. Environment and teenagers—California—Case studies.
5. Architecture and youth—California—Case studies. I. Title. II. Series.

HQ796.C458237 2000
305.235' 09794—dc21

10 9 8 7 6 5 4 3 2 1   99-087617

Contents

Contents

Foreword

In the spring of 1999, two teenage boys in Littleton, Colorado, shot to death twelve of their classmates and one teacher, then killed themselves. A few weeks later, my mother called from the upstate New York village where she lives to express her outrage at two local teenagers who had set fire to a lumber yard and the high school bleachers, which both burned to the ground. "What's wrong with kids today?" she asked plaintively, posing a question currently asked by many other Americans as well.

In *Landscapes of Betrayal, Landscapes of Joy*, Herb Childress provides no direct answer to this question, but he does describe the everyday world of typical American teenagers and provides clues as to why some young people feel overwhelmed by their lives. In his book, Childress studies how teenagers in one small Californian town renamed "Curtisville" use and find meaning in the routine places and situations of their everyday lives. Childress's approach is ethnographic and narrative. He "lives" with the teenagers of his community for over a year, interviewing them, observing their behaviors, and "hanging out" with them. Most importantly, he participates in the worlds of eleven student "volunteers," each of whom becomes his "escort through a life in Curtisville." The result is a detailed portrait of the more personal, private aspects of teenagers' lives—for example, a series of chapters that insightfully describes the homes, bedrooms, and family life of these eleven young people.

In this regard, one of the most effective aspects of *Landscapes* is its *concreteness*—its gritty picture of teenagers' lives at home, at school, at work, in public. There are chapters on the importance of cars in teenagers' lives, the ways in which classroom teaching succeeds and fails, the places that give teenagers pleasure and the places they avoid, the situations that stimulate self-worth and what Childress calls *joy*—"that action that makes us feel as though we are, perhaps, finding ourselves in the world."

Throughout the book, Childress demonstrates the crucial role of social, economic, and educational institutions in the lives of teenagers and their positive or negative, active or passive responses. He suggests that, too often today, these institutions undermine and destroy the places and situations where teenagers might find joy, with the result that many young people become manipulative, cynical, or angry. In the last chapters of the book, he points to the shift in adult values, perceptions, and actions required to make American society more supportive of teenagers' needs and possibilities.

Though Childress does not claim a phenomenological method in his book, his discoveries and conclusions illustrate the best kind of phenomenology, if by that word we mean accurate and insightful pictures of human experience out of which arise broader patterns and significances not thoroughly seen before. In phenomenological terms, this book is an explication of the teenage lifeworld and some ways by which that lifeworld might become more sustaining and joyful through changes in policy, planning, and design. What we make is what we understand, and Childress's book is important because these teenagers' stories stay with us and make us adults understand their lives, dreams, and predicaments in a new, more empathetic light.

DAVID SEAMON

Acknowledgments

Now is a moment for true joy: the offering of gratitude to some of those who have made this story possible to tell. To begin with those most distant, I have debts to pay to some friends whom I have never met. Whenever I speak of hangouts, for instance, those beloved places where we meet our friends for no special purpose other than to be with them, I am expanding on the ideas of Ray Oldenburg and his book *The Great Good Place*. My central strategy, that of examining places through asking what sort of societal conditions could have brought them about, is a direct result of knowing Murray Silverstein and Max Jacobson's article, "Restructuring the Hidden Program: Toward an Architecture of Social Change."

Once I understood that I was studying emotions as much as the places and events that stirred them, I discovered that Jean-Paul Sartre had creatively examined the core of what our emotions mean to us. Robert M. Pirsig appeared to me many times, telling me to trust what I saw, to record Quality wherever I encountered it, and equally to understand it by knowing where and when it was absent.

Before I ever began this project, I knew that ultimately I would be faced with a rough, bulldozed hill of data to be turned into an orderly and fruitful landscape. My guides and inspirations were Henry Glassie's *Passing the Time in Ballymenone*, William Least Heat Moon's *PrairyErth*, Joan Didion's *The White Album*, Jon Carroll's daily columns in the *San Francisco Chronicle*, and almost everything that John McPhee has ever written. Through them, I saw that it was possible not only to be a strong and vigorous thinker, but to bring kindness and grace to the task as well. My shortcomings should not dissuade others from reading their work.

I thank three people who stand closer to my life: Paul Groth, Doug Paterson, and Mike McDaniel. Paul taught me—along with hundreds of other students at Berkeley's College of Environmental Design—to look both at and through the world around us, to be literate in the cultural facts and origins of our streets, parks, buildings, and communities. His deep sense of responsibility, his urgent need to pass this literacy along to others, and the gentle force of his writing all combined to set me onto my current path.

I see Doug once a year or so at an academic conference, and I always know what to expect—a broad smile bursting through his beard, and an insistence upon joy even when he's in the middle of a heated argument. He centers his thinking on our experience of places, not on their stylistic formulae or on rational codes of development. Vancouver is fortunate to have him as an advocate, and I have been fortunate to make his friendship. Doug also acted as a reviewer of this book for SUNY Press, as did Stuart Aitken of California State University at San Diego and Lynn Paxson of Iowa State University; their comments have enriched the final product, and they deserve your thanks as well as mine.

I met Mike when we were both entering ninth grade, and he kept me from wasting my high school life. Through his example far more than that of any teacher, I learned what it could mean to be a successful adult. He later went on to teach high school and then college math; if I could populate our schools and community boards with him, this book never would have needed to be written. For twenty-five years, he has been my harshest critic and best friend.

In the foreground, there are my colleagues at the University of Wisconsin–Milwaukee. I was fortunate to come to grad school along with the most remarkable set of peers that I could imagine. Mallika Bose, Yasser Elsheshtawy, and especially Jeff Lackney and Maggie Calkins became a whirlwind force, catching me up in their enthusiasm, their energy, and their wisdom. Later, I expanded that galaxy of students, meeting Matt Roberson in English and Julio Rivera in Geography, being introduced to postmodernism on the running track and theology at the drinking fountain.

Linda Krause and Gary Moore taught me the joy of thinking on the run, the improvisation of new ideas in collaboration while drawing from the firm basis of deep learning. John Goulet pushed me to write, and to write, and to write again, all the while letting me talk my way into a strategy for bringing this project into life. Tom Hubka has the most extraordinary knack for asking just the right question at the right time, and his motto, "It's the *place*, stupid!" has never been far from my desk. Jerry Weisman shares my interest in the emotional resonance of whole places and whole experiences, and he also shared his classroom and his experience with me so that I could learn something about successful teaching. And Judith Kenny was a serendipitous teacher and friend from the Geography Department, keeping me attuned to the larger issues of culture and power in the environments we inhabit. I am proud to know them all. In addition, the University itself supported this project with a one-year fellowship, giving me time to follow kids around.

My friend and colleague Laura Hall served as a consultant on this project, eagerly responding to hundreds of pages of questionnaires and crazed journal ideas. Even more important than the material work on this project, though, has been ten years of her friendship and inspiration, as well as the professional examples she has set as landscape architect, urban designer, and writer. If we are ever able to bring about an architecture of kindness, Laura will be at the forefront.

Series editor David Seamon has been a creative and generous guiding force in my thinking since I met him eight years ago. His work in environmental phenomenology has taught me to trust people's experiences of the places in their lives far more than any body of architectural theory, and has led directly to the way that I do my work.

Closer yet, I cannot begin to properly express my gratitude to my wife Judi. Through moving away from work and home; through ready and thoughtful support of my work from database management to graphic design; and through enduring my absences, emotional distance and frequent despair while at work, she has withstood more than Job himself. I can only assure her that the first one is the hardest.

Finally, though, my greatest joy is mingled with a burden. I have been blessed with the opportunity to meet several hundred people at Curtisville High School and to become good friends with perhaps three dozen. The fact that some of them are fifty years old and others are sixteen is utterly irrelevant; they are among the most breathtakingly open, wise, and honest people I have ever had the privilege to know. Because of the protective anonymity that cloaks this book, I cannot thank them properly. Their names are changed; the details have been blurred. But without their hospitality, their curiosity, and not least their willingness to forfeit their privacy and let this stranger into their lives, I would have remained on the outside with hundreds of questionnaires and no insight. My responsibility in writing this book is not to myself, to my committee members, or to some abstract set of intellectual standards. My responsibility is to the citizens of Curtisville High School, and it is to them that this book is dedicated.

Preface

Just before I began this project, I went to a lecture by an anthropologist who had done community research both in Africa and in the United States. I was terrifically insecure about how I was going to carry out my year's work among the teenagers of Curtisville; I was hoping for any clues that would make my job seem possible.

As she talked, I listened with interest—but growing doubts—to what felt like simplistic descriptions of living among and learning from new people. At the end of the class, I got to ask our guest a question that had troubled me for months: "When you go to a new place and gather information from people, they're giving you something of real value. How can you offer them something so that they benefit from your presence?"

She replied quickly and confidently, "Before I leave, I go to the dollar store and stock up on crayons. I give out lots of crayons, and the kids seem to appreciate them."

It wasn't the answer I'd hoped for.

I went off to do my research anyway, and took no crayons. About eight months later, Benjamin (a pseudonym[1]) and I were sitting in his computer room, formerly the garage. He was one of my "research subjects"—a loathsome and deceptive term—and it was my first night of following him around; he was trying to come to terms with how much he wanted to tell me, what was out of bounds. "I have like this artificial respect for you because you're my elder and all that, but you're like my friend too, so I don't know what to do sometimes."

Benjamin's confusion over my role wasn't uncommon; I was often as confused as they. My relationships with Curtisville's teenagers made a parody of the anthropological term "participant-observer." I was never a participant-observer; I was either one or the other. Whenever they were doing something that I could do, no matter how badly, I did it with them—losing at computer games, dancing, learning to play Hacky Sack, being an alien's victim in a newly scripted movie, running along the beach, playing cards, washing horses, playing basketball, taking a French test, looking for interesting rocks, sharing a cigar. I wasn't doing those things analytically, I was just doing them. When they did things that I couldn't share with them, whether it was surfing or dissecting a pig or taking a shower, then I stepped back with my notebook and recorded and thought.

I voluntarily surrendered my adulthood (which is to say my authority and encultured status of power over these people), and in many ways I succeeded. I don't know how many kids said that I was something other to them than "an adult," even though I was clearly not their age. They had no precedent to help them figure out who I was.

Instead of crayons, I gave Maggie lessons in stick-shift driving, taught Kirk a new throw with the Frisbee, and edited Julian's poems before he put them into book form. I offered innumerable rides to the carless, acted as a chaperone at dances, served refreshments at parties, and spent six hours flipping people upside down onto the Velcro Wall at Safe and Sober Graduation. I bought lots of sandwiches and burritos and chocolate.

I talked in over a dozen classes during the year. I talked about the nature of home; about the nature of science and deductive logic; about the change in European architecture (and, by association, European culture) from the Romanesque Medieval to the Gothic to the Renaissance; about how to edit short fiction and why to bother writing at all; about the landscape of modern America as the stage-set for the society Huxley described in the *Brave New World*; and about football. I gave a stage presentation on two nights in May, attended by about three hundred students, parents, and teachers.

All of this may have balanced the official scale somewhat, although the debts remain mostly on my side. But I think—I hope—

that there is an informal balance that might be more equal. The kids I spent time with got to tell me things that they couldn't tell other adults or each other, not so much to have me solve their problems as to hear themselves admit out loud what they already knew to be true. They got to see an adult who loved his work and wasn't afraid to tell that to other people, an adult who was curious and enjoyed himself wherever that curiosity took him. They got a new audience for all of their old stories.

They also got a friend who wouldn't make fun of their plans and their insecurity over the future, and who could answer factually, if anecdotally, about what an adult life might be like. As I went further in the project, I spent more Saturday evenings doing the basic work of friendship. After a Thursday and Friday and most of a Saturday with each of my volunteers, they generally trusted me enough to ask the questions that really mattered. "What will college and work be like?" was a big one, but it was far down the list when compared with more basic human questions like, "What is it like to be married?" "What is it like to have your own apartment?" Their questions were never this abstract, of course; they were asking about their own futures, but the questions were always phrased in language about my experiences: "Do you like living so close to downtown Union?" they would often ask. "Did you have a lot of girlfriends in high school?" "Do you still have sex after you're married?"

I opened my home to them in small return for being a part of theirs. They seemed to enjoy coming to visit, to listen to some odd music that I wanted to share with them or simply to sit on the couch and read and play with the cats, to see another version of adulthood, to add another scrap to their own collage.

The responsibility I started out believing was the important one—learning enough to tell the world about their lives and places, being their public advocate—disappeared constantly under the real responsibility of being a good friend.

I hope I have done enough.

ૢ**

For the most part, it is the teenagers to whom I talked over the course of my work. It was their responses and their beliefs that I was pursuing. I interviewed numerous teachers and had casual conversations with almost all of them; I talked with the principal about six times over the course of the year, though I never met the district superintendent whose office was on the same campus. I met quite a few parents, though almost no "community leaders." But the vast majority of my time was spent among people under eighteen.

In the beginning, I interviewed the kids, gave them questionnaires, and despaired of learning much of anything from them. But they—ignorant of the rules of research and thus wiser than I—taught me what I needed to learn by the simple human effort of trying to make friends with this strange person who roamed among them.

I came to understand that it is only through seeing specific people acting in specific circumstances that the social meanings of places can be read. Data is useful for examining concepts, but stories are the appropriate tool for understanding people. The following is a list of the people you will encounter most frequently in the stories to come; names have been changed, but nothing else.

Becky: Senior; seventeen; lives with mom and dad in an upscale woodsy area at the edge of Curtisville; cheerleader; Drama Geek; we say goodbye to Becky in chapter 9, but take a look back at her as a member of Julian's crowd in chapter 22.

Benjamin: Junior; sixteen; lives with mom, stepdad, younger sister in a middle-income section of Curtisville; punk; Drama Geek; we see him organize a concert in chapter 6, explore mortality in chapter 7, work in the school darkroom in chapter 15, and pee on the neighbor's fence in chapter 19.

Dan Jacobs: Teacher; English; fifty; scholar; gadfly; icon; we visit his classroom in chapter 14 and hear his unifying principle of education in chapter 23.

Duane: Sophomore; sixteen; lives with mom, stepdad, and younger brother (sometimes) at the outskirts of Curtisville; mechanic; Cowboy; never seen without his Rodeo King black hat; we meet him at work in chapter 4, drive with him at 115 mph in chapter 5, and learn a little more about his house in chapter 17.

Ethan: Senior; eighteen; lives with mom and stepdad in a middle-income area in Curtisville, just arrived from across the state; photographer; peripheral Surfer; loner; we take a ride in the "Swinger" in chapter 5, celebrate his eighteenth birthday in chapter 8, watch him in the darkroom in chapter 15, and spend some time in his room in chapter 18.

Irene: Junior; seventeen; lives with mom and older sister on ranchland in Curtisville's oldest house; scholar; Drama Geek; Band Nerd; horsewoman; Mara's best friend; she runs the theater sound in chapter 15, hangs out with Mara at Julian's in chapter 22, and discusses competition in the arts in chapter 23.

Ivy: Senior; seventeen; lives with mom in a working-class neighborhood in Curtisville; romantic; Drama Geek; we meet Ivy's car "Seymour" in chapter 5 and look from her driveway into the adjacent walled neighborhood in chapter 19.

Jeff Dawson: Principal; thirty-six; disciplinarian of students and faculty alike; he oversees the school in chapter 12 and takes us on a tour of the campus in chapter 23.

Julian: Senior; eighteen; lives alone, or sometimes with his younger sister, in a poor neighborhood in Curtisville; actor; Drama Geek; had eleven different hair colors in one four-week span during the spring; we meet him on stage in chapter 15 and spend time at his home in chapter 22.

Kirk: Junior; seventeen; lives with mom, stepdad, older sister and younger half-brother and half-sister in the upscale Sandstone Heights neighborhood of Sandy Cove; one hundred percent Surfer; we watch him at work in chapter 4, check out his car in chapter 5, and follow him through a couple of days of school in chapter 10.

Laurie: Senior; eighteen; lives with dad on the boundary between middle-class and working-class Curtisville; cheerleader; senior class president; chapter 3 is devoted to her, but she and her cars also appear in chapter 5.

Maggie: Senior; eighteen; lives with host family (two parents, two sisters, two brothers) during her year as an exchange student from Dublin; popular; Prep; I teach her to drive in chapter 5, she rules the Quad in chapter 11, and we see her room in chapter 18.

Mara: Junior; sixteen; lives with both parents in a middle-class cul-de-sac in Curtisville; scholar; Drama Geek; horsewoman; she duels with the school administration in chapter 12, runs the theater in chapter 15, wanders the neighborhood in chapter 19, hangs out with Irene at Julian's in chapter 22, and explains the role of the theologian in the high school in chapter 25.

Matthew: Senior; eighteen; lives mostly with dad, sometimes with mom, both ten miles out of town in different clearings of the forests of Flat Lake; runner; ponderer; we spend a weekend with him alternating between his homes in chapter 20.

Mrs. D: Teacher, Drama; fifty; actress; model; promoter of joy; we see her at work in (and through) her classroom in chapter 14 and look at some of the outcomes in chapter 15.

Tami: Senior; eighteen; lives with mom, stepdad and younger brother in a fancy area of Sandy Cove; Stoner; heavy metalist; we see a little of her room in chapter 18 and spend three days and 550 miles with her in chapter 21.

CHAPTER ONE

Woven Stories, Woven Lives

During the 1994–95 school year, I tried to learn what roles places played in the lives of the teenagers of Curtisville, California. I wanted to know how kids chose places; how they evaluated places; how they used places, and how they modified places. I wanted to learn about conflicts between teenagers and adults over places, and how those conflicts were managed and resolved.

In order to do this, I became an everyday resident of Curtisville High School, in part because I believed that school would be a place of both importance and conflict, and in part because a high school would easily afford a large collection of teenagers to talk with. I took no established role within the school. I made no attempt to "go undercover" as a student, a pose both ethically questionable and chronologically unlikely. Neither did I pretend to be a teacher, counselor, aide, administrator, custodian or coach. I simply walked the halls, stood on the Quad, sat in the back rows of classes, and talked with anyone who was interested.

Early in my study, I tried to perform the work in a carefully structured fashion. I distributed a questionnaire to all 800 students. I set up scheduled, tape-recorded interviews with over forty students, and had another forty fill out a detailed time-and-location report on a specific date. I did careful observation mapping of a different student every morning, tabulated the number and direction and occupants of cars leaving the parking lot at lunch each day.

Through these exercises, I learned what one might expect. I learned about frequency and location, about pattern and direction,

1

about likelihood and density. I learned almost nothing about meaning, almost nothing about what kids thought about all those places they used. Near the end of the first semester, looking through my hundreds of questionnaires, hundreds of pages of field notes, dozens of drawn maps, and a drawer full of interview cassettes, I started to realize that I knew a lot *about* the kids I followed and watched and interviewed, but that I didn't *know* them.[1] For that, I clearly needed a different tool.

The students themselves supplied it. As I sat on the concrete planters of the Quad, my notebook in my lap, kids would occasionally sit beside me and ask, "What are you *writing* in there all the time?" And I would show them some scribbled notes or a hastily-constructed tally sheet, and we would have a brief conversation terminated by the beginning of the next period.

As they gradually learned that I was neither malicious nor disdainful, our conversations grew longer, branched to other topics. They introduced me to other kids, explained to me why someone had said what he'd said or done what she'd done. They teased me to see if I could take a joke, and started including me in their activities.

They reached out to make friends.

In December, I gathered fifteen of these friends together—people who, in many cases, had no friends in common besides me—and asked them to help me make a change in my work. I was frustrated, I explained, by how little I had learned of the things that really mattered. I asked them if they'd be willing to open their lives to me, to let me be with them over a few days in order to watch them and feel them navigate through their world.

In the end, eleven kids (and their parents) said yes. They were six girls and five boys. They were six seniors, four juniors, and a sophomore. They were lifelong Curtisville residents and new arrivals, town kids and fringe kids and rural kids, inhabitants of seven distinct social groups within the school. I chose them somewhat on the basis of this "representativeness," but more importantly because I knew them well enough to care about the parts of their lives I couldn't see. They chose me as well, of course, opting to take the risk of extending our friendship outside the easy boundaries of our school personae. Each of them picked a weekend in the spring to escort me through a life in Curtisville.

Every week, I would meet my assigned partner as she or he arrived at school on Thursday morning, and I stayed close at hand throughout the school day. These Thursday mornings were usually the hardest for them; they (or their friends) would often glance over toward me in class or at lunch, and smile tentatively as though to say, "I know I volunteered for this, but *he's still here!*" In every case, though, we talked all day and grew more comfortable with one another; about half of them asked to see what I was writing in my notebook as we went along, and I always handed it over.

After school on Thursday, I went with them to do their chores or their extracurricular activities or just to hang out. I went home with them in the evening, met their families, usually had dinner there, saw their rooms and their neighborhoods. After dinner, I stayed through homework or television or back out into town with their friends. And at the words, "Well, I guess I'd better get ready for bed," I'd pack up my notebook, say good night, and drive home.

On Friday, we'd repeat the exercise. Fridays were quite different, though: the character of the classrooms was looser, students and teachers alike were preparing for the weekend, and my participants and their friends were usually far more relaxed about (or resigned to) my presence. Friday evenings were different as well. Family dinners were rare, replaced by dances or sporting events or parties. Friday nights were less constrained, more social, chosen freely.

On Saturday, the last day, I would come to their houses at a prearranged time and once again be their guest. Like Friday nights, Saturdays were freely chosen; unlike Friday nights, Saturdays were calmer, less frantic. We did fewer things for longer periods, saw fewer people and invested more of ourselves in them. Saturdays were the days in which both they and I learned the most.

Saturday nights were often spent alone at their instigation, just the two of us coming to terms with the fact that they'd be on their own again on Sunday, that their shadow would vanish. As part of that, they wanted to be reassured that I was still a friend, that I wouldn't abandon them now that their utility had been depleted. They wanted to talk about what I'd seen, to come to agreement on what the stories meant. And they wanted me to set their stories into social context, to know whether they were "weird" or "strange" in relation to the other kids I'd been with to that point. None of them knew many other teenage lives in such close detail as I had just seen theirs, and they wanted me to reassure them that they weren't alone, that their actions and desires weren't abnormal.

Somewhere around midnight or one o'clock on Sunday morning, I'd head home and try to rest. And on Sunday, I would spill out observations and ideas onto the computer's keyboard, transcribing and amplifying and trying to understand the three days' contents of my notes.

Finally, on Monday morning, I'd meet my participant one last time as she or he arrived at school, offer my thanks once again for their help, and hand them a twenty- to thirty-page account of the weekend. I did this for three reasons. The first and technically most important was that I wanted them to make corrections, and to offer alternative interpretations to the ones I had concocted (which many did). The second was that I felt it was important not to talk about them behind their backs—they deserved to know what I was saying about them before a wider audience saw their stories. And the third was that these stories acted as small gifts for their large service. At the very least, they were mementos of an unusual event; at best, they were portraits drawn by someone who cared about them and wished them well.

❧

The reader will perhaps have noted my repeated use of the word "stories," and wondered whether or not I was simply being colloquial. Perhaps I meant instead "evidence" or "empirical data." So it is worth spending a moment to talk about stories.[2]

In their 1993 anthology of narrative study, Ruthellen Josselson and Amia Lieblich asked, "What must be added to *story* to make it *scholarship*?"[3] In other words, what makes stories into ethnographic research as opposed to documentaries, travelogues, journalistic essays, or other forms of nonfiction? Their answer was that it had to make the move from a narrative to a conceptual mode.

My question in return is, why *should* ethnographic writing be set apart from those other fields? Why should we strive for a privileged position in the canon, some supposed area that lies beyond story? All well-told stories have a conceptual structure—there has to be a framework under all that data, whether the data is presented by Joan Didion or Henry Glassie, or else the data just remains the unreadable chaos we started with in our fieldnotes.[4] That framework, always created rather than found, provides clues to help us see, allows us to draw connections between events that seem distinct. Constructing that framework, making those connections, making *sense*, is the intellectual's job.[5] The difference between storytellers and social scientists is that storytellers use their frameworks—soft-pedaled, almost invisible—to build narrative links, to give emotional weight to the story, whereas social researchers usually use the stories—or more likely, snippets and quoted lines—to exemplify their frameworks.

Literature teachers David Bartholomae and Anthony Petrosky talk about "strong writing"—thick, dense, metaphoric, purposefully unclosed, not artificially unified—and say that it offers an invitation to "strong, aggressive, labor-intensive reading." They write in the early pages of their anthology:

> To say that [these essays] are challenging is to say, then, that they leave some work for the reader to do . . . To take command of complex material like the essays and stories in this book, you need not subordinate yourself to experts; you can assume the authority to provide such a reading on your own.[6]

When we tell stories whole, in plain language, with a minimum of explanation or exposition, we allow more potential readers to take an empowered and active stance toward the work we provide. When we write with strength, we surrender power.[7]

The construction of this book is my invitation to your strong and aggressive reading. The following chapter is a portrait of Curtisville, the spatial and cultural landscape within which its teenagers lived. The main body of the book is a series of twenty chapters, each based around specific kids' experience of a particular place. I have divided these stories and their associated places into three groups—"Around Town," "At School," and "At Home"—because those three most generic place types held fundamentally different social roles and standards of behavior. The interpretive and narrative voices vary from chapter to chapter in their proportion and predominance, but each chapter is, foremost, a story: scenic, temporal, reported in action and real-life dialogue, constructed to convey not mere facts but also meaning.

After an aggressive reading of these twenty stories, the reader deserves to ask questions, just as I was left at the end of my year in Curtisville with stories and questions. In the final part of this book, "After the Fact," I have tried to anticipate the largest of those questions—How do these stories make sense together? Why should others care about the unique case of Curtisville? Is there hope for change, and what would change look like?—and to draw out what I see as the dominant ideas of these stories in a way that offers one possible set of answers. Without minimizing the power of the stories themselves, I can say here that one major theme is the role of institutions in the lives of individuals, and the other major theme is the active or passive responses that individuals make in the face of these institutions. These two dimensions represent the warp and the woof from which modern lives and stories are woven—not just in Curtisville, and not just for teenagers, but for us all.

CHAPTER TWO

Reading Curtisville

If America had been settled from west to east, Timber County would have been a state. It runs over one hundred miles north to south and as much as fifty miles wide, roughly the same size and shape as Connecticut stood on its right side but with about 3½ percent of Connecticut's population. Most of Timber's 120,000 residents inhabit a forty-mile band along U.S. Highway 420 from Milltown at the south to Sandy Cove at the north—take that little ribbon out of the county and there are fewer than 50,000 people in all the rest, about ten people per square mile. A great deal of the land is owned in heroic parcels by the Coastal Lumber Company, American West Forest Products, Stevenson Timber, state and federal forest and coastal preserves, and two major tribal reservations.

As you might expect from that list of landowners, Timber County is a heavily forested place. Log trucks dominate the highways, and environmental politics dominate the news. Bumper stickers vie for our loyalty: "Save Ancient Forests" is about equal in numbers to "This Vehicle Paid For with Timber Dollars." The landscape runs from oceanfront up to a two-thousand-foot elevation within a few miles, from city to wilderness just as quickly. The county's ruggedness and dense forests have led to isolation; the closest city that most Californians would recognize by name is Redding, four hours away in the summer and impossible to reach in the winter. The closest cities other Americans might recognize are San Francisco to the distant south, or Portland, a day's drive north.

Like a lot of rural America, Timber County saw its greatest wealth in the late nineteenth and early twentieth centuries, during the great resource-gathering binges of the Western expansion. The downtowns of Milltown, Union, South City, and Port City became public centers, gathering places that offered business and recreation opportunities for a scattered population. Now the wealth flows mostly outward, and the county is torn between the rural and urban horns of its identity. Port City and Union set the tone and much of the policy for the rest of the county—hip, urban if not always urbane, revitalized by a great influx of newcomers in the 1960s and '70s who were escaping the craziness of Southern California and San Francisco. The county's outlying residents often feel that urban concerns over recreation and the environment threaten their ability to make a living from the diminishing stands of unprotected forest.

But urban and rural divisions, as sharp as they might be, don't explain all of the conflict within the county. There are a great number of homesteaders out in the mountains, more than a few of whom augment their incomes from logging, conservation, or welfare with a marijuana crop that gives Timber County most its fame in the outside world. And there are no conservatives more vocal than the older residents of Port City and Union who watch from their bungalows and see their established social order succumb to that of the hippies and transients. In short, Timber County is still contested territory, still wild and only partly claimed.

No community is a clearer embodiment of that contest than Curtisville, which by most estimations and nobody's admission is the second largest city in Timber County. Curtisville is an unincorporated community which has grown from about 1500 people at the end of World War II to ten times that number today. It is governed through an odd mix of jurisdictions, which means that things often happen to it from the outside. There is a local Community Services District which is in charge of water provision and wastewater removal, refuse disposal, parks and recreation. But planning and zoning services, roads and street maintenance and law enforcement are all provided by the county. Schools are managed through yet another set of districts, small and local for the elementary schools but spread across almost 500 square miles in the case of the high school.

Curtisville has had an "image problem" for a great many years. It has historically been a relatively poor community, settled by the rural working class who so often become icons of squalor when viewed through middle-class and suburban definitions of proper life and proper landscape. The mild but chronic poverty that leads to mobile homes and humble frame houses on unpaved roads—in combination with the many active ranches and other land-extensive businesses such as wrecking yards, nurseries, and a feed store—had pinned upon Curtisville the despised nickname "Oklahoma by the Sea." The name is instructive, not only about Curtisville but also about Oklahoma and about our collective images of good living.

Curtisville's business and real estate boosters are dedicated to improving the community's image, intent upon inventing a new collective story. This invention is also instructive, both about rural life and about business culture. The television commercial that advertises Curtisville as an ideal location for families and businesses closes with a view down the cypress-lined entry to town, the boughs framing the freshly five-laned Main Street in front of the new Kmart, not a trailer in sight.

Land has been cheap and regulations loose in Curtisville, and developers and home buyers have made the most of it. Families who found themselves priced into rentals in Union and Port City have been able to buy large new homes in Curtisville's comfortable, quiet neighborhoods. Most of the growth of the past twenty years has been in the most characteristic American suburban style—relatively modest single-family homes on wide culs-de-sac pulled well back from the main roads. This pattern of settlement, reminiscent of everywhere else in the country exactly because it has no identifiable regional origins, is also one of the reasons that so few people recognize that Curtisville is a fairly big city. Much of its population is invisible—a development of a hundred houses on a dozen culs-de-sac has only a single entry street, and shows just the few houses at its gateway to the rest of the world, hiding the rest. Curtisville's 15,000 people are spread around twelve square miles, with plenty of old ranch parcels still undivided. From the few main through roads, most of what is visible is the landscape of the 1950s.

Curtisville now has the highest per-capita income in Timber County, an aggregated measurement that conceals much division.

The rural laborers are still there, as poor and poorer than they were twenty years ago. The shambling neighborhoods of trailers and shacks still make up much of the western section of town beyond the freeway, but the new residents don't have to see them. The newcomers have their walled subdivisions with no businesses inside, one street leading in between the gates and no reason for old and new to mix.

The most obvious sign of Curtisville's new vigor is the redevelopment of Main Street, which seemingly went from the 1950s to the 1990s without any intermediate stages. Curtisville has always been a one-street town; there are about a hundred retail businesses in Curtisville, and exactly three of them are not on Main Street. Main Street had been part of US 420 until the 1960s when CalTrans ran the new freeway corridor parallel to it and a mile to the west. Many observers predicted the end of business in Curtisville when the freeway drew travelers off Main Street, and indeed, shopping in Curtisville has been meager throughout most of its history. But within the past five years, business has recognized what many of Curtisville's residents have not: that there are an increasing number of people here, all of whom buy things. Local business owners haven't been the ones to see this fact—they still have "Oklahoma by the Sea" as a part of their local narrative. The businesses that have "revitalized" Main Street are the same ones that have decimated other Main Streets all across the country. Kmart is just over a year old, McDonalds only a few months, Burger King even younger, Taco Bell just a toddler, followed by the infant twins Denny's and Kentucky Fried Chicken. The two older grocery stores along Main Street are struggling under the weight of a large regional chain of grocery-deli-espresso-video superstores which opened an enormous market in the same shopping complex as Kmart.

As Main Street becomes more mainstream, so too Curtisville gains new residents, seemingly in direct proportion. It is unclear which is the chicken, which is the egg.

❧

The act of architecture, whether that act takes the form of a ranch house or a drive-through restaurant, is really the creation of stage sets for everyday drama and comedy. We are constantly sur-

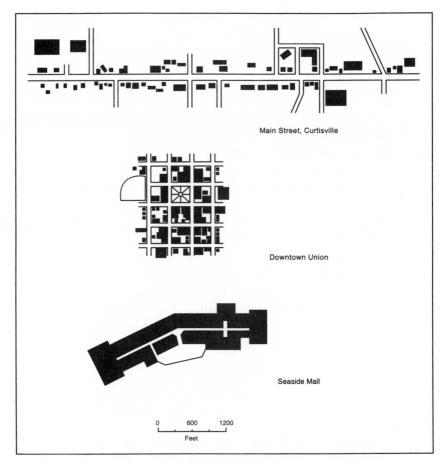

Main Street, Curtisville

Downtown Union

Seaside Mall

0   600   1200
Feet

Fig. 1. Three street plans

rounded by the things that we have built, from interstate freeways to neighborhood sidewalks, from city parks to parking lots. We built them all on purpose, and the purpose is often more interesting than the object itself. The things are just things, but the ideas behind them are a commentary on the future.

Reading a building or a landscape is as revealing as reading a novel. Characters reveal themselves little by little, showing us their strengths and their flaws long before they themselves discover them. And writing about those landscapes is no different than writing any story: people with intentions encounter other people with different intentions, set within a context of local customs and historical events and the manifestation of power.

Let's try a short reading exercise.[1]

On the top of Figure 1 is a map of downtown Curtisville's business district, along Main Street from Diagonal Avenue on the north to Kmart on the south. There are about ninety retail stores and professional offices in this area, which is a little less than a mile long. It would take twenty minutes to walk from one end to the other, though nobody ever does.

The middle map is Union's main business district: between Ninth Street and Thirteenth Streets north and south, A and D Streets east and west. It's less than a quarter of a mile square, and it takes about five minutes to walk from one side to the other. And in that small space, there are 132 retail businesses and professional offices. Plus there are plenty of apartments and quite a few houses, and City Hall and the Fire Department and the whole open block of the Plaza besides, and hundreds of people on the sidewalks at any hour between dawn and midnight. All of that stuff, the whole downtown of Union, isn't a lot bigger than the property that Kmart and its parking lot sits on in Curtisville.

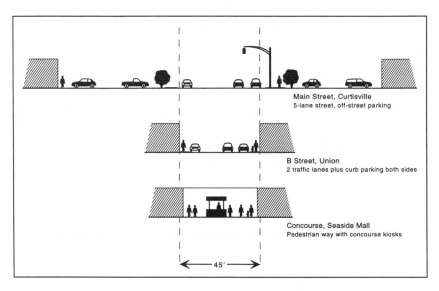

Fig. 2. Three street cross-sections

The lower map is a floor plan of the popular Seaside Mall in Port City, about twenty miles south of Curtisville. It's also about a third of a mile long from Penney's to Hudson's, and there are almost exactly 100 businesses in that space.

In each of these three places, there are a similar number of retail and service shops, the kinds of places people might go into on a whim. But in two out of the three, they're packed together into a condensed area; in the other, they're strung way out apart from one another.

Let's look at another set of dimensions in Figure 2. Again, the uppermost is Curtisville, a section cut across Main Street from one storefront to another. I've chosen the section between Pizza Hut and Timber Bank, because that's as close as the buildings come any-where along that strip, about 180 feet apart.

The middle one is the same kind of section across B Street in Union from the Union Theater to the New Leaf used bookstore. It's forty-five feet across, including the five feet of sidewalk on each side, and the store frontage is right on the sidewalk. The storefronts range from fifteen to twenty-five feet tall.

The bottom drawing is across the Seaside Mall, from Barnes Optical to Beachcomber's women's wear. It's almost exactly the same width across as B Street, forty-two feet, and the storefronts are right at the edge of the pathway, about fourteen feet tall. Mall developers are in the business of making places to which people want to go, and there have been volumes of research published on malls and mall behavior since Victor Gruen designed the first mod-ern shopping center in 1956.[2] What it has all lead to, more or less, is a replication of the density and dimensions of downtown Union.

One other thing to note about each of these places is how fast you're expected to go through it. In Curtisville, the speed limit on Main Street's business district is thirty-five miles an hour, though forty-five is often closer to the fact. In Union, the posted speed limit is twenty-five, but there's a stop sign at every intersection, so cars rarely exceed fifteen or twenty. That, of course, is for those who are driving, and there are a lot of people walking. In the mall, *everyone's* walking, so everyone's going two or three miles an hour. We have in our language the expression "running into someone," as in, "Oh, you'll never guess who I ran into today." At a couple of miles an hour, it's quite pleasant to run into someone, because you can stop and have a conversation. At thirty-five or forty miles an hour, running into someone is considerably less gratifying.

We are, all across America, making places—making so-called communities—that actually force people apart from one another, that put physical distance between us. We make it a lot more difficult to meet one another accidentally, to "run into" one another. Union was mostly built in the 19th century, when we didn't have cars to take us effortlessly from one place to the next. The street layout was built with the shops right next to one another and all of them right on the sidewalk, built with the expectation that people would walk from one shop to another and make several stops along the way.

For a closer example of what that spatial organization means to everyday life, let's consider two bookstores: Brooke's Books in Curtisville and New Leaf Books in Union. New Leaf is right against the sidewalk which is right against the street, exactly zero inches from the pedestrians who go past it. Brooke's is over three hundred feet back, hidden away in the corner of a 1960s shopping center.

Every week, New Leaf changes its window display, with a new theme and a new bunch of books and magazines. This is, of course, a sales tool—they create that display in order to get people to stop and look and come in. But it's also a gift to the people who pass by. Even if you don't come in, you get something new to look at all the time, you get a little treat every time you go past. Multiply that times the thirty or forty shop windows you might go past every time you walk downtown, and that's a lot of changes to look at, a lot of interesting information to take in, and a lot of options to choose from.

Poor Brooke's back in the corner of the parking lot has a shop window too, but it's hard to say why: it's hundreds of feet away from anybody who might go past. The only people who go to Brooke's are people who were already going there. No one drops in because they see something interesting in the window, because they couldn't see the window unless they'd driven there on purpose anyway. The people who run Brooke's weren't allowed to give their community the same kind of gift that the people who run New Leaf could.

The car-centered shopping is only a symptom of the car-oriented housing, of developments held beyond easy walk of work, stores, or neighbors. We have to put those cars someplace once we get where we're going, and store owners know that. That's why the parking lot is out at the street—it's an advertisement that the merchants are making, that their store will be easy to shop at because they're providing a place to leave our two tons of steel.

Of course, teenagers don't have the same kind of access to cars that adults do, so places that depend on the car don't work for kids at all. But they don't really work well for adults either—these places make us drive from one store to another, and then say, "look how easy it is, you can park right here." So we drive to one store, get out, do our chore, get back into the car, drive to the next place, get out, do our chore, get back into the car, and drive to the next place. It's much less likely that we'll run into someone we know and have a conversation; it's much less likely that we'll drop into a store on a whim or because we saw something interesting in the window.

The everyday mobility that Curtisville demands must be seen together with the larger rootlessness that has brought half of all of Curtisville's population to the town within the past ten years, and that has led almost half of its teenagers to live in four or more towns over the course of their lives. The most any kid told me was twelve, adding at the bottom of the survey page, "there were a lot of others, but I ran out of room." When you move that frequently, it's impossible to build a relationship with a place, to learn its nuances, its richness. Ivy, a Curtisville teenager who had moved a lot as a child, told me, "It doesn't really matter where I wake up." And that may be true; it may not matter much where you are. After all, you're still the same you, regardless of location.

But that's not quite complete. We define ourselves partly through our relationships, through intersection with those around us. Imagine saying those same words about our relationship with a person—"It really doesn't matter who I wake up with." Could we really leave someone every two or three years? Could we be so autonomous that we no longer need people and places to help shape us?

We have, for the most part, given up on the idea that place matters in our lives, that places can deeply affect us, that we can have enriching relationships with places. We leave our towns far more often than we leave our families, although Curtisville's adults were horrifyingly regular at that as well. And that rootlessness is another of the reasons we build landscapes that are as boring as Curtisville: we're constantly leaving them, moving from one anonymous place to another, from one auto strip to another, from one Kmart to another, and it really doesn't matter where we wake up. We almost don't want it to matter, because we know we might well be gone a few years down the road.

We build emotional shallowness into our environments, the architectural and urban equivalent of low-priced consumer goods like t-shirts or disposable razors: attractive on the surface and there for us to use, and we can walk away when we're finished and have no regrets.

Carl Coplin, a history teacher at Curtisville High and a twenty-year resident, told me early in the year that "Curtisville's changed a lot. It used to be a requirement that you had to have two junked cars in your yard, your mother couldn't wear shoes, and a muu-muu had to be a part of her wardrobe. They used to call it Oklahoma by the Sea. But now you don't have to go very far off the main drag to see new development, pretty nice houses. I call it Tulsa del Mar now."

As these pretty nice houses have come along by the hundreds, they have spurred two opposing reactions. Among the older residents and those who stand to gain from development, there is an embrace of "progress." Among the newer residents, those who moved here from the relative urbanism of Port City and Union, there is more often a "bar-the-door" mindset, a recognition that welcoming very many more residents will bring about the end of what they came to Curtisville to find.

This conflict plays itself out in image-making that becomes policy. At the inaugural meeting of the Citizens' Advisory Committee, a volunteer board that makes recommendations to the County Planning staff, all fifteen members stated in their introductory remarks that they were committed to maintaining Curtisville's "rural character." What they didn't say—I asked, to no effect—is what they meant by "rural." A community of 15,000 is no longer rural by our demographic definitions, so they must have meant something else. They may have meant the fact that you can see over the tops of the one-story development to the forested foothills; Curtisville, like many places in our country, is stunningly beautiful so long as you look about ten degrees above the horizontal. Another part of their definition of "rural" may have included the fact that the committee was made up of employed or retired white-collar homeowners. None were ranchers or loggers or mechanics. None had dead Chevrolets on their lawns.

During the discussion period at that first meeting, a young, bearded audience member told the rest of us about the open space of local ranches that made suitable habitat for the circling red-tailed hawks he had seen from his porch that weekend, and he wanted to know how we could preserve that. He told us that he could hear the ocean from his house a mile away, and he wanted to know how we could preserve that. But the committee's attention was quickly drawn to a vigorous embrace of the County Planning Department's Geographic Information Systems database, a computer mapping system tied to traffic flow data, utilities maps, and property ownership histories. As far as I know, Timber County doesn't maintain databases on hawk sightings or the sound of the ocean, so the committee members must have meant something else when they said "rural character."

In the early 1990s, the community services district issued a questionnaire to try to learn what Curtisville's residents wanted their town to be like, as a preparation for future planning and zoning. Some of the answers were compelling. "If you have moved to Curtisville in the last five years, what features attracted you, or were important to your decision? Please mark all that apply." Two hundred forty-eight people said that they'd been in Curtisville five years or less, and they overwhelmingly said that "rural atmosphere" was the primary attraction. The other features that mattered to more than half of them were, in order, the price of homes, the scenic views, "not much traffic," the large home parcels, the climate, the seclusion, the clean air, and the opportunities for outdoor recreation.

Those folks who had lived in Curtisville for longer than five years were also invited to rank those same amenities with regard to their own satisfaction with the community. Four hundred thirty-eight filled out this section and again, "rural atmosphere" was far and away the winner. More than half of the long-term residents also noted the clean air, the "price and value of your home," friends and family nearby, not much traffic, scenic views, and large parcel size.

For both newcomers and established residents, Curtisville's perceived values lie in the affordability of the single-family home in a "rural atmosphere" of clean air, large lots and low traffic. Shopping opportunities, employment opportunities, and rental prices were at the bottom of both lists. The respondents of this questionnaire chose Curtisville because it was a bedroom community, a place to drive away from the city jobs and city shopping they already had, a place to look out the windows and see forested hills. Sixty percent hoped that the 21st-century Curtisville would be "rural residential with minimum commercial areas." Even though these people already had homes in Curtisville, presumably in neighborhoods that were established and built out, they didn't want to have a downtown of any sort that implied "density" or "urbanism:" fifty-five percent agreed that "clustering housing to have more open space areas is a good idea," but only one percent thought that the current minimum lot size of five thousand square feet might be reduced, and almost seventy percent thought it ought to be larger.

Leaving aside the question of who got to answer this questionnaire, or even who knew of its existence, the responses portray a view of the good life that is distinctly middle-aged and middle-class. For teenagers, dense urban places (even as small as downtown Union) are popular and convenient because they offer lots of interesting social things to do and look at and touch and smell and taste, numerous places to gather that don't require a car to get to. For teenagers, employment opportunities are welcome. For teenagers, the possibility of affordable rental housing stands close to the foreground of their future concerns. Teenagers are defined out of existence in Curtisville, because their concerns and interests are counter to those of the people who matter. That there are teenagers in the community anyway is an awkward fact for everyone concerned.

PART ONE

Around Town

C H A P T E R   T H R E E

The American Dream

If you were the type of person for whom counting things was reassuring, you might want to know that the California Department of Education has mandated that a high-school year should consist of 64,800 "educational minutes," a figure that Curtisville High School exceeded by fewer than an hour's worth of minutes in 1994–95 due to a power outage in October and another one in December. This 64,800-minute total means that each of the 180 days of school must be at least 360 minutes long, which is why Curtisville High's schedule runs from 8:20 A.M. to 3:05 P.M. with a forty-minute lunch.

If you were a counting person, you might also want to know that on Thursday, February 9, 1995, Laurie Andrews spent 314 minutes in her six classrooms, including twenty-one minutes of counting the change from the Pepsi machines as part of her duties in Leadership class; eleven minutes of listening to the daily bulletin; thirty-four minutes of watching the end of *My Fair Lady* in English; thirty-one minutes reading *Cosmopolitan* in Silent Reading period; seventeen minutes of listening to the radio in Geometry class; and twenty-eight minutes of sitting on the sidelines while her basketball team played in Physical Education. She also spent sixty-four minutes talking with friends on the school Quad, thirty-seven minutes doing various chores as the Senior Class President, and eight minutes at her locker. All of these activities were tallied equally against her required instructional minutes.

You can begin to understand why I am not a counting person.

But let us continue. You might also be interested to know that she spent 289 minutes on that day in her gray 1986 Mitsubishi Precis that she called "The Beast," making fourteen trips totaling about sixty-five miles. Or that she spent thirty-six minutes in restaurants and convenience stores. Or that she spent 236 minutes at home and awake. You might want to know that in the fourteen hours I spent with her that Thursday, she was in over fifty places, only one of them for more than an hour at a time. Friday was about the same.

On Saturday, though, the day moved much more slowly. Saturday was the day that Laurie and Amy and Clair had planned all week, a day to be released from the mad pinball deck of bed - shower - breakfast - car - classroom - library - locker - Quad - classroom - errand - locker - Quad - gym - Quad - classroom - locker - Quad - classroom - Quad - conference room - Quad - car - home - car - classroom - classroom - Quad - car - Union High - car - locker - car - Union High - Northtown Yogurt - car - Taco Bell - car - front porch - kitchen - car - Taco Bell - car - school - car - gas station - car - Bryan's house - car - cheerleading practice - car - Rick's house - car - kitchen - living room - bed. In fact, Saturday was a far less hectic day for all eleven people I followed, and the relative calmness was vital to the heightened awareness that the kids had of their actions.

I called Laurie as requested at 9:37 Saturday morning, and arrived at her house about ten minutes later. She was just dressed, hair still wet, and was busily packing clothes for the rest of the day and overnight. It looked like it took her a while to pick the pastel yellow-beige shorts she had on—her bedroom was even more strewn with clothes than when I saw it for the first time on Thursday. "It's just typical for a teenage girl, that's what I tell myself," she said. Separated from the kitchen by a three-foot length of hallway, her bedroom was about eight by twelve feet; a third of the floor area was occupied by her twin bed, but both the bed and the floor were camouflaged by clothes and magazines and elastic ponytail holders, books and shoes and hangers. The nightstand at the side of the bed held a Bible, a new *Cosmopolitan*, and the remote control for the TV on the dresser.

Most striking, though, were the twenty-six separate pieces of Marilyn Monroe memorabilia on all four walls—posters, calendars, photos, a ceramic plate. "She's my role model, she left a print on society. And I just think she was beautiful." Laurie was about the same color blond as Marilyn, though bodily more in the model of an Olympic gymnast: just over five feet, strong, athletic. She smiled easily, a broad friendly grin. Her teachers used words like "perky" and "outgoing" and "honest" when they described her, and predicted that she would lead a solid American life.

Her dad Steve, a carpenter, was sitting at the kitchen table working on income taxes. He asked Laurie if she'd received a bank statement yet. "I don't know. What would it look like?" she said, rushing through a bowl of Western Family sugar pops.

I used the bathroom just before we left. A Marilyn Monroe calendar on the wall overlooked the sink.

As we drove away in The Beast, Laurie told me she wasn't sure how long we were going to be at the wrestling tournament, or even why we were going exactly. She was also not sure anymore if she wanted to perm her hair or not—"It's been doing so well lately"— which was the outward purpose that lay behind the long-planned gathering of her friends that afternoon. Once we arrived at school and got out of her car, she realized as though for the first time how short her shorts were: "You get dressed at home and look in the mirror, and then you go out somewhere and it just feels different."

At about 10:10, we walked into the Curtisville gym. The wrestling tournament had just started ten minutes earlier, and the very lightest wrestlers were on the mats as we took our seats in the quarter-full bleachers. The meet was a four-team tournament, common for schools with limited travel budgets and long distances to cover. Curtisville and Northern High were on the northern mat, Valley and South City on the southern. All four were rural schools, gathering their few hundred students from dozens of small hamlets apiece, and none would be strikingly successful at wrestling this year.

We seemed to have sat in an odd section of the bleachers— there were people around us cheering for Curtisville wrestlers, some others cheering for Northern wrestlers, and a couple of people sitting behind us who changed allegiances after each match. Wrestling certainly is an esoteric sport, like most I suppose, but it isn't the sort of general spectator sport that gathers an entire small town together like high school basketball or football. The two hundred or so fans seemed mostly to be parents, brothers and girlfriends of the wrestlers. Laurie herself really came only to be with her friend Amy, whose boyfriend Joel wrestled in the 155-pound class.

The woman hollering from behind us had watched a lot of wrestling in her life. "Oh, look, look, he's too high! Now, Colin, now, run him! Run him!" She could have been a coach. Some of the Northern High wrestlers probably wished she *were* their coach—the real coach was standing at the edge of the mat, shouting Generic Motivational Stuff at his kids. "Stay tough! Get in there! Think about what you're doing!" Whenever one of his wrestlers lost, the coach sullenly shook hands with the winner and had little to say to his own pupil.

Laurie and I weren't really watching the wrestling so much as surveying the entire gymscape. "I wonder where Amy is. She'd better get here before Joel wrestles. She's so funny when Joel's wrestling—she won't look, but then she looks, and she grabs onto your arm, and then she won't look again." Amy is the president of Curtisville's Associated Student Body, and she and Joel have been the Perfect High School Couple for several years. Joel and Amy remind me very much of a teenage version of the Reagans—Amy's very straight and controlling, self-conscious, a little whiny, and Joel is easygoing and loose, amiable, generally unconcerned about things larger than the personal.

Amy arrived a little after eleven, but we discovered shortly after that Joel wasn't wrestling that day anyway—he had dislocated a piece of cartilage between his ribs and his sternum, and wouldn't work out again for another week or so. We stayed through the last match of the first round only because we had no immediate reason to leave—Laurie's boyfriend Bryan wouldn't be home from Boy Scouts until a little after noon. Even then, we didn't really watch as Bear, Curtisville's All-County heavyweight, easily pinned his opponent; we talked with Joel and Rick and Jake and Joel's mom until the round had ended and the teams switched mats to take on their next set of opponents.

It was just past noon when Laurie, Amy and I left the gym to pick up Clair at her aunt's house. Clair stayed with her aunt more and more frequently since she turned eighteen. Her mom couldn't threaten her with being thrown out of the house anymore, because Clair could just stay with her aunt. Why Clair's mom might threaten to throw her out of the house went unsaid.

We drove just past the high school, north of Murphy Road, into a subdivision that hadn't existed two years earlier. Laurie and Amy filled the car with biting commentary on suburban patterns of housing and living.

"Everybody's house is like two feet apart, and they all look the same."

"If that house was like way out in the country, I'd be happy."

"You spend all this money on a house and you can still look right in your neighbor's windows."

When we arrived at Clair's, her uncle was washing their new Escort GT in the driveway, and his big powder blue Chevy pickup with the raised suspension and oversized tires sat parked at the curb. *"There's* a Curtisville truck," said Amy. Clair came out to meet us but went back into the house to pick up some clothes for overnight and the next day, and the architectural critics picked up where they had left off.

"Look how small the front yard is."

"People take such pride in their lawns. Don't they have anything better to do with their lives?"

"If I had, like, little rocks perfectly arranged around my driveway, I would just puke."

Clair returned with a gym bag and an outfit on a hanger, and we headed back to Laurie's. All three girls were in the front together, and I was in the back. Laurie said, "My legs are so fat." All three girls were wearing shorts in celebration of a rare warm February day, and discussed whether they were really fat or whether it was just the car seat. Clair was almost exactly the same size as Laurie, and Amy was twenty pounds lighter than either of them. All three were cheerleaders in the fall for football, as they had been for the three years before that, but Laurie dropped basketball cheerleading in the spring. "It's stressful just to be there, everybody just argues all the time. And the coach is like a total flake."

We spent ten minutes at Laurie's to pick up a couple of last-minute toiletries, a jacket, and a can of pennies to play blackjack with. She also begged ten bucks from Dad to buy her perm kit. I collected my car since I wouldn't be staying overnight, and backed down the gravel drive to follow The Beast to Bryan's house in Glen Ellen, about ten miles south.

Bryan was a junior at Union High, and he and Laurie had met the previous year at rehearsals for the two schools' joint production of "How to Succeed in Business without Really Trying." On Friday, Laurie had worn Bryan's gray sweatshirt at school, and she had every one of her girlfriends smell it over the course of the morning to see if they thought it had a Bryan-like scent. Nobody had any clue at all, of course, but they humored her. She wrapped the hood of his sweatshirt around her mouth and nose and inhaled deeply. "It smells just like him," she said, eyes closed.

Laurie wore a thin ring with a little red stone on the ring finger of her left hand, no other rings or watches or bracelets. Bryan gave it to her. She wore a leather thong necklace with three long oval moonstones. She got it from Bryan. Friday afternoon at Oyster Beach, a young couple with a pair of dogs had walked past on their way to the surf, and Laurie and Bryan talked about what kind of dog they would have, which was the sort of oblique way they talked about the possibility of their marriage. (On Thursday over lunch, Laurie told Brittany that Bryan had been talking about marriage the night before, to which Laurie and Brittany exchanged a high-five. Laurie described her wedding, which she will have two years from now in May. "I wanted it to be in the snow, like in Tahoe, but Bryan doesn't want everyone to have to travel. I don't care, it's *my* wedding! Girls start planning their weddings when they're about five.")

At Bryan's, the garage door was open, displaying years of disorganized storage. Bryan's older sister and brother-in-law were about to move back into the house for a while so that they could save money for school, so Bryan was moving out to the garage rather than share a small bedroom with his thirteen-year-old brother. Bryan had to make considerable headway on the mess in the garage before he could join us for the day, but Laurie told him that they would be perming her hair all afternoon anyway and that everyone else was going to get together around five or so. A little kiss for Bryan and a "Bye, Ellen" to his mom, and Laurie was ready to leave.

She pushed The Beast ten miles over the limit all the way to downtown Port City and Taco Bell (known to the occupants of the Beast as "Toxic Hell"—Friday night's dinner had been at the "Brown

Panty" rather than the Town Pantry). The primary marketing strategy of Taco Bell may be learned from knowing that the parking lot was laid out so that we had to walk across the drive-thru lane to get into the restaurant.

We sat in Toxic Hell for fifteen minutes, eating light, not more than a burrito or taco apiece. A young woman two booths over held a cooing baby, and all three girls cooed in return from a distance, as they had on Friday when an ex-classmate brought her infant to school for a Home Study meeting.

Once the tacos were dispatched, the girls piled back into The Beast and drove on to Long's Drugs for candy and perm-kit shopping. They wandered blindly though the store, picking up a bag of Peanut M&M's along their search, and finally discovered hair-care products in the furthest rear corner after several minutes. Perm kits lined the shelves in bewildering variety, and Clair (the group's appointed beautician) read the instructions from one kit while we looked at dozens of options and prices. Laurie said, "We might as well get the cheap one, they're all the same." Amy and I looked at each other, and Amy said, "That's right, Laurie, they're all the same, the ten-dollar one's not better than the other." Clair and Laurie decided on a middle-of-the-road kit that cost six bucks.

They stopped in the candy row on their way to the register to pick up a box of Alexander the Grapes. Little bite-sized repetitive food—M&M's, Skittles, sunflower seeds—was the overwhelming choice among this group, as it was among almost all kids I was with all year. The night before, standing in the Arco station before the basketball game, Amy and Brittany were critiquing the sad mini-mart candy selection made up almost completely of full-sized candy bars like Snickers and Three Musketeers:

"They don't have Nerds!!"

"And they don't have Runts, either!! What can they be thinking?"

Back at the checkstand, Laurie spotted a prominently displayed magazine called *Love & Sex*. She said, "Oh, look, *Love & Sex*! Somebody check it out!" But we were through the line and gone.

I followed The Beast another seven or eight minutes to Laurie's mom's house, where we were met at the door by her mom's boyfriend. It would be a cliché to say that the house looked like it had been ransacked, and it wouldn't be accurate anyway because burglars wouldn't go to the effort to spread that much dirt and dust behind them. It looked more like a crew of oil wildcatters had left it behind after a month of dry holes. We were welcomed into the back yard where Mom was potting flowers. Nearby, at the end of the grassless lawn, a six-foot diameter trash pile was adorned with dozens of empty Pabst and Olympia twelve-pack boxes.

We left after only three or four minutes. I'm still not sure why we were ever there—Laurie did give her mom a prom photo of herself and Bryan, but that felt like an afterthought. On our way back out to the cars Amy said, "Your mom seems okay today."

Back into The Beast one last time, off to our final destination, the promised land: Grandma's house. This would be the culmination of four days of planning, and even though Bryan wouldn't be able to be with her for the entire day, Laurie was happy, looking forward to being with her friends.

Grandma lived in an enormous house tucked back into the redwoods at the edge of town. The house lay down at the end of a eighty-foot-long sloped and landscaped driveway—the roofline was hidden below street level—and it went on and on and on. Two stories over the garages, an entry porch in the middle, and a three-bedroom guest wing closest to the front. The entire face was dark-stained redwood siding, with frosted leaves etched into the accent glass on all the doors. The doormat said, "Get Lost."

Nobody answered the doorbell, so Laurie unlocked the door and raced in to turn off the alarm. She was too late, but there weren't any neighbors close enough to hear it anyway. After disarming the alarm, Laurie let us all in; we walked to the furthest guest bedroom to drop off bags and clothes, then back out to the kitchen and onto the deck. The inside of the house, like the outside, was designed to impress rather than to be comfortable for two retirees, now one widowed retiree and a housekeeper. There were half a dozen unnecessary three- and four-foot level changes, sunken rooms and raised tubs, a wet bar and refrigerator in the living room with six leather-upholstered stools around it. There was a TV in the family room that was bigger than my car, and another one just as large in the laundry room that wasn't working because a visitor had broken it playing Super Nintendo.

The kitchen was a land of gadgets: a Braun electric carrot peeler on the tile counter, a cordless phone, a restaurant-sized double-bay refrigerator and freezer. A double range, an overhead microwave, a full pantry room. Out on the deck, Laurie turned on the hot tub heater to get ready for the evening. The hot tub was on a sort of sub-deck, down three steps from the rest of the deck.

Laurie often entertained her friends at Grandma's. She brought Amy and Clair and Brittany and Erica there to sleep over a couple of weekends a month, along with a handful of big parties every year. Laurie loved her grandma, and idolized her grandfather while he was alive, but she admitted, "My grandma stresses me out. I made dinner for about ten people before the prom, and she's all in the kitchen going, 'You should cook this *this* way,' and I'm all like, 'HEL-lo! I'm cooking, okay? Just leave me alone.' And when I do my hair, she's all, 'Oh, I like your hair curly, not straight, and I like it long, and it should be back to its original color.' And I'm like, 'HEL-lo! Whose hair is this anyway?' Like it's not gonna grow back out anyway . . ."

Amy turned on the TV in the family room and we watched the opening minutes of Spike Lee's *Do The Right Thing* on cable. They've all seen it before. "What is that stupid dance she's doing?" But before long, Grandma arrived home along with Dave the housekeeper. It took Dave four trips to the car to carry in the eight big bags of groceries, full of chickens and a five-pound filet mignon. Grandma told Laurie that her uncle Jim and his wife and four kids would be coming over that evening at about seven for a barbecue. Laurie was upset—"She *knew* we were coming over tonight," she said to us once she thought Grandma was out of earshot—but she didn't want to make a fuss. Grandma knew, and said, "If you're going to be here tonight, then they can come tomorrow night." Laurie replied impatiently, "No, if they're going to come tonight, then that's okay."

The girls and I moved to the kitchen to grate cheese and peel potatoes for dinner. Spike Lee worked unnoticed. Grandma knew everyone in the room except me, and she assumed I was Clair's boyfriend even though I was twenty years older. Everyone called her Grandma, including Dave, but she was a Palm Desert version of a grandmother, slim and hair-dyed, squeezed into designer jeans and a western shirt rather than a rounding out a modest checked dress and apron.

Once dinner was underway, we retreated to the laundry room to begin with the perm. There were eighteen steps to the instructions and hundreds of tissue sheets to wrap around the rollers and three chemicals to mix, but all three girls were laughing and talking, removed from all of the other little hassles going on around. The work and happiness was interspersed with complaints about Dave. He got room and board and $150 a week in exchange for shopping, cleaning, doing basic maintenance and some cooking. Laurie and the others didn't like him at all. Laurie thought he took advantage of her grandma terribly: running out of money on gambling sprees and hitting her up for more; always complaining that he was underpaid and overworked; and complaining especially that he had to clean up after Laurie and her friends. Laurie had another problem with Dave that she alluded to but never told me. She said, "We'll talk about it later." We never did.

After twenty minutes, Dave came into the laundry room to chat a little. He and I wound up having most of the conversation; the girls refused to answer him except for the most curt "yeah" and "no" responses. So instead he talked to me about his broken neck suffered several years earlier in a surfing accident and about living in San Diego and other parts of California. He said, "When I came in, I didn't know who you were, but then so many people come through here that I don't know half of them."

He also asked Laurie, "Did you turn on the hot tub heater?"

"Yeah, we're going to use it later."

"It isn't working right now. Both the gas burner and the motor are bad. It's going to cost a lot of money to fix it."

"Like my grandma doesn't have a lot of money. I mean, look at this house."

"Well, this house is a big upkeep expense."

Dave left the room, and Laurie gave me a burning look and said, "I hate him, he's such a jerk."

The perm consumed just a little over two and a half hours, keeping us in the laundry room the whole time. At 5:20, just as Laurie rinsed out and began to dry her hair, her friend Rick and Amy's boyfriend Joel arrived. Bryan should have arrived an hour or more ago. It was time to head to the grocery store for snacks and movies, and Laurie gave Grandma explicit instructions to ensure that Bryan stayed put if he showed up while we were gone. Grandma went to her purse and gave Laurie a twenty-dollar bill for our chips and videos, and the six of us all piled into Grandma's mini-van and drove off to the grocery.

Seven minutes of snack deliberations resulted in a box of Wheat Thins, a bag of white corn chips, a bag of Wavy Lays, a jar of ranch dip, and a jar of salsa (mild, after long discussion and two votes). Then we hit the movies at the front of the store. "Look, *Demolition Man*."

"I've seen that twice."

"How about *RoboCop II*?"

"Hey, *Predator*, that was cool!"

"Nah, we saw that last week."

The junk food decision seemed easy by comparison. We left the video racks holding two compromise candidates: *Man's Best Friend*, a horror movie about a genetically-engineered dog which at least had the advantage of being new to everyone; and a back-up, *The Secret of Nimh*, which everyone had seen between one and three times.

Back at Grandma's, still no Bryan. Laurie headed upstairs to Grandma's bathroom to spray some mousse into her hair—she was frustrated that her perm didn't come out the way she wanted, though she wasn't explicit about exactly what she did want. Clair and Amy reassured her as best they could ("my hair was really frizzy on the day I permed it, too," Clair offered), but without success. Laurie was tired and bummed and Bryanless, and Clair had a headache from creative stress and from inhaling all those perm chemicals.

The girls walked down to the family room to join Rick and Joel watching *The Butcher's Wife* on cable—they'd all seen it, but the TV was on and we weren't. We were waiting . . . waiting . . . waiting for Bryan. I sat on the floor while the kids sprawled across chairs and sofas with blankets spread over them. Joel lay on one couch watching the movie; Amy was in his arms, near sleep. Clair's eyes were scarcely open; Rick fell asleep on the floor, leaning against the loveseat; and Laurie just glowered from the depths of her over-stuffed recliner, a comforter over her legs and her arms crossed tightly over her chest.

Dave was at work on the deck supervising the steaks and chicken on the gas grill. Grandma walked into the family room and reached over the back of the recliner to put her hand on Laurie's shoulder. "Where's your Bryan baby?" she asked. Laurie jerked her shoulders in a brief approximation of a shrug, not uncrossing her arms, and didn't look up at Grandma. "I don't know, he'll be here when he gets here." Grandma retreated to the kitchen.

By 7:10, Joel had wrestled and ticked Amy awake, but Clair had fallen asleep. It appeared that dinner would be a while off, and Amy and Rick were both hungry but tried to be polite. Laurie said, "Go ahead and have something, I don't care." People started to meander into the kitchen to open up the salsa and chips. Laurie burrowed deeper into her chair, tucked all the way into the back corner.

Laurie's uncle Jim and his family arrived at about 7:30. Introductions weren't offered by Grandma or Laurie, and Jim had to do it himself. At the end, I don't think anyone was really sure who anyone else was or how they were related in family or friendship. Jim's family moved to the kitchen to leave us our space.

Ten minutes later, Bryan arrived. He hadn't been able to get a ride. "I just stood around and waited and waited, and they kept saying they were about to go, so I kept waiting for them." He kept apologizing over and over, to no response, until Laurie snapped, "Are *we* saying anything?? Do you hear anything??" She was really toasted, but pretended she wasn't by turning her attention away from Bryan and toward getting everyone else ready for dinner.

Just before eight, Erica and Chad showed up (completely unexpected as far as I was concerned; their names had never been mentioned over the three days I'd been with Laurie), and we begin dinner. Erica and Chad were another Perfect High School Couple: an honor roll/accomplished musician/beauty queen senior and her college freshman boyfriend, the previous year's star scholar/musician/actor/athlete. Laurie's anger began to melt under the warmth of so many friends, and we all laughed and ate well.

Grandma and Dave and uncle and family—eight people—were in the breakfast room; Laurie's group of nine filled the dining room. The only interaction between the two sets was at the serving platters and the refrigerator. Of the fourteen rooms in the house, only three were in use, and they were more than ample. The food was more than ample as well, plenty for the seventeen of us and another dozen more, had more arrived.

By about 8:20, most of us had finished eating and begun to dis-
perse—two or three hung around the kitchen, four or five draped
themselves across the three stairs leading to the guest wing, all of
us joining and departing groups to move around the house. Within
fifteen minutes, though, Laurie and Amy gathered us all back
around the dining table for blackjack. Nobody really knew the rules,
and all the pennies were Laurie's, so there was no real interest in
the game itself; like the television, it was just an excuse to be
together and talk for an hour. Amy was the big winner, collecting
$4.35 on the last hand. She counted it out, loudly announced the
total to collective indifference, and poured the coins back into
Laurie's cardboard box.

By quarter to ten, we gradually gathered in the family room to
watch *Man's Best Friend*. It really was a dumb movie, but fun to
watch with nine sets of comments going on. Jim and family left
about 10:30 with no goodbyes to our group. Grandma went upstairs
to bed shortly after, with a friendly "good night" from the kids, and
we settled in to eat chips and watch Ally Sheedy and her killer dog.

Dave's girlfriend stopped by to pick him up and go out dancing
at about 11:30. Just before they left, the intercom buzzed in the
kitchen—it was Grandma from upstairs. "Are there any M&M's?"
None remained. "Could you go to the store for me? I want some
M&M's and a Snickers, and we need some rice cakes." Dave and his
girlfriend left. I'm not sure if they returned.

The couples were tightly curled together under blankets: Erica
and Chad on the couch, Amy and Joel on the loveseat, and Laurie
and Bryan snuggled together deep in the recliner where she'd been
so cranky a few hours earlier. Rick and I played rummy on the floor.
Clair left, unacknowledged, to go to bed. When the movie ended,
they switched to *Saturday Night Live*. Nobody laughed for the
entire ninety minutes. They complained about the musical guest,
some Top-40 singer they'd all heard before. They complained about
Bob Newhart, the guest host. They complained about the skits. They
complained about the ads.

Of course, none of that mattered. Neither *Man's Best Friend*
nor *Saturday Night Live* mattered, as Clair knew when she left to go
to bed, nor did blackjack or grilled chicken or scalloped potatoes.
What mattered is that the romantic ties were whole, that the uni-

verse of Perfect Couples had no missing lights. What mattered is that Laurie and Bryan lay together under their blanket in the comfortable stuffed chair, in front of the fieldstone fireplace and the massive TV, surrounded by their friends in the living room of a big, beautiful house. It's what Marilyn would have wanted.

CHAPTER FOUR

The Working Life

Duane changed hurriedly after school, exchanging his beloved Western wear for black polyester slacks and his "fag shirt," the pink polo shirt that constituted the upper half of the Pizza Palace uniform. He tossed his apron into the back seat of my car and we took off for Union. We arrived at work a bit before four o'clock, and I left him; the plan had been for me to hang around and watch him work, but his manager wasn't comfortable having me there, and I didn't push it. Instead I went home and wrote notes for a few hours, and returned to Pizza Palace at 9:45. I found a booth where I could watch him clear out the salad bar and the under-bar refrigerator.

Duane wasn't yet sixteen, so he could only officially do the mundane stuff—he couldn't serve beer or use the ovens and knives, the slicer, the big mixer, the dishwasher. He was limited to pizza garnishing, restocking, cleaning, and handling the register. He worked steadily, not acknowledging my presence, not hesitating or dawdling. Only three of the thirty tables were occupied on that Friday night, and work in general seemed to have shifted from production mode to cleaning mode: wipedowns, table and seat cleaning, consolidating the salad bar ingredients, pushing the benches under the tables. Duane was running down the mental checklist, working through the closing routine.

He finished and punched the clock by 10:15, joining me at the booth with an order of garlic-twist bread and a plastic cup of ranch dressing. Duane liked the fact that he worked, liked making some money and having control over it. He wished, though, that they'd give him more hours—"Like, last week I only got seven hours."—and more responsibility.

The answers to one question from my survey showed that a little more than a quarter of Curtisville's kids worked at jobs for pay. Those jobs ranged from commercial fishing to dance teaching to heavy equipment mechanics. Girls held more jobs than boys, and twelfth grade girls were the most likely to have jobs: about two-thirds of them were employed.

We have tried over the last thirty years to break down work stereotypes in this country, to convince the military to accept women and nursing schools to accept men. We have tried to let all girls and boys know that they can pursue any career in which they have an interest. And yet, all of the jobs that Curtisville's teens told me about were so sex role-correct that my data might as well have been taken from a survey conducted in the 1940s. Of the eighteen kids who babysat or worked in child care, seventeen were girls. Of the fifteen kids who were maids or janitors, fourteen were girls. Thirteen of the sixteen clerical workers were girls. All four of the teachers and all four of the hospital workers were girls.

And the boys? All seventeen construction workers, nine of the ten landscape workers, nine of the ten manual laborers and eight of the ten farmers were boys. The only gender non-specific work types were retail (seventeen girls and ten boys) and restaurant work (twenty-one girls and twenty boys): even those jobs might have shown more sex division if the kids had been more specific about their roles (server vs. cook vs. dishwasher, for instance).

It's hard to get too worked up over this division of labor. This is just teenage employment, after all, and not college majors or true career choices. But the real question is whether this first foray into the work world isn't somehow predictive of the next step. It's certainly reflective of more than just personal interest and skills that no girls at all took construction jobs and only one boy sought out a child care job. Enculturation is far stronger than any school career program can ever be.

I bother with this introduction at all because I think teenage work can be vital to helping kids find an image of their futures (for better or worse). One thing that I saw a few times over the year was the importance of a workplace where kids could be in control, could be taken seriously and depended upon. There are teenage jobs that are unlike Pizza Palace counter work, for which the corporation tells you specifically what must be done, how fast, in what order, and with what clothes on. In a few cases, a teenager was essentially given the keys, given a job, and left alone.

ɻ💙

Kirk drove madly off to the Runway restaurant at the airport, using his right hand to towel his hair dry from his two-minute shower after surfing. I followed him in my car because I wasn't sure if I'd be welcome in the kitchen. At the employee parking lot, Kirk left his pass card in the parking gate so that I could get in behind him. We jogged across the parking lot, inside the terminal, up the stairs, and through the kitchen door. Kirk immediately ran around to the cook-line and checked the clock. "I'm a minute early—sweet!"

Three people handled the kitchen at the Runway, Curtisville's only fine dining room. Scott was the chef, Navy-trained, coordinating the show. Kevin had worked with Scott for about three years and seemed to be doing whatever Scott wasn't doing at any particular moment, an exact complement. Kirk was the general assistant, roaming from the dishwasher to the freezer to the cookline.

The Runway worked like a home kitchen: pans on the range, hand-mixed ingredients, no differentiation between prep area and cooking area. A four-foot by six-foot butcher block worktable dominated the middle of the room; on it, Scott assembled orders and garnished plates while Kirk stocked and chopped on the other side. Along the back wall from left to right were a two-basket Fryolator, a two-foot square gas grille, a four-foot wide griddle with two ovens below, and a four-burner range. All were clean but darkened by years of flame. A two-bay stainless steel refrigerator extended into the room at an L on the right end of the cookline. The appliances were old, the storage racks were wooden, the paint was patched, and a poster above the chest freezer displayed the menu from the Road Kill Cafe ("You kill it—we grill it".) The kitchen sang with the sounds of knives through onions and onions in skillets. Waitresses in their black dresses and white aprons laughed and called out orders.

Kirk started his evening by doing some dishes but quickly cleared that job and began to restock the reach-in refrigerator for Scott and Kevin. When the fridge was full, he washed some saute pans in the side sink. By 6:40, the backlog of preparatory work had cleared, and Kirk opened the bread steamer and ripped open a dinner roll for himself. He walked to the bulletin board, half the roll already gone, and pulled down Scott's work list, written on a napkin. The list read:

- Dishes
- Prawns
- Pull 1-1/2—2 flats 8 oz chx
- Check 6-oz
- Crush boxes
- Put mayo in 5-gallon bucket

Kirk started on the list by peeling and de-veining shrimp for twenty minutes, filling two half-gallon plastic pans, and then moved on to thawing chicken breasts. He stood across from the cookline at the butcher block, drinking a soda and pounding on the frozen chicken parts with a meat hammer to break them apart from one another. Once that was complete and the chicken had been transferred onto trays in the refrigerator, Kirk went to the bottom of the list and began to ladle mayonnaise from a cardboard box into a five-gallon plastic barrel—it usually came in a plastic bag inside the box, but for that shipment, the packager had somehow neglected the bag.

The mayonnaise finished, Kirk delivered Swiss cheese slices to the cookline, devouring one along the way. Scott took a break from the grille to teach Kirk how to debone snapper filets. Two examples later, he handed the knife over and reviewed Kirk's first attempt, calling it pretty good. Kirk continued for about fifteen minutes, deboning twenty more fish while Kevin did the small accumulation of dishes.

I stood well out of range during all of this, leaning against the chest freezer to enjoy people working together. There were none of the things I resented about my own long-ago kitchen history: no shouting, no frantic dashes to get things done ahead of the clock, no buzzers or bells going off like an endless demented game show. Whenever Scott wanted something, he called out, "Kirk-dude!" Kirk-dude refilled the cookline margarine tub and then made an order of French fries for the bar. He pulled the fryer basket from the oil and tossed the sizzling fries into a steel bowl with salt and grated

Parmesan cheese. He added a little unnecessary flourish, tumbling the fries from the bowl in his right hand through the air and onto the plate in his left hand a foot below, and passed the plate through the little window between the bar and the kitchen. He ate the extras that he'd left in the bowl.

At 8:05, Kirk diced green onions for the cookline. When he finished, Scott said, "Thanks, Kirk-dude." Scott thanked Kirk and Kevin for everything they did; Kevin thanked Kirk and Scott, the waitresses thanked the cooks and the cooks thanked the waitresses. The kitchen ran on rituals of courtesy, observed by all. Scott high-fived everyone after clearing a big bunch of tickets, including not only Kevin and Kirk but Betsy, the sixty-year-old head waitress.

At 8:23, Kirk scrubbed down the big cutting board after working with raw fish and beef. At 8:26, he took a phone call; Josh had left his wallet in Kirk's car at Quiet Cove when they were surfing. Kirk told Josh where the car was parked at the airport so that Josh could come get his wallet later in the evening. Then he returned to the sink to scrub saute pans and cookline tools.

The pace began to slow down, coasting toward the 9:00 close. At 8:47, Scott cooked Kirk a big plate of pasta alfredo. "Put a lot of garlic on it," Kirk urged him. Every employee got one free meal per shift, and Scott seemed to enjoy cooking for his friends, taking their suggestions and requests to be followed or improvised upon as he pleased. Betsy ordered fish (no butter) and grilled vegetables. Scott cooked it up as ordered, and he said to me as he slid it onto a plate, "There's no butter on her fish . . . but there's a shitload of it on her vegetables!" He grinned at me as he garnished her plate as carefully as he had for his patrons. "Keep 'em fat and they're happy!" He offered me dinner as well, but I declined—Kevin had already made me half a plate of fries earlier in the evening.

Two days earlier, I had taken Kirk for an interview to his favorite lunch spot, Chicago Pizza; he ran through all the ingredients as he recommended the pesto and sun-dried tomato Godfather pizza. "I love to eat. When I was little, Mom wanted us to help out with dinner, probably just because she was busy and stuff, but she says that ever since I was little, I wanted to help in the kitchen. I cook all the time. A couple of nights ago, I made dinner with some mushrooms that I found out on an alder tree on Scenic Road, and some crabs I found on the beach up at Harborville. I made a cream of mushroom soup. I've been thinking about going to school in Oregon or maybe San Francisco and become a chef, and then go on to the academy and become a master chef. All of the most beautiful spots in the world have a tendency to become, like, tourist traps, and they all have fancy restaurants and I could cook there."

I can't help but reflect on the differences between Kirk's work and school selves, differences you will see later as well. He was a hard, diligent worker whose best attributes—independence, conversational camaraderie, flexibility, and intolerance of boredom—were negated by school. He got his jobs done, and Scott and Kevin didn't mind if he ate or talked on the phone during his shift for a few minutes at a time. He loved to read, he worked hard, he surfed hard, he played soccer hard. His friends enjoyed him, his co-workers liked him, his little stepbrother and stepsister loved him, and he was a marginal student. I wonder which assessments were wrong.

A year later, Kirk dropped out of Curtisville High and prepared to take the GED. He also quit the Runway. His stepdad says Kirk is making his living by growing and selling pot with his dad. I have to admit that I'm angry with Kirk for not having the patience to last the final half of his senior year—he at least managed to hold on through soccer season, after which school held nothing at all for him—but I understand his choice. He's streamlining his life to include more time for the things that enrich him. More time for surfing, more time for his vegetable garden, more time for his girlfriend. And, as with the Runway, there's no artificial division between his responsibilities and his hobbies; he's making his living at something he knows and enjoys, working for someone he likes and who relies on him.

Meanwhile, Duane has also found a job that he likes. After a second restaurant job that lasted five or six months, he now works for a local dairy farmer laying irrigation pipe. He gets up at 4:30 and rides his bike five miles to the ranch, where he and a partner work to position and connect a quarter-mile of the wheeled pipe sections. No supervisors, no rules about the legal age of handling dangerous tools, just a cold field and a sunrise and a couple of hours of continuous work. He finishes at seven-thirty and has the day to himself until mid-afternoon, when he returns to disassemble the rig, move it to another region of the pasture, and connect it all again. Duane, too, has found a workplace that suits him, doing physical work outdoors around stock animals, making a difference on the farm. And he doesn't have to wear someone else's shirt.

CHAPTER FIVE

I Love this Car, Man

I'm talking on the school Quad with John and Cal at the beginning of lunch, discussing my practice of following people around. "Who are you following today?" asks John.

"Nobody, I don't start my next victim until tomorrow."

"You want to come with us to Foodland?"

I think about other responsibilities, other people I might have stayed to talk with at lunch. That lasts half a second. "Sure, let's go."

So we join the stream of students out to the parking lot and pile into Cal's car, an '84 Corolla called The Flymobile. Cal drives quickly up to Foodland, a supermarket two miles away on Main Street, where he and John spend five minutes standing before the bounteous rack of Little Debbie snack cakes. "Oh, man, what are we gonna get? They're all great." Finally, the decision is made— Oatmeal Creams.

We walk on the ridge of the curb back to the car, all three of us balancing successfully the hundred feet or so from the front door to the parking lot. The cookies remain unopened; the anticipation builds. We enter the Flymobile and head back to school with Cal driving, John up front in shotgun, and me in the back. John opens the package and leans over the seat with a cookie. "Herb, you have to have one of these oatmeal things if you're going to ride in the Flymobile!"

I take up the joke. "Oh, no, peer pressure!"

John catches it right away. "It's only one, Herb, it won't hurt you."

Cal says, "Yeah, nobody's going to force you to have any more."

I have half a cookie. It's gross, tasting like an oatmeal cookie with about a stick of butter laid on it. I announce this: "That's gross."

"Hey, you can't go dissin' on our cookies in the Flymobile, man."

We get back to school but stay in the car, eating more Oatmeal Creams while waiting for the bell. Billy Simmons bounces into the lot in his new '94 Ford four-wheel-drive pickup, and Cal and John make fun of him (from inside the safety of the Flymobile, Billy being a big and relatively unstable fellow) because, as we all know, his mommy bought him this truck after he'd wrecked the one she'd bought him before.

These guys do know how to have fun.

Space/Place through Time

•

Teenagers and their cars. The phrase brings back images of early rock'n'roll—the Beach Boys taking the Woodie on a surfin' safari; Jan and Dean bragging about gear ratios and racing on Dead Man's Curve; Ronnie Howard and Harrison Ford on the cruise in Modesto.

When we think of teenagers and cars, there are lots of things we could talk about, things which have already been discussed to death in a thousand other places. We could talk, for example, about new-found freedom, the self-determination of schedule and connections. Those kids I followed who had cars of their own were certainly more fluid and independent, able to go wherever and whenever they chose without regard to someone else's schedule. The car also enabled a more effective search for social life—if there was any rumor or possibility of gathering, the car allowed a broader and more immediate search for it. So many car trips were a sort of rummaging for connection, "seeing what's up" in a dozen places on a single trip, the embodied version of channel-surfing.

We could talk about the new extension of the personal range, being able to go great distances. This didn't happen all that often, though, at least not in the realm of things like weekend trips to Oregon or the Sierras, because their schedules were still constrained by their parents. It's one thing to have a car that might allow you to drive to Lake Tahoe, but another thing to be allowed to be out on your own for three days in order to do it. This aspect of car ownership, for me one of the most gratifying, was rarely exploited. Teenagers used their cars overwhelmingly for short local trips—to school, to work, to the beach, to the restaurant, to a friend's house.

We could talk about responsibility, the hesitant entrance to adult life marked by insurance payments and the nagging scratch for gas money, the need to attend to the car's maintenance. Most of the kids I met at Curtisville who had their own car had gotten it for little or nothing—a hand-me-down family car or a low-priced used car that came as a gift from the folks. However, the kids were usually responsible for everything after that: insurance, gas, repairs, traffic tickets. The car acts in many ways as a hook into adult patterns of living—it links you irretrievably into the money economy. It offers freedom and immediately provides constraints. These constraints are often looked forward to prior to car ownership; car and work are correctly thought of as concurrent events, concurrent adult roles for kids who heretofore haven't had any.

Another aspect of that responsibility came through the car owner's service to their carless friends. The Curtisville kids who had cars spent a great amount of their driving time picking up and delivering their friends around town, performing an adult service for which they received gratitude and occasional gas money. They were needed and depended upon, another adult role which they got fairly little of in other places.

We could talk about speed and danger, about racing down the freeway or spinning long, loud circles on the beach. Driving can be terrifically gratifying—something that adults often forget in commuter traffic or in hectic trips to do household shopping chores. Having a large machine to amplify the sensations of speed and vertigo, sensations that are so much fun on bicycles and when running through the woods, is an intoxicating experience.[1] Duane and Curt and I rode twenty miles or so from Stony Beach with Duane's friend Steve driving at a little better than 115 in some stretches of the highway. The combination of fear and exhilaration left all four of us laughing and wordless, as though we were riding the Grizzly at Great America.

But driving, even at legal speeds, is also a skill to be mastered, one that gives immediate sensory feedback about success. That mastery offers a legitimate sense of pride and hierarchy among the initiates. After school on a Thursday, Maggie and I were driving in my two-month-old car to visit friends of hers who turned out not to be at home. (She had a lot of friends for an Irish exchange student who had only been in the country for seven months.) On our way back to her house, Maggie was briefly quiet and pensive, and then she blurted out, "You can say no if you want, and I'll totally understand, but would it be possible for me to drive your car?" Once I didn't say no immediately, she put on the pressure. "I really need to practice on a stick-shift . . . I've got my permit with me." Well, sure, what the heck.

We pulled into the new and only partly completed Pacific Heights subdivision. It was very quiet at 4:30 in the afternoon, and the one broad and freshly paved street that ran through the development was P-shaped, so that the inner loop didn't connect with any cross streets or traffic. I drove a couple of times around to coach her a little bit and then pulled over so we could trade sides.

Maggie was tentative at first, not willing to bring the clutch pedal up at all for fear of killing the engine. I had her break down the job into segments, not worrying about steering but just rolling the car from a stop to ten miles an hour along the curb, stopping, letting the clutch out and rolling along the curb again, stopping. After about five minutes of practicing starts, she'd gotten pretty good at it, only jerking a few times, and we started the loop course. Her steering and braking were fine, as were her shifts from second to third and third to fourth; it was just the feel of the clutch engaging and the engine revving under no load that were hard for her to gauge.

At one point, after about twenty minutes of fair success, she had a couple of tough starts and shifts in succession. Frustrated, she started to think about what she was doing rather than just doing it, and she got progressively worse. I asked her to pull over to the curb, and we switched seats so I could drive. "Close your eyes and listen to the engine when we shift," I said, and she did as I drove one loop around. Then she took the wheel again, and was much better. "Have you ever taught anyone to drive before?" she asked, pleased with her regained dexterity. "You're a very good teacher."

After three or four more successful laps, I had her pull over again. She left the engine running, set the parking brake and put the shifter in neutral, and started to open the door. I said, "No, you're staying in. I'm getting out."

"What?! Really? No, I can't do that!"

"Sure you can." I got out. Maggie, staring ahead in grim determination, released the brake, put the shifter into first, turned on the left-turn signal, and slowly pulled away from the curb. That tightness lasted about two minutes, but then she began to realize that she really could drive a stick; her driving was smoother and more relaxed every time she went around the loop. Even now, I can still see my little purple car scooting along the back straightaway, Maggie smiling broadly as she downshifted from fourth to third to make the last corner.

She kept turning back into the loop over and over—we'd still be there if I hadn't called a halt to it at about 6:40 and driven us back to school for her French Club presentation. "God, I love driving! That was so much fun!"

We could talk about the car as a way to proclaim both adulthood and (especially) manhood through transference of the car's attributes to its driver. The modifications boys made to their cars were immediately evident—huge suspension lifts on their pickups, big tires on their muscle cars, easy-flow exhaust systems that made the car sound fast just at idle. Nobody talked about better brakes or fine-tuned suspensions that allowed better handling—those were invisible and inaudible, and thus not worth bothering with. Boys talked in numerical code: putting in a set of 4.11's and switching to R60/15s, maybe installing a pair of Holley 750s and doing a thirty-thousandths overbore when they rebuild their 350 in Mr. Fischer's class next year. And for boys who really loved cars, no conversation was complete without sound effects; to be a part of this group required the ability to imitate car sounds, especially spinning tires. They lived for the sound of burnouts, or in their words, "big ol' monster smoky burnouts" or "lockin' up the hubs and diggin' in."

The car also acted as a social marker, a group identifier. When we talk about cars as status symbols, we most often refer to the status of the individual as wealthy or stylish. There was some of that, certainly, but the decoration and modification of the car had a more important status-marking role: it told others what group an individual was part of. Kirk's car, for instance, was representative of the Surfers—the Green Party bumper sticker and the surfboard rack on top of the car with its foam pads wrapped in old dishtowels, the Aerosmith and Ziggy Marley CDs piled on the back window deck. Parts of the car didn't work, and no one cared. "You can't roll that window down—it's off the track and it just falls into the door."

The music inside the car was another social marker. Cars without radios or tape players were extremely rare; on nice days, the parking lot was a sequence of five-second concerts as cars and trucks drove by with their windows down, proclaiming the allegiance of each body of passengers. Even in a radio market as small as Timber County, there are strictly formatted stations, and kids tended to land on one of the seven or eight options and claim it as their station to the exclusion of all others. Mistakes in music were immediately commented on—sometimes severely, as when Laurie hit an unfamiliar station in passing, and Amy cried out, "Country music! My ears are bleeding!"

For some groups, the actual name-brand of the vehicle was an important part of group membership. Duane was a Chevy guy, and took that seriously. "Some guys swear on Chevys and some guys swear on Fords. There's a few guys who like Dodges, like my friend, he has a Dodge truck, but he likes Chevys, too, and hates Fords." This is sort of like our relationships with sports teams: we love the Packers and hate the Bears. But with brand names it's more immediate: you can actually own a Chevy truck and be part of the team, even if only in a limited way. And this desire to identify isn't limited to teenagers. Kurt, the thirtyish manager of the Arco station up by the freeway, had come out to survey his lunch crowd over by the picnic tables just as some recent Curtisville grads came careening around the highway off-ramp in their Ford Bronco, bouncing into the parking lot. As they passed by Kurt, he hollered out, "Hey, buddy! No Fords in this lot!"

Ritual belonging to mythical groups is a common feature of American life, from indistinguishable political parties to indistinguishable sports teams to indistinguishable consumer brands.[2] Republican/Democrat, Pepsi/Coke, McDonald's/Burger King, Marlboro/Winston, Skoal/Copenhagen, Nike/Reebok, DOS/Mac, Chevy/Ford. We don't just choose one or the other based on their objective qualities—we choose the community to which we want to belong. We attribute magical qualities to our chosen selection, qualities which don't reside so much in the product as in our imagined selves with regard to those products and their other adherents. We become part of a social group that has no human contact, that exists only through media like "Hot Chevies" magazine and the decals on the sides of our favorite NASCAR racing team. We replace community with product placement, belonging with brand loyalty.

But even though I saw all of those things, I want to talk about two other characteristics of the car that I haven't read much about in the past. The first is that the car allows extraordinary privacy, more than any other place in teenagers' lives. In the car, they're sealed off from others who can no longer reach out to affect them. When they drive at thirty-five or forty miles an hour, others no longer see them within their cars, but rather the cars themselves as potential hazards or facts of navigation; the occupants inside become invisible and untouchable.[3] Their cars allow them to remove themselves from the places where people know them, to go to other cities where they will become anonymous, to leave behind the prying of neighbors and parents and teachers and spend an hour off campus or in the woods, or a day in a larger town.

Kids could also use the car for their secret hiding spot, a place to hold forbidden cigarettes and magazines. The car was really the only room in many of these kids' lives that they had complete and total control over. Their folks wouldn't think twice about going into their kids' rooms, whether to clean or to put away laundry or just to look around; and there were rules set on just what the kids could do to their rooms, from the volume of their music to the color of the walls and ceilings. ("I wanted to paint my bedroom black, but my mom wouldn't let me." How many times have I heard this—and wanted to do it myself when I was fourteen—and what does it mean?) Those rules, and that invasiveness, didn't exist for their cars.

The car was the parlor, the seat of entertainment and visiting. Access to the car was by invitation only, a privilege extended only to their closest social group. The close personal distancing—you sit much closer together than you stand in public, much closer together than you ever sit in your house—lends an intimacy that often spurs intimate talk. I learned more secrets in cars than I learned anywhere else; we're together, we're close, we're confidential, it's natural to talk about things that are close and confidential. We're allowed to have anyone we want to join us for as long as we want, and we can do anything we like. Adults take this for granted because they have the house or apartment over which they hold complete control of access, but kids have no such control over home or even their portion of the home. The car, though, was all theirs. It was an expression of self, an environment built slowly through habitation and wear and the accretion of gum wrappers, a relationship redefined and reinforced every time they encountered it or shared it with someone else.

❧

The other thing I want to talk about is why kids named their cars. Over the course of the year, I rode not only in the Flymobile, but also in Seymour, the Beast, the Swinger, the Stang and the Big F. Because I finally had my own car (Raspberry), I offered lots of rides to lots of kids and didn't get to encounter the insides of all that many of their cars, but so many that I was in had a name.

Did kids name their bedrooms? No.

Did they name their lockers? No.

They named their cars.

Naming a car makes it different from all the others, and takes it away from its status as mass-produced object. The act of naming invests uniqueness in the object, as well as infusing an element of self into it, a name that the owner selected and their friends approved.[4] The names were usually sort of ironic, a way to say "this car is me, but it's not as cool as the me I could be." The Beast was Laurie's way to simultaneously proclaim and deny her self-image through a relatively staid and disheveled gray Mitsubishi with a transaxle problem. The Big F was a pretty grand name for a beat-to-hell Ford F-250 pickup.

The Swinger got its name from Dodge; in its late-60s/early-70s rush to be hip, Dodge had advertised the "Swinger" edition of the Dart, with its bucket seats and large but nonfunctional hood scoops, as the vehicle for the fun-loving young adult. For Ethan to call his car the Swinger was his distancing from that carefree teen role, his admission that he was a loner and that it was ironically funny that he was driving a car proclaiming him "the Swinger" in chrome script on the front fender.

Naming a car goes along with decorating it, which the kids almost invariably did in some manner. Usually, they started from the inside, with stickers on the visors and strings of beads hanging from the rear-view mirror, custom gear-shift knobs and steering-wheel covers. The stereo, of course, was an obvious statement of self and group, filled as it was with personal choices about music. Most often, the girls embellished only the inside, perhaps going as far as to put on a bumper sticker or two and maybe a personalized license-plate frame ("No, This Is Not My Boyfriend's Truck," for instance). Boys were more overt, with their decals and custom wheels and unmuffled exhaust.

When I asked Ivy to describe her favorite place, she immediately talked about her white Nissan pickup Seymour (named for the plant store clerk in "Little Shop of Horrors"): "My favorite place . . . I like to be in my truck. It's me, it fits me, my truck is like the perfect size for me, even though the seat is messed up and I have to like sit on my jacket." She laughed. "But, I don't know, it's . . . I'm used to my truck, I know how it works, it's an extension of me. And my antenna is an old coat hanger, and it's getting all rusty, and it's tied in a knot,"—she laughed again—"it's really pathetic, but I really like it. There's a little rubber chicken hanging from the rear view mirror. It's mine when I'm in it by myself, 'cause I don't have to worry about the other people in it, are they cold or are they hot, or anything, and I don't have to adjust the temperature or the radio, it's just me and I don't have to worry about anyone."

Ivy graduated from Curtisville High last spring. While she was attending a graduation party, her father and sister painted a mural of entwined ivy across Seymour's hood and sides. It was the best graduation present anyone could have gotten.

ॐ

I got the word on a September Thursday that Saturday was "cruise night," and again on Friday afternoon two guys mentioned that it was almost time for "American Cruise Night" in Port City.

I got to town at about 8:00 P.M., and already there were a fair number of people making the loop—south on 4th to D and the carwash parking lot, back north on 5th to P and the Circle Burger parking lot or to 5th and R and the Burger King parking lot. I made the loop a couple of times on my motorcycle (I didn't own Raspberry at that point) to get a feel for the protocol and then parked the bike and walked the circuit several times.

At Circle Burger, there were half a dozen customized cars already gathered, along with a pickup whose bed opened out into a massive stereo cabinet with banks of flashing red and blue lights. Spectators were setting up lawn chairs on the sidewalk and taking places on retaining walls and benches, as though it were a Fourth of July parade. Two pickups full of cowboys and cowgirls in their mid-twenties were parked in front of the New West Saloon on 5th, and they had barbecue grills on the curb behind the tailgates.

The trucks in the promenade were almost all modified: raised-suspension Curtisville mud trucks or chopped and lowered urban cruisers. The cars were a much more mixed bag. Some were custom or restored cars, some were hot rods, but a larger number were beaters, Japanese econo-boxes, Mom's cars—it didn't seem to matter so long as there was a stereo and room for six.[5] There were a fair number of high-school age kids, both in cars and on the curbs, but a larger number looked to be post-high, early twenties. The custom cars were often driven by guys in their thirties and forties.

A rusty Ford Escort passed by me, and I heard a girl's voice—"Look, it's Herb!" Then I heard more voices—"Hey, Herb! Hi, Herb!" All six occupants were leaning out the driver's-side windows and waving at me. I recognized them from school but knew only one by name. They certainly weren't this demonstrative on the Quad at school, but their protection within the car, their mobility, their safety in numbers and the unlikeliness of our meeting had made them bold. They never greeted me as enthusiastically again.

The police were a visible part of the cruise as well. Apparently, Port City had a "cruising problem" in the recent past, and was trying to work with car clubs to remedy it by allowing them to have an official car show with a parade. But that was three weeks earlier—this night's cruise wasn't part of that. Nonetheless, the cops were tolerant, knowing that they couldn't hold back the tide but merely regulate and channel it. They did fine.

The cruise felt familiar to me, even though I'd never done it when I was a kid. Sitting on the sidewalk, watching the pickups and overpacked sedans roll by, I tried to think of where I'd seen this event before. It took about forty minutes to realize that it felt like a bowling league. Anyone was welcome to participate, and hundreds did at all different levels of skill and commitment. Sociability was the key, hanging out with your friends on a regular night and at a regular time and doing something that you all appreciated. It didn't much matter whether you were the best or not, because it was fun to see those who were.

And to some extent, it didn't matter whether you even liked the game all that much—in this case, custom cars—because there were little pockets of people all along the sidewalk for the whole thirty-block loop, a series of mini-parties in the cool September night. Cars or bowling—there's no difference when the real reason is to see friends and watch people go by.

A year after I left Curtisville High, I ran into Laurie. She was full-time at Timber State and half-time at a big department store in the mall, and she had gotten rid of the Beast in favor of a brand new sea green Toyota Tercel.

"I saw you've got a new car."

"Yeah, it's great, I love it."

"What's it's name?"

Laurie smiled. "It doesn't have a name, it's just my car."

"Doesn't have a name?! How can your car not have a name?"

"Well, none of my friends are here to help me name it."

CHAPTER SIX

---

*One Night in Manoa**

The Manoa Community Center used to be a grade school: two buildings, one story each, surrounded by overhangs covering the connecting walkways, high windows delivering light without view into the classrooms. It was no different than Curtisville High, just smaller. The buildings are surrounded by a gravel lot and a bunch of picnic tables, the whole scene ringed with a chain-link fence. It's located well off the highway in Manoa, fifteen miles from Curtisville, out where the mobile homes and perpetually parked busses meet the dunes.

At 6:30 on a January Friday night, I drove out to Manoa and gave five dollars to Benjamin at the folding table just inside the door. He and his partners Quentin and Allen from Curtisville and Wally from Union High were putting on a punk music show. Benjamin had given me the flyer two days earlier at school in the Drama Room. It consisted of the names of seven bands, a hand-drawn map to the Community Center, and a date and time, all photocopied from a felt-pen original. Three or four of the bands were local, including the current favorites Gaucho, but the others were traveling from as far south as the suburbs of San Francisco and as

---

*An earlier version of this chapter appeared as part of Herb Childress, "Kinder Ethnographic Writing," *Qualitative Inquiry*, vol. 4, no. 2, pp. 249–264. Copyright © 1998 by Sage Publications, Inc. Reprinted by Permission of Sage Publications, Inc.

far north as Seattle. Five bucks for seven bands. "You ought to come," Benjamin said.

There were about fifty people in the room ahead of me, including the high school jazz band saxophone star I'd seen on stage at the school a month earlier playing Duke Ellington and Tommy Dorsey. The band onstage wasn't on the bill; they'd just brought their gear and started playing before the first real band got underway. They were a bass player and guitarist, both of them girls of about seventeen or eighteen, and a male drummer in his early twenties. The bass player never looked at anything except her fret hand. Her fingering was sure, if not fluid, and the effort showed on her face.

We occupied what had once been the gym/auditorium, with painted concrete floor, plywood walls, and a distant acoustic fiber tile ceiling. A continuous wooden bench with thin coarse-cloth padding, like the pews of a hard-luck chapel, ringed the room against the side and rear walls. The fluorescent lamps, covered with metal screens to avoid damage during dodge-ball, were all turned off so that just the stage lights were on.

Under those lights stood a plywood platform, twenty-five feet wide and about two feet tall. Off to the side was a mixing board and two big monitors, owned by Gaucho. They were the only band that had made enough money to afford professional sound equipment. As expensive as it was, though, it wasn't treated as a precious object; the other arrivals, including even the first nonband, freely patched their guitars and microphones into Gaucho's amplifiers and mixing console without supervision.

By 7:00, the first official band was setting up—a group of high schoolers called Stub, who'd driven 250 miles from their hometown for the show—and the crowd had grown to about ninety. They, too, were high school kids; a few were in their early-twenties, and one couple older than me was there with their teenage son. Lots of pierced nostrils and septa, one pierced eyebrow, a couple of pierced lips. One muscular early-twenties guy had dressed in full '70s glam-punk: long stringy straight black hair, white makeup with a black harlequin star painted over a third of his face, black leather jacket, a silver-studded black leather choker about an inch and a half thick, black and white rock band t-shirt, shredded denim shorts with a thick leather belt around his right thigh. He talked briefly with a girl who had three piercings in her nose and a hooded sweatshirt declaring "Pussy power" in iron-on letters across her upper back.

Once Stub seemed to be running smoothly, Quentin and Allen and Benjamin left Wally at the door alone and found me. "Come on," they said, and we ran together up the dunes behind the community center, rolling and diving in the near-dark down the sandy slope. After about fifteen minutes, Quentin stopped, looked out over the parking lot and called out, "Truck!" Benjamin replied, "See any cowboy hats?" The cowboy/punk opposition had periodically come to blows in the past, but this particular pickup rolled back out of the lot with no menace.

As we descended from the dunes, I asked Benjamin and Quentin whether there were any bands at Curtisville. Benjamin immediately said, "Nah, I don't think so . . ."

"Unless they're like, twang, twang," added Quentin.

Benjamin laughed. "Yeah, 'My cow wasn't very good last night.' "

Back in the gym, Stub was so loud that I couldn't hear Benjamin shouting at me from about a foot away (well, I could *hear* him, but I couldn't make out any words). There were over a hundred people in the dance hall, with maybe twenty-five more outside, and I decided to go back outdoors for a bit. Groups of two to six kids leaned on posts and walls near the door, and a couple of clusters of two or three sat out in the dark against the back of the classroom building. I saw only a handful of beer bottles, but lots and lots of cigarettes.

At about 8:00, Stub finished their set, and I came back in. By 8:10, the local band Boxing with Timmy was on the stage. At a big arena show, there might be an hour's gap between the opening act and the headliners, but not here; the equipment was simple and the bands were eager to get onto the stage. Boxing with Timmy consisted of a guitarist, bassist, and drummer, all boys about eighteen, and a female singer of about the same age. The first song, "Chocolate," had only one line that I could make out, and I heard it several times: *"I don't care I don't care I don't CARE what you say . . . I . . . don't . . . give . . . a . . . flying . . . FUCK about you!"* A not especially polished lyric, but it lay close to home for its writer. Punk isn't about learning someone else's material.

Dancing to punk music isn't about learning someone else's moves, either, nothing like the choreographed country line dancing so popular at Curtisville High. I followed the basic educational pattern of "learning by doing," and found that slamming is conceptually simple. You just crowd into the mosh pit, leaping through the loose and timid fringe toward the stage and into the dense core; keep your arms up tight against your chest or down against your hips and your elbows tucked in against your ribs as best you can; and bang the hell out of whoever stands close to you. You bounce up and down until you can aim at someone and try to contact them with as much of your side/upper arm/shoulder as you can. Of course, while you're aiming at someone, somebody else could blindside *you*. When you fall, someone else will fall over you; when you fly out of the pit, someone will push you back in again to bounce around like a hot electron. Imagine bumper cars at the county fair, but without the glitz (or the padding). People with glasses left them at the table in the back.

After fifteen minutes in the pit, I went outside to get some rest and air, and to take down some notes in my little shirt-pocket spiral notebook. I perched on a picnic table to take down some of the outdoor scene; I'd already been writing on and off inside for forty minutes. I could hear people up in the dunes playing tag; small groups sat on the concrete patio in back of the building, sharing cigarettes and small talk. I'd hardly started noting all this when a very large and sturdy-looking fellow—shave the goatee and put him into uniform, and he'd have looked like a college baseball player—appeared beside me in the darkness. "You know, you're making a lot of people nervous with that notebook," he said quietly.

"Yeah, I do that."

"Well, I just want you to know that if a whole bunch of people decide to start pounding on you, there isn't a whole lot I can do." And he walked away. I put the notebook back into my shirt pocket and went inside, and when Boxing with Timmy finished their song, the singer said into the microphone, "The security guard just told me that there's an authority figure here tonight who's writing down names of people who are drinking underage. So if you're drinking underage, just be inconspicuous about it." That got a big laugh, but I figured that enough people had seen me writing that I should clear things up before I got thumped.

I found Benjamin and explained my situation. He said, "Do you want me to clear your name?"

"Please."

"Okay, who talked to you?"

I pointed him out, and a couple of minutes later I was outside talking with the big guy again. His name was Blake, and he was in charge of keeping the peace at these events. I don't know what Benjamin said to him, but it must have convinced him. "I really didn't mean to threaten you, I was just telling you how people felt. There are a lot of old-time punks here who are used to getting harassed, and they just don't put up with it." We had a real nice ten-minute conversation, my questions interspersed with Blake apologizing again every twenty seconds.

Blake's narrative of teen social life:

See, I'm from Redding, and over there when you're sixteen, your dad sticks a beer in your hand and says, "Welcome to manhood." And he keeps handing them to you until you pass out or puke. There's nothing like that here—maybe in Curtisville, but the Union kids got nothing to do, no place to go. There's no parks or anything. So we've been doing these shows for a little over a year now. There's never been any problems, never anything bad happen. Well, I broke a guy's nose once, he was diving off the stage and I head-butted him, but it was an accident. But basically, we just want a place where we can listen to music, smoke cigarettes, and get drunk if we can. The people that rent us the place want us to have Pinkerton guards, regular security guards with uniforms and radios and stuff. When we've had them before, the kids just stand around and don't dance or do anything. Now we do security ourselves, and we never have any problems.

We parted as friends. Later, Blake dragged me back into the pit, saying that I had to get the full experience if I was going to write anything good. I ended up on the floor a couple of times and got my nose flattened again, but I was getting a clue and doing as well as a small person can do in the pit.

By 9:30, there were well over two hundred people in the gym, and another fifty or more outside. Benjamin was still in charge at the door, but he occasionally nabbed one of the other three to cover for him while he went off to dance in the pit or check out some potential problem outdoors. At five dollars a head, well over a thousand dollars had been stashed into a little cardboard mailing box on the folding table. The box went unwatched for ten or fifteen seconds at a time during shift changes or when Benjamin was collecting more money and stamping someone's hand. Whenever the box got too full to close, he grabbed a handful of cash and put it into the safe (the trunk of Wally's car). By a little after ten, Benjamin stuck the cash box into the trunk, folded up the table, and opened the show up for free.

There was constant motion in and out the single door, a steady thirty or forty people a minute between 8:00 and 10:30. Most teen dances have a strict no-exit rule; once you leave, you're gone for the night. In Manoa, we all flowed in and out like bees. Crowds of people stood and leaned near the door, around the entry, out in the parking lot, in and on people's cars. We were all submerged into a single stream, exuberant and barely controlled. We banged into other people, danced on chairs, and didn't quite know where our hands were until they were stopped by a solid object.

Tactile immersion carried its price: not purposeful damage, but damage nonetheless. I got popped in the nose by a guy who was vigorously hugging a girl he'd just run into—as they continued past me, he thumped me on the shoulder a couple of times by way of apology. The paper towel dispenser in the men's room was lying in the wastebasket, and one of the bench seats had cracked from its support a little bit because there were eight people dancing on it while Blade was playing. Late in the evening, Quentin said, "I don't know hardly anyone here, which is funny because I've been smashing bodies against almost all of them and in a big pile on top of about six of them." I encountered one of Quentin's smashees mopping up his bloody nose in the bathroom; Quentin had been flung out of the pit, a human Scud landing on top of this fellow and his girlfriend as they made out on the side bench. Shortly thereafter, that same couple was in the same spot, as deeply intertwined as before.

I left at eleven, exhausted and pounded and two-thirds deaf. Benjamin later told me that the show had closed up about one in the morning. "You should have stayed for Tsunami. They were awesome—and the pit was huge. I was on my ass so many times." He said that after the show ended and the last kids had driven away, the promoters and the band members stood in the parking lot and divided the receipts. They started with five hundred dollars to pay for the Community Center. The seven bands each got a one-eighth share of the remainder, enough for gas and food to get their vans and station wagons to the next town; Benjamin and Quentin and Wally and Allen and and my new pal Blake shared the last eighth, and went off to breakfast at a twenty-four-hour Denny's.

For about eight hours, with few resources and no adult assistance, four high school kids and their friends had brought forth out of the darkness an amazing chaos in pursuit of a clear and orderly set of goals. Human contact. Conversation. Movement and abandon. Sensory overload. Control and authority. Doing it yourself. They weren't part of the rock'n'roll empire, but they were part of its spirit. They didn't have much money, so their efforts were rough, but they got the job done. No grown-ups had to tell them what to do.

I never saw another example like it all year.

CHAPTER SEVEN

The Dead Zone

During the week of school immediately before the Christmas holidays, the citizens of Curtisville High observed their own festival: Curtisville Students Against Drugs, Alcohol and Tobacco. During lunch period all week, the SECS Club (pronounced "sex," and standing for Students Exhibiting Common Sense) promoted different activities to stand as alternatives to drinking and smoking: on Tuesday, a bubble-gum-blowing contest; on Wednesday, a "virgin drink" booth on the Quad; on Thursday, a motivational speaker.

On Friday, the capstone day, the central data byte drilled into us all morning at the beginning of each class was that a high school student was killed every ten minutes because of drinking and driving. It didn't sound right to me, so I did the math: six students per hour times twenty-four hours per day times 365 days per year equals 52,560 dead teenagers annually. Our nation's total automotive death count in 1993 was 40,300; Common Sense was apparently interspersed with a bit of hysteria.

Also on Friday, the Grim Reaper—a SECS Club parent dressed in a death mask and a sheet, carrying a big plastic scythe—summoned a preselected victim out of every class over the course of the morning in an attempt to dramatize the suddenness with which a friend could be taken and how many could die in alcohol-related accidents. Later that day, all of the victims were gathered at the center of the gym floor at the afternoon assembly to reinforce the potential for danger over the holiday party season.

Twelve hours later, Parker Mays was dead. He'd been driving home from a party at about 2:30 in the morning and was unable to handle the long curve on U.S. 420 heading north. His pickup flipped over in the median. He was thrown out of his truck and onto the southbound lane, and was run over by a van while lying in the road.

Within two days, a wooden cross with a wreath appeared on the grass at the edge of 420, marking the spot of Parker's death. Once school opened again, a memorial service was held in the multipurpose room at lunch.

Four months later, I was at track practice. The distance runners had taken off for the airport, and I was standing at the rail of the track talking with Bear, the winter wrestler turned springtime shot-putter and discus thrower, and Sally, a sprinter. Bear asked me if I'd been to any big parties lately. "Haven't heard of any," I replied.

"Me neither," said Bear. "Probably won't be any until graduation. It was really quiet after Parker died. People kind of quit drinking, we were all like, 'poor Park.' " Bear smiled kind of sheepishly. "Then it was like, 'Oh, poor Park . . . but there's nothing to do anymore.' And then it was, 'Let's have a drink to Park.' "

"You know what really pissed me off is when those guys went and drank a bunch of 40s at Parker's wreath," Sally said. 40s, by the way, refer to the 40-ounce bottles of beer or malt liquor that are cheap and plentiful at convenience stores. "That's so sick, going and drinking beer where a person you knew died from drinking. That's just stupid."

Bear looked at me like he was going to say something, but then he looked at Sally and then down at his shoes. "Yeah," he said quietly.

Benjamin found me in the halls at school. He was jittery and quiet, a far cry from his usual outgoing self. "Herb, I need to ask you to do something for me."

"Sure. What?"

"My uncle Jeff killed himself yesterday. Can you come to the funeral this week?"

"Sure. I mean, yeah, jeez. What happened?"

"I dunno. He was over on Saturday, and his wife, my mom's sister, was staying with us because he was beating her, and he found out where she was, and he came over and was trying to get her to come back with him. He was yelling and stuff. And then he killed himself." He was getting paler even just telling me this much. I thought Jeff had killed himself at Benjamin's house, which wasn't true, but the story wasn't coming out clearly. "I'll talk to you about it later, okay?"

"Yeah. Tell me where the funeral is, and I'll be there. Call me if you need anything." I gave him a hug and he walked away to class.

Two days later on Thursday, I drove to Port City and the Saint Francis parish church. Benjamin's stepfather Jim greeted me at the entry and handed me a memorial. I went to be with Benjamin because he'd asked, but I still think Jim thinks I was there as an observer—"let's see how kids handle trauma"—and I'm writing this, so I suppose I was after all.

Benjamin and his sister Nicole were ushering. I shook his hand, but I don't know that it registered much that I was there. He was somber and official as he led me into the chapel. There were about a hundred people in the room, all facing the closed casket. It was surrounded with flowers. Two studio photos of Jeff and his wife stood on easels in front of it. The men wore their best suits or their Georgetown basketball t-shirts; the women wore their business dresses or their tight new country-dancing jeans.

Benjamin never did talk to me about his uncle or about the funeral, but he gave me his research journal at the end of the school year. I'd given all of my volunteers a journal to fill out for the semester, with goofy cartoons photocopied all through it just as my research methods instructor had suggested three years earlier. In it, I had a space for every day from January through May, with the instructions:

> *Pick one place and time from your day today:*
> *This was a _____ place / event. (Describe in a word.)*
> *The part of being there that made me feel best was:*
> *The part of being there that made me feel worst was:*

Benjamin's journal for the weekend had looked like this:

Date: *4 / 08, Saturday*
Time: *Morn.*

Place:	*w / Tasha & cops*
Description:	*angry, frustrating, annoying, surprising, depressing, discouraging, tense.*
Best:	*There was no best. I guess it's that he (Jeff) was going to get help.*
Worst:	*Uncle Jeff beat his wife. He was always "the man"—Never hit girls—things like that ya know.*

Date:	*4 / 09, Sunday*
Time:	*Morn.*
Place:	*living room*
Description:	*frustrating, sad (kinda), annoying, surprising, tremendous, depressing, calm, tense, humbling (ya know)*
Best:	*There was no best.*
Worst:	*Jeff tried to kill Tasha then he killed himself. . . .*

Date:	*4 / 09, Sunday*
Time:	*later*
Place:	*Jeff's bedroom*
Description:	*sad, surprising, tremendous, humbling (ya know), lost senses, fucked up*
Best:	*I guess it was that I got to see it (& to keep parts)*
Worst:	*It was my Uncle's blood that coated the ceiling (whatever) and, well, it really sucked.*

I found out later that the "parts" were in fact two shards of Jeff's skull that Benjamin picked up from the carpet and took home.

Date:	*4 / 10, Monday*
Time:	*12:45*
Place:	*School*
Description:	*Frustrating, sad, annoying, surprising, discouraging, tense (kinda), strange*

Best:	*No best. Just getting it off my chest and them (Suzanne and Diane, the school attendance secretaries) being understanding enough to let like Jim or Willy or someone else clear the absence.*
Worst:	*They knew about it! HOW! It pissed me off.*

Date:	*4/11, Tuesday*
Place:	*School, like the whole thing*
Description:	*fucked up, challenging, frustrating, sad, tired, depressing, tedious*
Best:	*Um, well, I could tell people what was up, and they showed some compassion/sympathy.*
Worst:	*The events of the weekend pummeled me all day.*

Date:	*4/12, Wednesday*
Place:	*Aunt Lucia's house/ranch*
Description:	*working, clear and cleaning, challenging, dull, okay, so-so, annoying, boring*
Best:	*I was helping to make the funeral reception better. (We were treated to lunch at Lucia's Mexican restaurant, Aunt Lucia & my Uncle Reynaldo own it.)*
Worst:	*D.Z. [Benjamin's cousin] was bugging the piss outta me.*

Date:	*4/13, Thursday*
Place:	*Funeral*
Description:	*time for me to be strong for my family, angry, challenging, dull, frustrating, sad, depressing, interesting, tense*
Best:	*Being there to help my family cope with such a loss of life (sounds cliche but....)*
Worst:	*It was a funeral (also I broke my VOW not to enter a church . . . But it was for a good cause . . .)*

Three days later, he wrote:

Date:	*4 / 16, Sunday*
Time:	*12:00* A.M.
Place:	*Room, going to sleep*
Description:	*weird, frustrating, sad, annoying, depressing*
Best:	*Nothing, I was . . . funked up . . . .*
Worst:	*I kept thinking of Jeff, & his 2 pieces . . . & his spirit locked in my room since I have those pieces. . . . I was scared (kinda)*

We try to shield kids from the pains of the world. But part of the development of a self is the beginnings of the awareness that the self will end, that all life will close with a death. The chapels and cemeteries where the dead are memorialized are useful for distancing death, useful also for remembering the life that came before the end of life. But the end of life itself is an important fact, as uncomfortable a fact as it is. It was important for Bear and his friends to sit at the spot of Parker's death, at night, as the freeway traffic rushed past. It was important for Benjamin to see Jeff's bedroom, to literally put his hands on death. Both kids were taking their first steps toward learning death, and they both sought out the places where death appeared. These visitations were honest pilgrimages—in Bear's case, a pilgrimage accompanied by a group that would have felt threatened by admitting to one another any spiritual overtones, so they took beer and pretended it was recreation instead. Like a Civil War battleground, this modest bedroom and this dark highway had become urgent, had become necessary, had become sacred.

CHAPTER EIGHT

Birthday at Oyster Beach

On a Friday morning, Ethan asked me before history class if I'd come to his eighteenth birthday party that night out on Oyster Beach, partly to help him celebrate and partly to be a driver afterwards. I told him I was following Laurie all day and evening, but that I'd come out later if he was still there. He looked discouraged; he was already concerned that the turnout would be small, and he didn't think they'd be out all that late. But Laurie left the basketball game before nine to go home to bed, so I drove out to Oyster Beach. Sure enough, the Swinger was in the parking lot along with seven or eight other cars.

I walked out through the dune grass and onto the beach. The February night was mostly clear and the moon three-quarters full, so I could see pretty well. I walked toward a large bonfire straight ahead, but it was home only to a snuggling couple in their mid-twenties. The night was warm and the ocean sounded wonderful, though, so I stayed on the beach to walk along the hard-packed wave slope. After about ten minutes, I saw another fire glowing a little farther south, at the edge of the brush where I'd been to a party months before. As I walked up toward it, bottle rockets whistled and popped over my head. I stayed low and walked through the artillery fire; sure enough, it was Ethan, along with and Damien and Nick and Damien's older brother Paul who had bought the two twelve-packs of Miller. Once Ethan could recognize me in the firelight, he smiled in pure pleasure. "Herb! You came for my birthday, man! That's cool."

They hadn't seen me coming until I was twenty feet away. "Man, we must have been shooting those things right at you!" I had a can of beer to celebrate Ethan's birthday, and shot off a handful of bottle rockets across the beach toward the ocean.

We sat on a driftwood log in front of the fire and talked for forty minutes. The bottle rockets were good at covering any brief lapses in the conversation. I held my empty beer can to ward off further beer while the others drank at a leisurely pace. Ethan was quietly disappointed at the small turnout for his birthday, and a little resentful that some of his friends who had promised to be there hadn't arrived. When we got up to stretch our legs for a second, though, we could see a lot of people around the other fire I'd seen at the start. We gathered our empty cans, kicked sand onto the dwindling flames, and walked the hundred yards or so to see if the other group had intercepted any of Ethan's guests. Sure enough, we recognized about half of that bunch of thirty. They had a bigger fire and more people, so we stayed there instead.

As with the last beach party I'd been to, several kids were leery of the fact that I was there and kept their distance from me, but most of them were calm about it, and a few enjoyed having me around. Firecrackers popped next to our heads. Small groups of three to eight kids walked off to smoke their pot away from the big crowd, huddling together in the night before meandering back toward the fire. Ethan said to me, "I'm gonna have a bowl[1] for my birthday, and someone said they had a hit of acid they'd give me. Keep an eye on me, okay?" He walked off toward the grasses.

An older guy (maybe thirty) was there with his guitar, and played for almost an hour in exchange for a beer and a small pipeful of pot. A small batch of kids stood quietly around him as he sang "Hotel California."

By 10:30, about fifty people milled around the fire. Although there was no keg nor any more canned beer, several kids had bottles of liquor in varying types and sizes. That made me a little nervous, because there's really no reason for straight liquor other than to get badly drunk. It tastes horrible on its own, and it's not as though anybody brought any club soda to make mixed drinks with. But for the most part, the bottles seemed to act as props rather than as serious drink—it was cool to have a bottle, but not many people actually took much from them. Every bottle I saw started out and stayed three-quarters full.

Ethan continued to investigate the possibility of finding a hit of acid. As it turned out, though, he stopped with his five or six early beers and a few shared pipes of weed. He was pretty high, but a calm and smiling high.

At about 11:15, one of the guys came up to the fire and said, "The sheriffs are coming." We thought he meant in a few minutes, and one guy said, "Nah, the sheriffs never come down here." Actually, he meant within about fifteen seconds, because the sheriff's deputies had already arrived. The four of them were cool about things, and they just walked around the fire telling people, "Time to go home." The park had officially closed at dusk; though camping and nighttime walks were informally allowed, Timber County also had a 10:00 P.M. curfew for minors. The deputies looked at us all as we went by, checking for kids who might have been dangerously intoxicated, but didn't find any.

As the deputies stayed behind on the beach for a minute to shovel out the fire, the group I was with walked out to the parking lot, picking up other people's cans as we walked along the trail. We arrived at the parking lot; a few kids took the opportunity to toss a couple of the crushed and dripping cans onto one of the sheriff's cruisers, and Jake spit on the hood.

Jake, a wrestler, had pulled a muscle in his back a couple of weeks earlier and was on anti-inflammatory and muscle-relaxant drugs. Thus he wasn't drinking or smoking pot, so he volunteered to drive Ethan's car. I took Ethan, Nick, Damien, and Paul to Damien's house in my car, and Jake followed in the Swinger. Damien and Paul both thanked me seven or eight times during the five-mile drive for getting them home safely. I think Nick was asleep. Ethan sat beside me in the front, his lanky six-foot-four body wedged into the space where my five-foot-five wife usually rode, quietly watching the passing houses lit up against the dark woods.

We pulled into the trailer court where Damien lived, and we all stood around the cars and talked quietly for a few minutes. Ethan said to me, "I'm glad you came, man. I really appreciate it."

"I enjoyed it, thanks for asking me. Happy birthday."

I shook his hand, and Jake and I got into in my car, leaving

Ethan and the Swinger behind—Ethan was staying with Damien overnight so as not to get bugged by his parents about drinking on his birthday. Jake and I stopped at the 7-11 to get him a midnight Pepsi and then drove quietly out to his house in the country.

There was nothing special about Ethan's eighteenth birthday. On the day of his brand new adulthood, he had gone to the same six classes and sat in the same undersized school desks as every other school day. On the verge of a new role within his family, he avoided his family as he always did. At a celebration at least nominally focused on the occasion, he and his handful of friends were absorbed into just another Friday night beach party. On the first night of adult privilege, he and his friends were dispersed for a curfew violation.

Ethan was looking for something new, looking for a way to change. At the end of the school year, he said, "I mean, here it's the last two days of school, and we're just taking some finals and then we're gone, that's it. I could just blow off the next two days, fail all my finals, and I'd still get into Coastal College, so there isn't much motivation." He told me that he was tired of the pot he smoked four or five times a week, and with the dozen or so cigarettes he smoked every day. "Like tomorrow night is Prom night—I don't *want* to get high, and I know I shouldn't want to. I'm not like Tiffany and all the stoners who say, 'Hell yes, of *course* I'm going to get high before I go.' But it's like, when I look back in twenty years, what am I going to think? Instead of being a special night, it's going to be like, 'Yeah, I was high.'"

Ethan stood at the confluence of legal and educational emancipation, and hadn't the faintest idea how to use that new freedom. The shackles of the six-period schedule would soon be broken from his days, but he had no other schedule in mind. He no longer had to muddle through things like chemistry that other people found important, but had no sense that he'd seen anything worth devoting his newly-certified intelligence to. He had learned to navigate the educational system, but not his community, because he had never been asked to encounter his community. His passivity in the face of the school's desires, a passivity which had served him well within those boundaries, had left him unequipped to make serious and difficult choices.

On the Saturday of the weekend I was with him, we went for a walk through the marsh near Timber Bay, and we stopped along the trail to watch a seagull soaring low above us in the wind. The bird looked content, somehow, carried along on the warm breeze under his still wings; I said that he must be doing that at least in part for fun. Ethan told me about a dream he had several times: he stands on the ground, spreads his arms and starts to fly. But as he flies farther and higher, he suddenly can't fly any more, and falls. "That's supposed to mean I'm insecure."

I wish that there were a way for us adults to tell Ethan that he could fly. I wish that his status had officially changed because of something other than turning enough calendar pages and spending enough hours in ill-fitting desks, because we thought he had accomplished something worthwhile and shown us that he was ready to handle more. I wish that there were a way for his community to welcome him, his family to see him fresh, his friends to wish him goodbye and Godspeed.

Happy birthday, Ethan. I'm sorry.

CHAPTER NINE

They're Breaking Up that Old Gang of Mine

The fact that Becky had asked me to go to the midnight movie had little enough to do with me *qua* me, I think, and more to do with the resulting increase by one in the number of people who would be there for her farewell party. She had been planning her good-bye night for three weeks. Every time I saw her during August, she was either playing the *Pulp Fiction* soundtrack CD or quoting a line from the movie or asking yet another person, "Do you want to go see *Pulp Fiction* at the midnight movie on the 18th? It's the night before I leave for school."

Within a week, Curtisville's Drama Geeks would be a looser and less intense group. Becky would be at San Francisco State; Mara would be at UCLA; Carrie would break up with Julian in preparation for moving to UC-Irvine; and Rosalynd would start her high school teaching job down in South County. Relationships were cooling off, friendships being recast in a more detached mode. The midnight movies and the next night's surprise dance for Mara were the Geeks' last real chance to be a group.

I got to the Union Theater at about a quarter before midnight, with already nearly 200 people in line for tickets. The sidewalk was the court for standing and talking, and the car-deserted street was for walking. The young crowd, almost entirely under thirty, dressed in casual punk—torn jeans and leather jackets, thrift-shop turquoise sport coats and skinny ties. No cowboys, no jocks. It was still more than a week before the autumn tide of TSU students filled Union's sidewalks and apartment houses, and the kids who were at the movie were all locals.

I knew very few of the people in line, but came across Becky, Julian, and Laurie about halfway up the block. "Herb! Come on, get in line here with us." I felt a little sheepish about doing it—back in cool and urbane Berkeley, cutting in to join friends induced an ugly murmuring in the rest of the line that suggested imminent stoning—but in punk Union, I saw my hesitant entry repeated much more casually two dozen times in the next ten minutes. The Union Theater is huge anyway, and nobody had to worry about being left on the sidewalk for lack of tickets.

An extraordinary number of people seemed to know one another, and there was a real party atmosphere under the streetlights. We had as much fun watching other people as we did talking.[1] In fact, watching each other gave us all something to talk about. Calling out to passing friends, stepping into line for momentary conversations— a few people seemed somehow to know everyone in line and have a word or two with each. Three guys shared pizza slices from the take-out next to the theater, deciding while eating who was going to pay for whose movie tickets.

Once again, the physical interaction of people was fit to their social interaction; in this case, a big party in a linear space.[2] With everyone we know, we find ourselves on a continuum of acquaintanceship that spans from nodding recognition to intimate friendship, and there was a matching hierarchy of spatial behavior that went with it that night. Simple acknowledgements were taken care of while maintaining physical distance—a nod or a wave or a called-out "Hey, Glenn!" was all that was needed to say, "I know you and ought to let you know that I see you, but I don't need to impede your progress or mine in order to do it." Closer friends crossed the street or walked down the line to say hello, stopping briefly for a conversation, usually about matters at hand:

> Have you seen this movie?
> Yeah, seen it twice, it's terrific.
>
> Big crowd, hey?
> Yeah, well, it's a nice night out.

Did you see Jimmy?
He's here? When did he get back?
A couple of days ago, I think.

Well, I gotta get back to Tom, he's in line.
Okay. See ya later.

Even though the assembled community of theater and music types certainly felt comfortable with one another, these kinds of non-extended couplets of conversation were most common: bids opened, filled and closed. The distanced engagement was reflected in body position as well; the person in line was to the building side of the sidewalk, the interloper to the street side, and the arrangement of the conversation turned perpendicular to the line for its brief duration. Those who were stationary offered no invitation to stay; rather, by facing outward and holding the visitor toward the street, they offered a sort of disinvitation.

Closer friends made a more thorough spatial disruption. The person or people in line had to make adjustments to their group shape in order to accommodate the new arrival(s), who then stayed with that new group up to the ticket window. Once I arrived, our group was four. But then Ryan and Stacy showed up, and then Ivy and Mara and Larry, and then Lauren and Stephen, and then Rosalynd and Kelli and Giselle. We were never really a "group" of fifteen, of course; the sidewalk wouldn't have permitted it, nor the conventions of conversation. We were half a dozen subgroups of two or three, continually reconstituted through eavesdropping and entering new topics of discussion that we'd heard over our shoulders. Any gap in talk could be filled by entering a new and interesting subgroup within our larger crowd; that new topical allegiance brought with it a shift in location and orientation within the mass. Over the ten minutes I was in the line, I'd at least said hello and caught up on a few sentences of news with all fourteen others, and entered three or four interesting conversations.

Once we got inside, we claimed seats in a close pod about two-thirds of the way to the front. We sat (without discussing it) five across in three consecutive rows so that any one of us might still be able to talk to any other, but our closest neighbors were the people we most likely wanted to talk with for two hours. Becky sat between

Stephen and Julian, right in the geometric center of the rectangle of Geeks. I sat behind them next to Rosalynd, a Curtisville student teacher and honorary Geek, and we talked about how scared she was to be a week away from teaching five high school classes on her own. The theater churned with a hundred conversations, none loud on its own.

The movie's start was delayed considerably in light of how many people were still waiting outside to get in. But at about ten past twelve, the lights dimmed and a roaring cheer went up. Showtime had arrived.

The crowd quickly displayed its willingness to get involved in the night's proceedings. The conventions of midnight-movie behavior had been set by the undisputed champion of the genre, *The Rocky Horror Picture Show*, but those expectations had extended to all midnight movies at the Union Theater and represented an odd return to the audience conventions of the earliest movies. Cheering the hero and heroine, booing the villain, shouting out comments and adding to the dialogue: attending the midnight movies was a public act. The previews were roundly and almost indiscriminately cheered, as were the first couple of minutes of *Pulp Fiction*. Once the tense but funny opening sequence in the diner had played itself out, Dick Dale tore into the surf-guitar opening theme and the audience whooped as though the stage lights had come up at a stadium concert.

As the movie went along, the cheering just to be a part of the movie diminished and people lost themselves in the film, but whenever something either gruesome or exciting happened, the crowd was not at all shy about expressing itself. Uma Thurman getting her adrenaline shot, the gangster taking revenge with a shotgun against his hillbilly tormenter, the accidental brain-spill in the back seat were all greeted with loud groans of grossed-out and happy disbelief. At *Pulp Fiction*, Union's kids were among friends, a group with whom they identified and felt safe in, and commenting was a way of committing to and enhancing that group's experience. Friends *talk*, even during movies. For those of us who weren't a real part of the group, the group itself became part of the show, something for *us* to comment on within our own friendship group, as Rosalynd and Laurie and I did over the evening more than once.

This expectation of participating and commenting is part of the programming of the midnight movie—a good cult film has to have a surplus of those kinds of moments in which the audience can participate. *Rocky Horror* is the ultimate example, with its nationwide phenomenon of audience-based acting companies, but *Emmanuelle in 3-D*, *Akira* (a violent 21st-century Japanimation), *Midnight Cowboy*, *Harold and Maude*, *Drugstore Cowboy*, and *Cheech & Chong's Up in Smoke* (to name a few of the Union theater's prior midnight engagements) are all loaded with enough in-jokes or sudden twists to keep a hip young audience engaged and active, especially if many of them had already seen the movie and could anticipate what they should do next. It wouldn't do to program *My Dinner With Andre* or *Babette's Feast* at a midnight show.

Public reserve is a hedge against contact, a drawing into anonymity to protect the insecure self against unknown surroundings. Public expression is a welcome of contact, a statement of belonging and common beliefs, an affirmation that behaving as a collective is possible and desirable. During the regular shows over the rest of the week, the act of going to the movies is increasingly just the act of watching the video on a really big high-fidelity system, attended by an anonymous and isolated crowd that expects its aural privacy.[3] The midnight movie may be yet another expression by young people that they expect a public life more vigorous than rule-bound, one that rewards witty contributions over safety and passivity. It displays a different conception of movie-going that goes beyond the content of the movie itself, which may well explain why all these young people were willing to come out at midnight and pay full price to see a movie that had already hit the video stores.

If, as is often suggested, Curtisville gets a theater of its own, will its owners program a midnight movie? Will it be a culturally distinctive, "lifestyle-specific" movie, or safe and mass-market like everything else in Curtisville? Will it take place in one cell of an octoplex, or in a cavernous room that allows 400 like-minded people to cheer? All theaters are not created equal, which is why the midnight movie is at the huge Union Theater and not at the chopped-into-thirds Avocet Theater two blocks away, owned by the same company. If Curtisville gets a theater of its own, following the scale and program and ownership patterns of McDonald's and Kmart and

Burger King and Taco Bell and Kentucky Fried Chicken and Denny's, it isn't likely to be a single screen theater. That has ramifications for its physical and social characteristics: if we want the option of a dozen simultaneous movies, we end up with exactly one kind of theater.

And all theaters do not interact equally with their streetscapes, which is a part of why midnight movies at the imaginary Curtisville 8 Cinema would be very different than at the Union. Standing in line for a block to see a movie isn't a bad experience when in fact you're standing on a city block, against storefronts, with foot traffic going by at close quarters, people walking into and across the street, gatherings taking place all along the sidewalk, people passing by just to see whether other people are there. The fact that it's all in the middle of an already-active town makes the whole scene easier to escape (or to choose). Bringing someone in a car out to a movie at an isolated single-use theater makes it more of a "date," and makes the decision harder to back out of if something seems to be going less than well. With dozens of friends and other attractive alternatives close at hand in an active downtown, a kid can bail out on the theater without making a real "departure." Driving or walking into Union at 11:45 P.M. on a Friday could lead to any number of destinations, and thus reveals less and is less threatening as a statement of personal interest.

Becky's decision to have her "going-away party" at the midnight movie was at least in part an expression of insecurity at the end of her membership. Would her friends like her enough to come to a going-away party? What if nobody came? Those are dangerous questions, uncomfortable questions. Rather than put herself on that black-and-white line, how much safer to declare the midnight show of *Pulp Fiction* her going-away party, especially within a group of people for whom midnight movies are vital social events. She ensured that her friends would all attend and that a party mood would prevail, while at the same time being able to identify through association both with Union's artsy crowd and with Uma Thurman and John Travolta and the dancing patrons of Jackrabbit Slim's.

At 2:30 in the morning, the movie ended and the exhausted audience tumbled out onto the sidewalk and said our tired goodbyes. I hugged Becky and wished her good luck at school. Her round face was shining—her going-away night had been a huge success, and she was ready to go off to San Francisco State secure in knowing that she had many and good friends. The Geeks split up for their separate cars and separate plans, and I walked four blocks home to bed. I was too tired to think much about it then, but now I can recognize that the whole night, from the late hour to the long wait outside for tickets to the loud music to the constant "interruptions" of the movie, would have been pure torture for a lot of people—particularly for most of the people we put in charge of public life and teenagers.

It was the highlight of Becky's summer.

PART TWO

At School

CHAPTER TEN

Kirk's School Days

Thursday

Kirk wheels in at 8:16, parks at the curb in front of school rather than in the parking lot in the back, and walks quickly toward his locker. He looks through the office window to check the official digital time on the bell control panel. At his locker, he deposits a couple of books and a lunch bag, withdraws two notebooks, and then scoots to French. He's seated at his desk with a notebook out and ready to go at 8:19.

French begins at 8:20 with five minutes of silence to review the week's work, and then a quiz. Kirk's done with the quiz in five minutes, while others are taking as long as fourteen. He waits quietly, hands folded, elbows on the desk; he periodically doodles on the back of his quiz sheet. At 8:40, the tests are collected and the conversations begin. Kirk asks his neighbor, "How do you think you did? I got like four spaces filled in. I think I got the first three and like maybe one more." It doesn't seem to concern him much.

They look at slides of a French twelfth-century tapestry representing the Apocalypse, as Mme. Landers reads a French-language description of each one. Kirk looks at the pictures for a few seconds each but isn't really listening, just sitting patiently. The word "wormwood" catches his attention, though, and he volunteers, "Wormwood is like really bitter and they used it to wean babies— they rubbed it on the mother's nipples so that the baby wouldn't suck any more. I think they said that in *Romeo and Juliet*." Kirk doesn't follow the classroom prompts very often. He's more interested in expanding the discussion outside the confines of "the lesson." Mme. Landers tells of the angels laying waste to the Earth, and Kirk says, "Angels don't kill people." When people are shown elsewhere on the tapestry cowering before God, Kirk asks, "Why would people be afraid of God?" In neither case did Mme. Landers pick up *his* discussion prompts, but merely waited until Kirk had finished, and then turned once again to her script.

At about two minutes before the end of class, with slides still being shown, the room fills with the sound of twenty-nine notebooks being folded and packed away, none of which had been inscribed with anything anyway. At 9:20, Kirk talks with Angela and Gwen about the quiz as they leave. He stops at his locker, drops off one notebook and picks up a granola bar. We go to Geology ("the *best* class"), where he talks surfing with Phil and Dan until class begins.

Kirk is first and foremost a surfer. He picked it up about three years ago from a soccer friend, and now surfs fifteen or twenty hours a week. When Kirk took me to his favorite surfing cove, he said as we walked to the trailhead, "Surfing is the best thing in the world."

"Better than soccer?"

"Yep."

"Better than sex?"

A long pause. "I don't know. I suppose I could live on a desert island without anybody else. I guess they're about equal, you've got to have both of them. I couldn't live without surfing, but if I had to go without sex for whatever reason, I'd be hatin' it." Then we got to the log stairs and he bounded down the hill three stairs at a time, surfboard under his arm.

The Geology assignment for the next few days is to form a mining company and extract mineral resources for profit. Each group of four students is issued an envelope containing a balance sheet and about half a million dollars in photocopied currency, which they will use to buy a land claim—a wooden box the size of a shoebox, full of sand. Small clumps of PlayDough ore are buried in the middle of each claim, and its open top is covered with white paper. The miners will also have to buy mining tools (an aluminum pipette "drill," a pen; a drafting triangle), a set of mining and environmental permits, and pay the incremental costs associated with each drilling expedition. Their job is to find the ore in as efficient and economical fashion as possible through experimental drilling and then to extract and sell that ore back to Mr. Lyon. Profit equals passing grade; loss equals failing grade. It's one of the few lessons I've seen that talks overtly about the resource extraction that drives Timber County's economy, and that links the subject matter at hand with some sense of how people use it in the world beyond campus.

There's a great humor about the exercise among the students and teachers alike (this class has Mr. Lyon plus two student teachers, about an eight-to-one student-teacher ratio), a class event that acts as both lesson and reward. The room is loud, but they're on the job. While trying to decide what mining supplies to buy from Mr. Lyon, who's busy gouging the prospectors just as his mercantile predecessors did a hundred years earlier in this same community, Kirk looks up at me and says, "I hate this!" But he's laughing when he says it.

At 10:15, people pack up at the last second and leave quickly. Kirk walks back to his locker, grabs another granola bar and some fruit leather, and then dashes into the Hacky Sack circle on the Quad, entranced both by the cooperation and the challenge of keeping the little woven ball in the air. While hacking, he's also showing off his new pocket pipe to Dan and Damien, talking about pot and surfing and girlfriends. In the circle, people join and leave all the time—there are five or six people hacking at any moment, but not the same five or six. At 10:26, Mr. Peterson hollers down the hallway, "Hey, if you guys want a referral, just stay down there!" The circle breaks up and heads for class.

Mr. Peterson always starts his course, The Individual in Society, five to ten minutes late because he's also the coordinator of the Continuation School, the district's last-chance program for kids in academic or disciplinary trouble, and they run on a slightly different schedule. In fact, The Individual in Society is the sort of class kids take just before they go on to continuation school: it's an elective chosen by kids who neither want greater academic rigor nor another shop class, an educational cipher used for balancing the schedule and delivering some vague "good behavior" material on abstinence and smoking. Matthew, a good student who had signed up for this course "because I thought we'd be learning about psychology and behavior and stuff," waits in vain every day for something to learn.

Mr. Peterson is big and loud and tough-spoken, but he just likes to hang out and be social in class, and his lenient policies have really thwarted him in running this course. "Let's have some quiet in here!" he booms, and the ten concurrent conversations diminish in volume but none disappear.

Today, the class is really playing him. The discussion is on paternity laws, and Rachel says, "There was this guy on Rikki Lake that was the father of, like, four babies with four different girls and he wasn't living with any of them, and . . ."

Connie says, "That's such a dumb show! How do they get those people to be on that show?"

Dave adds, "Oprah's a lot better than Rikki Lake."

Rachel responds, "No way, Rikki Lake is cool, they get into fights all the time on that show."

Kirk, like most of the other students, leans back in his chair with no notebook out.

The room is geopolitically divided, with surfers/hackers in the southeast corner, cowboys on the north side, the two studious and quiet kids in the back center, and the gangsta girls in the front center. Thus there are lots of small conversations all around the room. Kirk gets caught conducting one of them, and he's moved to the front of the room, away from his group. Mr. Peterson wants to break these groups up, and on Monday he'll have a seating chart. They've heard that before.

Mr. Peterson gives up on the discussion at about 10:45 and hands out a worksheet. The class (mostly) falls to work, but there are still a few discussions. Within minutes, most of them have handed in the first worksheet and picked up the second. After about fifteen kids have turned in the first worksheet, someone notices that there's a second side to both the first and second worksheets, and they all dive back to the pile to get their first sheet back.

Just before eleven, Mr. Peterson announces the final assignment for the paternity unit: to create a public service announcement on video to try to persuade absent fathers to pay child support. Mr. Peterson talks about this for maybe ten minutes, with the class again not listening to him, jerking him around. "So what are we doing?" He's explained it about four times, and they're still asking questions that have already been answered. They're not listening because he's set up the expectation that they don't need to listen. The last sound I hear as the class packs up at 11:10 is one girl in front asking her friend, "So what exactly are we supposed to be doing?"

Kirk rushes back to his locker again, buys a fundraiser candy bar from a girl standing next to him, and then off to English where they're reading *The Old Man and the Sea*. Lars, the student teacher this semester, is trying to get them to analyze and dissect Hemingway's characters and worldview as they read about a chapter a day, and they're participating—it's a loud start-up, a very discussant class with no references to what Rikki Lake might think about Hemmingway. They talk together for about twenty-five minutes, with Lars enthusiastically leading them along with questions about what the kids think they know so far of Santiago and his independence and stubbornness, and then he lets them get back into reading the next chapter. At about 11:50, he regroups them for more discussion. The class works well, helped along by a good story, but the talk ends five minutes early in order for Lars to distribute report cards.

At 12:05, Kirk's got his grades: A-, B, B-, C+, and F for the grading period (the F is in French for "excessive tardies"). Overall semester GPA is 2.833, cumulative for the two and a half years so far is 2.61. He leaves his notebook on the heater in the classroom, since he has Journalism during fifth period in the same room, and we scoot out to his car. After buying gas at the mini-mart, we drive back to his house to set his wetsuit out to dry in the sun and grab a quick lunch.

Kirk lives about eight miles north of the school, uphill in the fancy Sandstone Heights section of Sandy Cove, in a big modern redwood house with apple and pear trees all around, flower and vegetable and herb gardens lining the porch and driveway. There's a ranch fence all around the lot, cats on the roof and the porch, and half a dozen huge redwoods west of the house near the garage.

Kirk's nineteen-year-old sister Paula is sunbathing in a purple bikini out in the backyard, lying face-down on their trampoline, reading a magazine. It's maybe seventy degrees with almost no wind, on the second of February. His stepdad is asleep in the master bedroom on the second level—he's a TV broadcast engineer and works evenings. Kirk shows me around the house a little, particularly his room in the basement. There are two bedrooms downstairs, his and Paula's; they share a bathroom and a family room ("This is my living room," he says). Kirk's room has clothes all over the floor ("I don't have a closet"), his varsity letter from soccer and his summer soccer camp certificates on the wall. A few sketches and paintings by his grandmother sit on a ledge. A futon rests against one wall and a couch against the other; a stereo, bookshelves, and a few plants are below the small window. The room has the seven-foot ceiling typical of converted basements, and the room altogether might be eight-by-ten feet. His living room has a big sectional couch and a large TV, an eighty-gallon fish tank, a floor-to-ceiling bookshelf jammed with paperbacks ranging from pop fiction to *100 Chinese Poems*, and a full-sized "Star Wars" arcade video game.

We say hi to Dog, the golden retriever, as Kirk drapes his wetsuit across the porch railing. He shows me his bucket of decomposing redwood scraps in which he's growing a few mushrooms (yes, those kind), and we take a drive to Honda Point to check the waves from the overlook. "Pretty messy. Maybe I'll go out after school, maybe not." Then we drive back to school, with Kirk wondering if the clunking sound from the front suspension is serious, "cause I have NO money. I just gave my mom my whole paycheck for insurance. It's, like, $75 a month."

We park again in front of the school, walk onto the Quad, and Kirk immediately spots a Hacky Sack game—"I see a circle!"—and joins in. The circle runs for seven or eight minutes, and then the first afternoon bell rings at 12:45 and people scatter for class. Kirk looks curious. "Everyone leaves when the first bell rings . . . I don't get it." Kirk continues to hack with one last guy for the five minutes until second bell, then dashes to his locker and grabs a book to read. We make it to Journalism only a minute late, and Kirk talks with the four kids sitting on the heater as he picks up the notebook he'd left there. He had continued to hack by himself all the way down the hall and is still doing it in the room while he's talking. Ethan enters the room, and Kirk takes the opportunity to show off his pocket pipe again. But by 1:00, almost everyone is reading.

While the class in engaged in Silent Reading period, I take the opportunity to sketch Kirk. He's about five feet, eight inches tall, pretty fit—I'd guess about 140 pounds. He wears his hair short, in an explosion of loose curls. His hair is darker below the crown and lighter brown above, not from peroxide but from constantly being in the sun and water. He has a ruddy complexion—both his face and his hair lend to the impression that he's just come in from a strong wind. Muscular forearms emerge from his heather gray t-shirt, ending in prominent wristbones and big hands. A faint scar on his left wrist is the remainder of a childhood accident. He wears no jewelry on his hands and only a short, thin gold chain on his neck. The t-shirt is baggy and untucked, drooping across the lap of his straight-leg jeans. There's a frayed hole about the size of a quarter on the seam at his right thigh. White socks, well-worn black canvas Vans skateboard shoes. He carries his heavy cotton purple-gray hooded sweatshirt with him all day, but hasn't worn it since first period.

At 1:20, Silent Reading is over. Kirk is hacking by himself again while waiting in line to talk with Mr. Springs about his newspaper assignment. Then we're off to the gym to interview Coach MacArthur about the basketball season to date. Kirk is supposed to write an overview article about the winter sports season as a whole, and borrows the team's scorebook to get the dates and scores of the games so far. He's having trouble deciding which information will be relevant—he doesn't have a sense of what the overall article is going to be about yet. Coach MacArthur returns to the office and talks to Kirk about two particular games, one win and one loss. This format was Coach Mack's idea—Kirk's question was, "Can you give me a couple of quotes about the season or something?"

After talking with Coach Mack, we're off through the locker room and weight room again and back out into the halls, hacking the whole way to Mr. Dover's room. The idea is that Mr. Dover would do the same thing for wrestling that Coach MacArthur did for basketball, but he's in mid-lecture when Kirk opens the door, and he gives us the "just a minute" signal. So Kirk and I stand outside the door, Kirk again hacking by himself the whole time we stand around: "Hacking is great. Sometimes you can get a rush if you've got a sweet hack going." After about ten minutes, we're still waiting, and Kirk and I play pitcher-catcher with the hack.

Mr. Dover never does emerge from his room, and we're back to Mr. Springs' room by 2:05. Mr. Springs counsels Kirk about the structure of his story, and then Kirk walks to his locker with Ethan. They're going to meet after school out at Oyster Beach. On the way to Geometry, Kirk's former girlfriend Jenny stops him near the library. "Can I have the keys to your car so I can sit and listen to music after school?"

"No way, you'll just drive it off somewhere." This, I later learn, has happened before.

"No I won't. You don't even have to give me the key, just let me listen to the radio."

"How will you listen to music if you haven't got the key? You can't turn the radio on."

She just smiles endearingly. "Come onnn, let me . . ."

Kirk says no one last time and we walk to sixth period. At 2:16, Kirk's late for Geometry, but no big deal, it's just conversation so far. Mr. Niesen's a hollering sort of coach/teacher—he works the room of forty chairs as though it were full, even though this class only has about sixteen people in it. He refers to everyone by their last name.

They're working on converse logic in proofs. Within three minutes, Kirk's completely slumped into his chair, and spins a piece of binder paper on a mechanical pencil through the punched hole. Each slow, fluttering rotation of the paper says, "bored, bored, bored . . ."

After one proof regarding congruent triangles, Kirk challenges Mr. Niesen as to why you need logical demonstrations for something which appears evident from the drawing that accompanies the problem. "I mean, you can just look at that and know it's true."

Mr. Niesen pushes for why logic is necessary in business, in law. "Let's say you were a salesman and you were trying to sell me something. You can't just say something is true and expect it to stand. You have to back it up, prove it."

Kirk presses his case: "I don't think that solving these kinds of proofs helps you with that kind of logic."

Mr. Niesen: "They do." He has been pressed to the limits of his own understanding of logic and can no longer back it up or prove it.

Eddie, sitting beside Kirk, chips in: "I don't see how you can learn logic. I mean, logic is just something you're born with."

"You can learn anything, Rooney," barks Mr. Niesen, clearly not believing it in this case but having no other intellectual ammunition at hand.

Eddie, in his best go-to-hell voice, replies, "I guess so, yes, sir."

At 3:05, they turn in their homework and get ready to go. Mr. Niesen stops Kirk on the way out the door and says, "Kirk, quit drinkin' coffee or Coke or whatever you're drinkin' at lunch." We leave the room. Kirk says, "Man, I hate that class. And Mr. Niesen's *such* a great guy . . ."

We go back to Kirk's locker, meet Ethan, and hack in the student store. They're joined by Nick and Damien, and the four of them stand in the doorway and admire a new girl leaned over the counter across the room. "Doesn't she have a nice ass? That girl in the white flowered shirt?" Kirk says, and gives me a huge grin. "Man, that's nice."

We leave the student store and sit on one of the concrete planters, where Kirk eats one of the enchiladas that he's brought back from lunch. He gets talked into giving a girl a ride to her house in Heartwood, but he's going to meet me and the other three guys at the second parking lot at Oyster Beach as soon as he drops her off. Kirk and the girl go one way, Ethan takes Damien and Nick out to the Swinger parked in the back, and I drive off on my own.

I get to Oyster Beach before anyone else. The parking lot is deserted, and the high fog has pulled in across the dunes, obscuring the warm sun we'd enjoyed earlier. I shiver and use the outhouse. After about five minutes, Kirk drives in, and we go look around in the iceplant to examine a small patch of mushrooms. He pulls one up and does an ID, looking into the gills and the cap for color, and pronounces it edible. We sit on the rail for a couple of minutes, and then Ethan's car arrives. Kirk once again shows off his pocket pipe and then goes out of the wind into the corner of the outhouse to light up a hit. He emerges coughing.

We walk out onto the beach and form a circle on the wet waveslope, and Kirk pulls out his Hacky Sack once again. I figure if I'm going to stand there in the gray and cold for god-knows-how-long, I'm going to learn to hack some. They're very generous with the hack, and tolerant of the old guy, too. A *very* fat joint emerges, as big around as my little finger—not one of those little toothpick-thin disco joints I remember from years back. It gets lit up and passed around. I decline. Nick asks if I ever smoked weed. "Yeah, from maybe when I was twenty-three until I was about, I don't know, maybe thirty or so . . ."

Damien asks, "Why'd you stop?"

"I just didn't have time anymore."

"That's cool." He laughs. "That's all we've got is time."

The circle goes on for a little over an hour, consuming that first joint and an identical twin. Damien is clearly the best athlete of the bunch, with very calm, controlled, elegant moves. Ethan and Kirk are both more abrupt, energetic but with less control. Nick's down the list a little farther, but still competent. The less said about myself, the better, although I manage to put my boot on more and more as we go along.

Around 4:30, we start to head back up the beach. Ethan, holding the hack, says to me, "Go long." I run up the beach and catch the hack over my shoulder about fifty yards away, and turn to throw it back. That precipitates a game of long-range catch with me on one end and all four of them on the other end, climbing all over each other to fight for every catch. After about twenty minutes of that, my arm is aching and we walk out into the parking lot. The other three leave in the Swinger, and I follow Kirk's car back to Sandstone Heights and dinner with his family.

Friday

Kirk arrives at school eleven minutes late, having gotten a last-minute phone call to pick up Dave. The two of them head straight to the attendance office to get their late-entry passes, and then Kirk immediately walks on to French. He goes in first and I'm behind him, and the only open seat is all the way across the room in the northeast corner. Mme. Landers stops her lesson as I walk through the center of the room and ponder once again the role of the unobtrusive observer.

Kirk told me about Mme. Landers last night over dinner, saying "all of the examples she uses are like full of God and religion, because she's like all into that. She says she's not bringing religion into the school, but she totally is." Well, this may be true—she's on her second day of using slides of a twelfth-century French tapestry depicting the Apocalypse to do a French lesson, and she keeps talking about the "Good News," capital letters in her pronunciation. She has a very sing-songy delivery, like Miss Winteringham, my kindergarten teacher. This is not particularly to say that she's talking down to the kids—she talks more or less that way in the teacher's lounge to Mr. Bauer and Senora Poore too, but in class she accentuates it.

At 9:05, they're done with the Apocalypse and take a brief break—Kirk immediately starts talking about tomorrow's soccer practice and the game this Sunday. Then they play Pictionnaire. The seat layout is divided into five clusters all vaguely aimed at the front desk, and each of those clusters becomes a team. A student is assigned a word like *"dejeuner," "bureau," "apres-midi,"* or *"voyager;"* he or she must draw a picture representing it on the blackboard, and the teammates must guess the word. The class mostly sits quietly or talks a bit during this Friday recess, and Mme. Landers doesn't prod them, but rather sits back in the corner and enjoys her Friday vacation as well.

At 9:20, we walk to the locker, drop off the French notebook and grab the Geology. Then it's off to class, where Kirk buys another almond candy bar from another school-band fundraiser and looks at Mr. Lyon's pictures of mining on the bulletin board. Mr. Lyon's classroom is wholly personalized with photos and magazine articles of geological things he's interested in and rock samples that he and his students have collected, classified, and labeled over the past twenty-one years, as well as pictures of his house in the forest and his various motorcycle trips. As he put it to me earlier in the year in terms a natural scientist might understand, "The room is completely mine. I've peed in all four corners."

Today's work is a continuation of the mining project started yesterday. Kirk takes charge—not particularly logical, but eager and enthusiastic. He's a "jump in first and look second" kind of guy. He and Dan grid the paper landscape and then flag down a student teacher to buy their first mining permit. Rosalynd tells them the price. Kirk is astonished. "Five thousand dollars?!"

"Yep, and that's just for the permit. It's gonna cost you ten thousand dollars an inch when you drill, too." Rosalynd has a completely guileless smile, cheerful as can be as she watches them squirm over the price.

"Man, that's horrible. Can we work a deal?"

No deals are worked. Kirk pushes the pipette drill through the paper and into the sand, creeping downward, feeling money leave his pocket with every push. He hasn't felt any resistance yet, but of course the ore might be at any depth. Finally he quits, and they mark the pipette's depth and draw it back out: 1.7 inches of drilling plus the original permit equals $22,000. Rosalynd smiles again as she pockets the money. "Thank you very much. Call me when you're ready to drill some more." As she leaves, Kirk taps his meager column of sand out of the pipette onto the table. No ore. Rosalynd spots him and reappears over his shoulder. "Is that an approved dump site?" she gloats. "It's going to cost you twenty thousand dollars to get a dumping permit."

They drill four more times over the class and locate two ore-bearing areas. They'll return on Monday to try to establish the boundaries of those areas and begin their extraction.

At 10:15, Kirk dashes out to the Quad. "Man, that is the best class! We're gonna get rich from all that ore in there!" He meets Eddie and starts hacking, and before a couple of minutes are up, the circle contains seven guys. Interesting that there are almost no girls who hack or surf. The circle is over near the attendance office, and thus the group can't see Mr. Peterson's classroom to know when he's arriving. They hack as long as they feel safe—"We should all just walk in late, you know? What are they going to do, write referrals for all of us?"—but finally do move to the proper hallway, running once they see that the door is waiting open. It turns out that Rachel got the keys from Mr. Peterson to open it, and that he's not even there. (That's how they phrase it: "Man, he's not even here yet. We could still be hacking.") Kirk sits down and gets out the daily log sheet that I've given him as part of his volunteer's work. He realizes that he hasn't done Wednesday or Thursday yet. He works on today's log anyway so that he'll get that complete.

Mr. Peterson arrives, and today's lesson plan is to watch a video on paternity laws produced by the state Board of Education. He pokes around campus for five minutes to find a television, finally borrowing Mme. Landers', and plugs in the tape. The spokesperson drones on about the ways that California courts establish paternity status, and Kirk reads a surfing magazine. Today's video actually has a legend which comes up for a couple of minutes that says "Stop the Tape and Discuss." After the legend, the second half of the video shows the same spokesperson giving the class their assignment to make a public service announcement about paternity laws (and here I'd thought that the project Mr. Peterson announced yesterday was his idea . . . silly me). Then another legend comes up—"Stop the Tape and Make a PSA."

What a contrast to have this busywork right after Mr. Lyon's unique and handmade project. The basic idea is the same, and if you wrote down the instructions, they'd look the same on paper ("a hands-on learning experience," it would probably say, the same as it would say behind the French version of Pictionary), but the spirit in which they were conceived and carried through are entirely different. It doesn't even matter if Mr. Lyon thought up the mining project on his own or not. It's okay to borrow someone's ideas if you think they're good, but you've got to make them your own, invest your life and energy in them, which he clearly has done and Mr. Peterson and a great many other teachers have not. Just pulling stuff off the shelf makes a statement to the kids in the class, a statement to which they respond in kind.

But with fifteen minutes left in the period and the weekend coming up, Mr. Peterson turns to another page of the paternity "unit" and, instead of getting them psyched up for the creation of this PSA video and giving them time to come up with a strategy and form teams, he gives them yet another busywork handout: "Write an essay about paternity from one of these three points of view. Use all of the points about paternity laws that you have learned so far." It's clear that the video is no more and no less interesting to Mr. Peterson than any other element of the curriculum package; it's all just part of the linear checklist.

The assigned essay was to be finished within this last few minutes, and it's hard to imagine that anyone ever got started with serious intention. Jerry handed in his essay within five minutes, and it was so far off the topic that even Mr. Peterson got a kick out of it, and read it in its entirety to the class: "I would like to have a cat. I would name it Bob. I would teach Bob how to disco dance, and buy him one of those mirrored balls that spins from the ceiling."

Kirk didn't do the assignment that was due today: to ask nine different people about their views on paternity responsibilities and child support. (Right at the beginning of class, four of the kids in the class came up to me and asked me to say what I thought, so that they'd be able to fill in one more of the blanks.) He and Eddie are passing the surf magazine back and forth. Kirk gets to an ad with a great back shot of a girl in a thong bikini. "Man!!" he says to himself involuntarily. Then he looks over at me, smiles sheepishly, turns back to the magazine and says, "What a great wave."

After The Individual in Society, there's a big fifteen-minute hack on the Quad—it's a beautiful, sunny day and nobody's worried about tardiness. At about 11:20, Kirk rushes back to his locker and then off to English, five minutes late. Lars chews him out briefly and asks him to stay at the end of class. The period had begun with a short lecture, then twenty minutes of silent reading. After that, small groups of three and four work on their interpretation of the Hemingway Code. Kirk wants to keep reading instead—"I didn't write any quotes, I just read."

After class, Kirk waits to talk with Lars (who's also been his soccer coach for the past three years). "You've got two T's already. I don't know what Mr. Springs' policy is on tardies. You're doing well on participation and contribution, you have a lot of that, but the T's just negate it. Not to mention that they disrupt the class." Properly chastised, Kirk vows not to be late again, although he'll be fifteen minutes late for Lars's soccer practice tomorrow morning.

At 12:12, we're off in the surfin' sedan again. We drive to the automatic teller and then across the street to the Main Street Deli, wherein we find perhaps two dozen other students waiting for sandwiches. The time pressure really shows when there are so few places to shop and so little time to spare. Kirk spends $4.89 of his just-cashed $5.00, and we're back in the car and returning to school. He parks at the curb, jogs onto campus and immediately scoots into a circle at the edge of the Quad's lawn. Kirk's turkey sub sits on the planter next to the group, and he rushes over to take bites every couple of minutes when someone drops the hack.

At 12:50, we return to the English/Journalism classroom. The first arrivals sit four across on the coveted heater, and the rest sit on top of their desks, perching and swiveling to talk to several people rather than sitting in their one-directional seat/desks. Journalism is being shepherded today by a sub, who introduces herself as Miss Jan Ellis. It's a very quiet reading period. At 1:20, almost everyone scatters for various parts of campus to work on projects for the next week's newspaper *Cat Tracks*, a name drawn from the school mascot Curtisville Cougars. Kirk and Adam and Tanya just sit against the heater and chat. It's a very lazy day, with wonderful sunshine, warm air, and substitute teachers all over campus as eight teachers attend a conference on Advanced Placement courses.

After seven or eight minutes, Miss Jan Ellis addresses the three students on the heater, telling them to get cracking on *something*, she doesn't care what. Kirk proceeds to Mr. Dover's room and interviews him on the wrestling season. He doesn't really care, and just gets the facts loosely along with a couple of snippets of quotable matter.

But Kirk's hatched a plan. He still needs to interview Mr. Cooper, the girls' basketball coach. Mr. Cooper has sixth period open as his prep period, and sixth period is the dreaded Geometry (with a sub, no less). So Kirk returns to see Miss Jan Ellis, asking for a pass to the Journalism room for sixth period so that he can interview Mr. Cooper and then type up his article. She's dubious, but Kirk is very persuasive. He carries the pass to the Geometry room, where Mrs. Borger—a sixty-ish woman quite likely wearing a toupee—is riding herd over a bunch of students doing math problems. Her entire responsibility for the day is to keep people quiet and contained while they do problem sets that Mr. Niesen has assigned. We enter Mrs. Borger's domain, and Kirk persuades her that a) he's already done the Geometry homework that's been assigned, and b) today is the last day that he can possibly interview Mr. Cooper. She smiles at me while I stand in the doorway—I look at her name written on the blackboard, subtly revised to read "Mrs. Booger." She tells Kirk, "Since your teacher has come with you, I'm sure it's alright. If he hadn't been with you, I wouldn't have signed it." I remain silent, and am now implicated in Kirk's scam, liable to be arrested for impersonating an adult. The gullibility of substitute teachers is legendary, but Mrs. Borger has just added a new twist.

Kirk high-fives me as we leave the room and return triumphantly to Miss Jan Ellis with the paper in hand. He pulls out his notebook and attempts to render the sketchy facts he's written into some shape, to incorporate it all into an article that overviews the entire winter sports season. The fifteen *Cat Tracks* journalists are all proudly non-jock. At a meeting almost a month ago, Mr. Springs had been trying to get someone revved up to write the story about the dramatic come-from-behind won-in-the-last-match one-point wrestling victory over the arch-rival and perennial powerhouse Union High team; they all shunned it as though they'd been asked to review a polka record. As the other journalists all straggle into the room, though, Kirk does confer for a few moments with Ethan about the overview article, and they work at it together for a bit.

At the end of fifth period, they walk out to the Quad to talk and meander off to their respective classrooms as sixth period begins. Lars, the student teacher, is in charge of the empty journalism room for sixth period, and he's checking to see what sort of games come on the Mac. I teach them how to play Iago—I win, and then Kirk wins. At 2:55, Kirk goes to Mr. Cooper's room and does a cursory basketball interview that takes less than five minutes; we then return to Journalism where I teach them how to play Brickles. All of my four years of grad school have come down to knowing how to play the games that come installed on the Macintosh.

At 3:05, Kirk checks quickly into Geometry to reassure Mrs. Borger that he's done his duty (and to tease Eddie for having to sit through the class), and then, the weekend begun, moves into another circle on the Quad.

CHAPTER ELEVEN

Free Public Assembly

Before school on Friday March 10th, Maggie and I met several of her friends just off the edge of the curb in the Quad, directly at the end of the walk that passed in front of the 300 Building. They talked about who was going to the Sadie Hawkins dance that night; Kate and Kara seemed a little uneasy that I'd be following Maggie even then. Nobody ever said as much, but there were times when they'd have preferred that I wasn't around.

After French, we stood there again to talk about plans for going to Pizza Palace before the dance. Maggie put in her vote for a pineapple and ham pizza, an item likely less available in her native Ireland than at an American corporate pizza hall. After History, we were in the same spot as Marshall told us all how late he and Brad and Ben had stayed up last night. They'd all been consoling Brad's older brother, whose girlfriend had "cheated on him." For some reason, Maggie enjoyed this conversation, listening intently and smiling the whole time.

After Health, Maggie met her friends again, left them for a moment to go to her locker, and returned quickly with nine dollars for tickets to the dance. After Spanish, we all met there to divide riders and cars for our trip to lunch at Edie's Hamburgers on Main Street; upon our return to campus, we reconvened in that same spot for another five minutes. Stephanie told us about the traffic accident out on 420 that she'd seen still scattered across the northbound lanes.

After Drama, we found the Quad again, same place, talking with Stephanie and Anne. "Are you going to Ben's party tonight after the dance?"

"Maybe . . . Ben's trying to keep it quiet, he doesn't want a whole bunch of people there that he doesn't know." Ben's parents were out of town for five days.

After Gym, at the end of the school day as people scooted off for cars and busses and the weekend's freedom, we rejoined a huge puddle of people out on the Quad. Stephanie was taking photos for the yearbook, so about twenty friends crowded around on the middle planter. And at 4:30, after track practice, we claimed Maggie's spot one last time and watched the softball team run a few laps of the school as we talked with Coach Fitzpatrick.

Maggie and her friends returned nine times that day to the same unmarked piece of asphalt, gathering each time within a foot or two of the previous meeting. Over the 180 days of school, she would be there well over a thousand times. It is likely both her favorite and her most enduring memory of Curtisville High School that she took back with her to Dublin.

During class periods, the hallways were theoretically free of students. Not empirically, of course, but theoretically. There were always five or six people wandering around, heading in pairs toward a bathroom or a locker, moving in the slowest possible manner.

In order to be in the halls during class time, it was necessary to ask a teacher for a hall pass. Some teachers were liberal in the use of the hall pass—one student would return, and the next would simply take the pass from his or her predecessor and leave without asking permission. (If this sounds as though the teacher were being irresponsible, consider for a moment what we would think of the kind of job in which a supervisor would have to grant permission to use the bathroom.) Other teachers almost never issued a hall pass, and students simply learned not to ask them.

"Hall pass" conjures up an image of paper—a ticket, perhaps a laminated card allowing the bearer to move from one specified location to another specified location at a specified time. Best to remove that image early on; hall passes at Curtisville were great lumbering objects. Joe Lyon in Geology used a chunk of granite the size of a bowling ball. Aaron Weimer in Biology used a elk's shoulderblade, though he would have preferred that his students called it a scapula. Al Lawton in Social Science used a canoe paddle. But whatever the object, possessing it made one a free agent, able to move through the halls at will. They were get-out-of-jail-free cards, carried with panache and defiance.

The buildings of Curtisville High School represented the common-sense campus, the "educational program spaces," the ones we could inventory. For fifty minutes at a time, Curtisville High existed as a set of thirty-some divided, discrete spaces; thirty cells in a honeycomb, each inhabited by its allotted drones and queen. But for the five-minute periods between classes, both the schedule and the campus reversed form, turned inside out.[1] The leftover spaces became a seamless, connected arcade filled with almost 800 active individuals; the sealed boxes had disappeared, at least for a moment, replaced with the playing field of free will.

The unallocated time—the negative spaces between the positive blocks of class time—also became visible. A lot of living went on in the five minutes between classes: secrets shared, makeup refreshed, snacks consumed, books exchanged, loves renewed, pent-up energy and aggravation released. Just as the point of the shopping mall for teenagers is not contained in the stores but rather in the promenade, the point of school for most students is not the classrooms but the halls. The entire human agenda of most of the kids at school found expression in this indeterminate place and time: owned by the school but occupied exclusively by students, half hallway and half sidewalk, places that were open and connective but still held away behind closed doors for most of the day.

At the last teachers' meeting of the year, on the morning after school finally ended, the administration put forward a few alternative plans to get kids to class on time more reliably the following year. The old standby, timed bells between every period, was trotted out and debated, as were more esoteric solutions such as issuing every student a large backpack instead of a locker to minimize the need for exchanging books. Lily Chase was adamant about getting kids to class on time. "What they don't realize is that the five minutes between classes is educational time. It's not social time, it's not eating time, it's time allotted in the school day to go from one classroom to another."

Not in this universe, Mrs. Chase. Not in the inside-out world of the hallways, not in the five minutes of old jokes and fresh news and human contact that provides so many kids with their reason to come to school every day.

ॐ

The Quad lay at the heart of the circulation patterns of the school, the O'Hare International of campus travel and public space. There were no traffic controllers and no labeled terminals, but specific groups claimed specific spots and met there almost unvaryingly. The Preps and the Jocks claimed the visible core intersection, while the Hacky Sack circles of Surfers and Hippies formed every fifty minutes at the edge of paving and grass. Groups of Cowboys peppered the western perimeter near the lockers and steel I-beam columns against which they leaned. The Drama Geeks and Band Nerds favored the grassy eastern side, closer as it was to their refuge classrooms within the school. The freshmen boys who would later become Jocks and Preps gathered at the far southwest corner next to the gym and the soda machine. The good campus citizens, studious and frugal, ate their paper-bag lunches close to the office. The Stoners, not surprisingly, had left the campus altogether.

All of these people used the Quad to divide themselves into the groups through which they filtered the larger world, and could identify other groups and their territories easily. Although there were relatively few fights here, no Crips and Bloods prepared to kill one another over group identity, it's a serious misconception that all of these white kids were homogeneous. There were (by most students' sociology) several recognizable groups at Curtisville. Perhaps the largest faction in this school were the Cowboys, also known (by non-Cowboys) as the Hicks. The Cowboys, boys and girls alike, favored big trucks and big belts. Their boots and Wrangler jeans and western shirts were new—there's no romantic chic among farmers and ranchers for old worn-out clothes. Hair was short on the boys, long and curled high on the girls.

"Prep" was the outsiders' term for those kids who seemed to be wearing the idealized media-flavored teen lifestyle, especially athletes and cheerleaders and student governors. That may sound like a small subculture, but when you consider the number of sports the school offered and the fact that there were Frosh and JV and Varsity cheerleaders (wearing different versions of the same $250 uniforms so as to be distinguishable from one another), the Preps amounted to about a quarter of the school. If the Cowboy was distinctive to Curtisville High, the Prep was distinctive to nowhere—a Prep at Curtisville would look equally at home in a high school in New Jersey or Alabama. They're the ones you'd see in the teen magazines like *Sassy* and *YM* and *Seventeen*, trim and clean-cut with casually expensive hairstyles, wearing nationally recognizable brands of t-shirts, baseball caps and sneakers. An Esprit sweatshirt might *look* just like any other sweatshirt, but it isn't—it's a symbol of taste and of resources, of being tuned into consumer culture.

The Surfers were more like the Cowboys, locally relevant but still influenced by national trends. They were the devotees of vertigo, the boys (almost always boys) who loved nothing more than to dive headlong into some physical act. If they played a school sport it was invariably soccer, but their real passion was for surfing. During school hours, they'd be found playing Hacky Sack in circles of two to six or seven, the closest dry-land approximation of the unpredictability of the wave. Their hair was longer than the Preps would wear theirs, and some grunge influences could be seen in the early stages of goatees. Footwear among the Surfers wasn't Nikes or Reeboks, but rather Teva sandals or Vans skateboard shoes; the brand names on their t-shirts were Boolabong and O'Neill and RonJon.

There were a significant number of Nerds at Curtisville, smart misfit kids who voluntarily lived on the fringes of pop culture. Often they were loners, but there were two large and identifiable subgroups: the Drama Geeks and the Band Nerds. They were the most unpredictable in dress and hair, the most openly searching. Lauren could look like a Prep one day and come to school wearing a yellow maxi-dress and a bright turquoise streak in her hair the next. Julian changed hair colors eleven times in a four-week span during the spring, and wound up shaving his head by the end. They often favored a sort of thrift-store chic, affecting things like Bing Crosby hats and satin vests simply because they knew no one else would wear anything like it.

There were a smattering of Hippies, wearing several layers of shirts and sweaters, old floppy pants, long and asymmetrical hair, displaying a conscious rejection of the outward symbols of consumer fashion. There were a very few Gangster-Wannabe's, almost all girls, wearing their sharp-creased pants or baggy jeans with the waist-band almost off their hips and their t-shirts above their navels, accessorized with chunky suede tennis shoes and dark lipstick, their hair tall and teased and sprayed-up. The Stoners were a harder group to recognize visually, often taking cues from the Hippies but putting a darker heavy metal edge on it.

If most kids could recognize and name these groups, then I think they existed—and probably mattered. Each group attributed different degrees of intelligence and ill motives to one another, not recognizing that they were distinct subcultures with different val-ues and rules. Each group had physical artifacts that identified and differentiated them from the others: not only clothing and hair-styles, but also types of vehicles; the slogans and drawings and notes they wrote on their binder covers (Stoners had not mastered the smiley-face in the ways that the Prep girls had, nor could the Cowboys draw pot leaves with the facility of the Surfers); their choices of drug paraphernalia, from Diet Coke to Skoal cans to ciga-rettes to ingenious pipes and places to hide pot; and their reading material—a Stoner reading *Seventeen* is an outlandish thought, as would be a Drama Geek with a well-worn copy of *Four Wheelin'*. They also had auditory cues by virtue of the music they favored.

All of these things were manifesting differences in the ideal futures of their owners—the local and working-class goals of the Cowboys included a steady job, sharp western clothes, and a status truck; the more media-driven middle-class goals of the Preps includ-ed broad popularity, a belief that college was an inevitable duty like thirteenth grade, a romantic relationship between equals, and mass-consumer notions of attractiveness. The Drama Geeks stood outside that dichotomy to some extent, looking for fulfillment in independence and ideas and involvement in creative life; some were eager to try college, while others had abandoned the notion that school could be a source of ideas. The Surfers were always in search of the next rush of adrenaline and vertigo, while the Stoners had surrendered any hope of real power over their lives and simply pur-sued a rush of a different type.

The groups at Curtisville High were groups that were defined around different hopes and expectations for their lives to come, dif-ferent fundamental measurements of success. Here at the end of the twentieth century, we have come to believe that inclusiveness and broad diversity are globally good, and distrust those who have chosen some degree of social or physical isolation. One concern about cliques and their associated hangouts is that these kids could just reinforce their own narrow beliefs. But we all do the same thing with churches and political parties: we gather together to reassure ourselves and each another that we have a community that thinks somewhat like we do, that other people believe that our life goals are both sensible and attainable. Both teenagers and adults choose a lot of their freely selected life spaces because those spaces are filled with people who are a lot like them. That's what *places* are about—enhancing a self-image, enriching a self-narrative—and belonging and group identity are a strong part of any social place.

During the forty minutes of lunch, the Quad was continuously occupied by perhaps 150 students, but several hundred others flowed through it at least for a few minutes on their way to and from other destinations. Even between classes, in the five-minute breaks during which they are allowed some humanity, kids flooded the Quad, gathering like swallows at their invisibly marked spots. Any chance for human contact with friends was welcomed. Of course, it's terrifically uncool to admit that, to say, "I need human contact." That's why the school, and especially the Quad, worked so wonderfully to meet their social needs—it brought them together in a way that was seemingly beyond their control, and allowed them to gather without having to make an admission of emotional need.

The effectiveness of the Quad was dependent on the presence of several important attributes, attributes that will be seen wherever people gather together voluntarily.[2] First, hangouts are created from negative space, what adults think of as unplanned, underutilized or "vacant" areas. Teenagers have no resources to build anything for themselves, so they claim the leftovers in the planned landscape. This act of claiming is socially important, a group choice that reinforces membership and autonomy. Places that are planned for them, such as "teen centers," are often shunned, implying as they do someone else's schedule, someone else's limited palette of planned activities, someone else's power of creation. Kids simply want places to be with friends, away from adult-defined roles; the more that they can create these places themselves, the more they appreciate them.

Teenagers' places are usually small and strongly bounded. They are often enclosed on two or even three sides, and offer a real sense of being "inside" or "outside." This allows the users to know their territory, and makes entering the space a definite social act to be welcomed or repelled rather than ambiguous or possibly mistaken.

Hangouts allow for both the stable and mobile aspects of gathering, as well as easy exchange between the two. They're located near paths or roads that facilitate frequent arrivals and departures, and will typically have broad and active gateways filled with impromptu conversations between those arriving and those leaving. The Quad, of course, was right at the school's pathway center, and the intersections were jammed with stationary kids holding brief meetings.

Hangouts have anchoring objects. The stable conversations in gathering spots take place around some physical element like a bench, a planter, a wall, a parked car. This does not mean that these objects will be used for long-term sitting; teenagers typically use benches and planters as location references, perching briefly on them or leaning against them. Kids who talked on the Quad were in constant and shifting contact with the pillars, wall corners, signposts, and curbs that bordered their group.

Hangouts offer both high visibility *and* privacy control; they tend to be in highly public locations, but allow individual users to move into the limelight or to fade back into the periphery. They thrive in noise-tolerant areas, away from potential complaints.

Finally, a good hangout has to bring people together in a way that allows the gathering to seem accidental, and it has to allow for easy escape. By being part of the path system and ringed with lockers, the Quad was a natural habitat that let kids search for friends without having to make verbal agreements on where and when they should meet—they simply knew that friends would be there automatically between classes. The fact that Maggie and her friends met hundreds of times at exactly the same nondescript chunk of pavement was clearly no accident, but it maintained the necessary illusion of accident; they were just moving between classes. If conversations grew strained, if the talk ran dry, there was no admission of failure. It was time to go on to class, after all. "Gotta go" is a more graceful closure, implying a desire to stay if only circumstances would permit, than some variant of, "Well, I guess that's all we had to say."

These are the basic requirements of a good hangout, and the Quad met them all. It lay at the center of the campus' broad walkway system, and the intersections were filled with brief conversations. Individual visibility could be had by claiming central locations or standing up on the planters, or could be avoided by sitting or moving toward the perimeter. There were planters, curbs, gutters, pillars, gates, and walls to lean against, and several natural spatial subdivisions that different groups could claim. Those gatherings that weren't physically bounded were always in the shape of a tight inward circle, their own backs forming the No Trespassing sign. Teachers never went onto the Quad except to pass through at full speed on their way to the teachers' lounge, and nobody managed it directly; supervision was at a minimum. Very few classrooms opened onto it, so that noise was rarely an issue even when a group inhabited the Quad during class times.

The Quad was a luxury in functional terms: it had no manifest purpose of its own, no educational mission to perform. It wasn't supervised by anyone and wasn't planned for much of anything. Unprotected and unenclosed, it cost almost nothing. It could have been left out of the plans with no harm to the agenda of the Board of Education.

It was the single most important spot on campus, the town square that Curtisville itself didn't have.

CHAPTER TWELVE

Pay No Attention to that Man Behind the Curtain

On the back of the Curtisville High administration building—if a building which faces the general public on one face and the school's public on the other can be said to have a back—are four blank green doors, a mural depicting a Native American man holding a blanket overhead in one raised hand, the ubiquitous high windows bringing light into restricted places, and a pair of large gray rectangles about five feet wide and three feet tall.

The gray rectangles aren't abstract decoration, but rather two deeply-tinted surveillance windows from the principal's office out onto the Quad. Curtisville High was unfortunately sold a particularly low-quality grade of one-way glass. If Principal Dawson was in his office and the lights were on, he was visible as though in a dense morning fog—one could see the pattern but not the colors in his sweater, read the title but not the author of the book he kept on his desk for Silent Reading period, recognize the current visitors that sat in the guest chairs across the desk.

Nobody ever acknowledged that they could see through the windows. Neither teachers nor students waved or made rude gestures as they walked by, even if Mr. Dawson were clearly looking directly at the windows and thus, by extension, at us. We knew that we weren't supposed to see in, even though we did. We all pretended that the windows weren't there.

ε⁂

At every possible entrance to the school grounds, there was a large sign bolted to the doors requesting that all visitors proceed to the main entrance on Murphy Road and register with the principal's office. That office was the single lawful public entry to the school, centered in the public face of the administration building. "Curtisville High" was painted in black Helvetica letters above that double glass doors, and not over the other six entries to campus that the students and teachers used. A flagpole rose from the concrete planter in front of that door, and no other. The administration building was the ceremonial gateway, the greeting of school to community, and played no part in the experience of the school for most of its inhabitants.

The administration building acted as the campus' filter, catching potential hazards and releasing them in appropriate directions and volumes. The flow of visitors and administrators crossed at the desk of Nancy Anderson, the principal's secretary and the school's first line of defense. She controlled the public intake system, shunting visitors toward the counselors and record-keepers down the corridor to her left, the teacher's lounge and mailboxes down the corridor to her right, the principal's office immediately behind her, or the purgatorial lobby back toward the door.

Like a nightclub bouncer, Nancy had an unwritten but clear hierarchy to help her determine who got access to information and people. She handled the educational establishment—the Superintendent and district staff, school board members, law enforcement, various county vocational and educational specialists, the visiting accreditation committee—promptly and accurately. They were familiar. They knew the language and the schedules. They had clear and unambiguous roles. Parents and students were much harder to read, and were far less likely to have quick or easy access beyond the checkpoint. Parents waiting to pick up a kid or to talk with the principal could spend considerable time in the lobby, leafing through the principal's monthly newsletter kept in a short stack next to the padded but armless chairs near the door. The newsletter contained no musings, no pensive thoughts; it was businesslike and optimistic, filled with advice on handling teen problems written by professionals who knew how. The lobby was an extension of the newsletter, the physical media of public relations—efficient, competent, polite but not welcoming, decorated with pleasant faculty pictures that suggested community.

Students who visited the office were most often simply deflected, though always with a polite smile. Mara, a student in the Yearbook class, asked Nancy early in the Spring semester for a set of teacher photographs for the yearbook. Nancy said, "I'm sorry, but we don't have a set of photographs other than the ones framed on the wall."

Mara returned to her classroom and reported this to Mr. Dover. He told her to try again, and said, "Make sure that Nancy knows you're from Yearbook, and that you need the set of small photos." Mara visited the office a couple of days later, and again Nancy said she didn't know about any such photos.

About a week later, Mr. Dover and Mara went to the office together. He asked Nancy for the set of photos. She said, "Oh, sure, they're right over here," opened a file drawer and handed the folder of photos over to Mr. Dover within twenty seconds.

Mara was still furious when she told me this story four months after the event. "Why couldn't she say that she had to give them to a teacher? Why couldn't she say that she didn't know which ones I was talking about, and try to figure it out with me? Why was it so easy for Mr. Dover to get them, and impossible for me?"

One reason that students were so easily dismissed from the central office is because they had a separate domain at the opposite end of the administration building: on the internal face of the building and at the far west corner, a pair of doors led to the Attendance Office. The student end of the administration building was the equivalent of a county courthouse: a place to go for permits and for sentencing, for guidance and for indigent care and services.

Like Nancy at the general-public entrance, the school secretaries Suzanne and Diane made the front-line decisions in the Attendance Office: they decided who got an off-campus pass and who did not; who got to use the phone and who was told to use the pay phone by the gym; who got beyond the partition to see a counselor or Mr. Phillips, the assistant principal; and who had to wait on the supplicant's side of the counter in the crowded waiting room.

This end of the administrative world held the hardware that kept the school running—schedules and attendance records—and it was governed by the assistant principal. Assistant Principal is an interesting title, suggesting (as is generally the case) that the assistant principal may become the principal down the line. But the assistant principal has a very different sort of job than the principal. A principal's role may be likened to that of a small-town mayor: responsibility for long-range planning, for receiving information from his or her departments and prioritizing the needs of the school, for coordinating the local with the regional, and for meeting foreign dignitaries. The assistant principal's role is more closely akin to that of a combination of sheriff and district attorney: law enforcement and surveillance mixed with counseling and the pronouncement of sentencing.

There is no particular reason to believe that a good sheriff would be a good mayor, but the progression of command in high schools most often runs this way. In the education world, you cannot become the mayor without having been the sheriff somewhere, and you cannot become the sheriff without having expressed a desire to leave the classroom and become involved in campus discipline. This necessary linkage of dissimilar jobs leads to circumstances like that of Curtisville High, in which a former (and by all accounts good) sheriff became a mayor embattled by faculty and students alike. He had a lawman's distrust of the public, and took on a job that required careful human relations. He had never fully made the shift to the other end of the building.

ॐ

The year before I arrived, the school gave its kids a forty-two-item questionnaire about their satisfaction with different aspects of the school, in preparation for the following year's accreditation process. Each item of the survey took the form of a positive statement about the school with which the student could "agree strongly," "agree," "disagree," or "disagree strongly." Lukewarm support was the general consensus for almost every statement: "strongly agree" wasn't checked often, but "agree" accounted for forty or fifty percent of the responses. The overall warm glow, in which every question rated fifty to eighty percent positive, was one of the reasons I was handed the results in my very first week in the school. All in all, the results seemed to suggest that Curtisville High was nothing to rave about, but not a bad place. If there had been a middle category between "agree" and "disagree"—something along the lines of "yeah, sorta"—the responses would have been more revealing.

Question forty-two was the most interesting to a qualitative researcher: an open question asking what could be done to improve Curtisville High. It was messy data, as important data always is; the school couldn't tabulate it, and it never appeared on any of the summaries of this questionnaire.

A lot of responses were predictable. "Fire Mr. Bauer!" "Kill Phillips and Dawson and get a new principal who isn't unfair and doesn't play favorites." These were rash but understandable comments born from the intersection of two people who disagreed within a context of power and subjugation. Names were named, and the suggested remedies were drastic and hot.

There were, however, a large number of comments about an unnamed power, comments that reflected smoldering frustration and confusion rather than live anger. Not one of these remarks was directed toward a named person, but rather toward a role and a system:

> I think if the counselors asked you as a freshman what you might want to pursue, you would have more of the classes you need.

> The counselors don't know their jobs, make career assumptions on the basis of sex, have made extremely poor suggestions on classes, and are generally difficult to deal with.

> I think that we should have a better counseling program. At our school you have to sign up, then practically "beg" to get help from the counselor. Not once have the counselors just called me up to see if I was making the right choices about my classes.

> I think that there should be more help from the counselors. Many of us need help planning out classes and college careers. I hate bugging them all the time, but it is the only way to get anything accomplished.

The school desperately needs new counselors. I have to take an extra year of science because the counselor "accidentally" told me the wrong class to take.

The counselors at this school should take more time out to help the students with ideas and choices. Don't just work with them for a few minutes because you have to. Show some interest and concern. Help them understand their future choices.

We need better counselors. We need people who can spend more than just 30 seconds with us when we have a question. I don't feel like I get any worthwhile advice that I didn't already know when I ask a question about my classes.

I think we need more electives, and the counselors need to actually know what they're talking about when giving students advice.

The repeated themes here—in paraphrase, they are "the counselors don't care about us" and "the counselors don't know their jobs"—are both based on miscommunication and improper assumptions. To say that the counselors don't know their jobs implies that the student has an idea of what the counselor's job is: to help that student make smart, personally enriching class and career choices. That is, unfortunately, a low priority on the counselor's job description, falling well below balancing the schedule, administering standardized tests, and maintaining the hundreds of cumulative files that become the *de facto* student body. The two counselors were charged above all with the efficient distribution of Curtisville's eight hundred students into cost-effective parcels of thirty per room per period.

The counseling offices were trapped at the core of the administration building, reflecting counseling's role as an administrative function rather than a student function. Adrianne Gable's office was just down the narrow corridor from the assistant principal, next to the storage room that was used as the detention cell. "The kids never come to see me," she said, "and I think in part that's because I'm next to the principal and the assistant principal. This is not a friendly hallway for a lot of kids, and it's uncomfortable for them to be here. I'd love to have my office out by the Student Store so that kids could just drop in and borrow a college catalog at lunch or ask me a question between classes."

In early May, I sat in on an English classroom that had been given over to Ms. Gable. Her job for the week was to go to all of the classes to help kids become familiar with the registration materials for the following fall. She passed out everyone's transcript to date and then gave each student a registration form and a course catalog. She then went on to talk in considerable detail about the choreography of registration itself, about how to fill out the form and when it was due back at the Attendance office. In her course descriptions and suggestions for next year's work, she was very bland and general. This makes sense; she was talking to twenty-eight people at once and repeating the same talk in classroom after classroom all week. But it was also clear that she simply didn't know what all of these classes were about. She knew that Geometry comes after Algebra, but not what might be entailed in taking it, and it was still too early to know who would teach it. Thus she didn't answer specific questions very well, telling kids to either look in the book or come talk to her later in the office. One kid asked, "My family's buying a house in Union this summer, so I'm going to Union High next year. When do I register there, and how do I get a form?" Union High and Curtisville High are in the same district, and the schools' counselors work together on common programs, but Ms. Gable had no idea how to answer his question and told him to call the school directly.

I place little blame for this on Ms. Gable herself. It simply wasn't her job to deal with individual problems, but rather to make sure that each of the school's thirty-student cylinders was firing properly, and to ensure that each student was registered toward state-mandated graduation requirements. The gross design and allocation of the class rosters are done during the last two months of the spring (along with emergency stop-gap counseling for seniors in danger of failing a required course), and the fine tuning is performed for the first two or three weeks every fall, leaving a relatively diminished block of time for simple academic counseling. Subtract from that the time spent on designing anti-tobacco and abstinence and zero-tolerance campaigns and orchestrating Career Day and administering and recording standardized achievement tests and simply maintaining student records, and it's a wonder that each of the four hundred students Ms. Gable was assigned got any contact at all. No surprise, though, that the students don't have the sort of emotional reactions to her that they do to their teachers with whom they interact for nine thousand minutes apiece each year. For the students, she is simply "the counselor." For her, they are simply their "cume files," the paper likenesses that have grown between the leaves of alphabetized manila folders.

Career counseling at this scale is as ineffective as course counseling. I sat in on a mass-counseling session for fifty kids who had just received the results of their Armed Services Vocational Aptitude Battery (ASVAB) tests. This group was run by the school's other counselor, Ms. Corelson, who simply read from the provided script and put up the provided overheads at the prompts (displaying them upside-down more often than not). The kids were far ahead of her, having already drawn their highlighter-blue stripes in their Occu-Find booklets, having already discovered which careers were appropriate based on their scores on a test devised by the military for allocating new recruits to needed functions. There was much quiet joking around me regarding Tim's newly-discovered potential as a radar and sonar operator.

Some of the kids were reading the "Exploring Careers" workbook that accompanied the test results. "Exploring Careers" is an advertisement for military recruitment in the guise of a comic book and guide to the test. In it, four cartoon students—the standard characters of diversity: a white girl, a black boy, an Hispanic girl and a white boy—are led through their ASVAB reports and associated career counseling under the hip guidance of the Asian counselor Mr. Lee. In one sequence, Karen, the preppy white girl in the buttondown shirt and tasteful stud earrings, said, "I'm not sure I want to go to college right after school. I'm thinking about entering the military."

Alan, Karen's preppy black male friend in the buttondown shirt and navy pullover sweater, replied, "Really? Why would you do that?"

"The military is a great place to get training and work experience."

Alan said with distaste, "I wouldn't skip college. The military's not for me."

"You don't have to skip college just because you're in the military. You could go to college first and then enter the military as an officer."

Alan was immediately intrigued. "An officer? That's pretty prestigious!"

"Yes, I know. My uncle's a major in the military. That's his officer rank, but he works as a surgeon."

"I never really thought about the military before."

"Well, you should look into it. I hear they give tuition assistance and scholarships."

Alan packed up his books and said with a smile over his shoulder to Karen, "That sure gives me something to think about."[1]

During all of this, while we were reading about Karen and Alan and Maria and Brian or laughing about our own predicted futures as religious professionals or chiropractors or artillery crew members, Ms. Corelson read on from the script, completely oblivious to what the punks, cowboys, and surfers in front of her were actually doing or thinking, doing her utmost to replicate the video that will replace her in a few years.

è&

Patricia Maher, a first-year teacher, talked about the troubles she was having with her first-period World History class. "I just went off on them today. I was the Terminator. You know how in most classes there's one kingpin? Well, in this class there are seven. I just have to beat them somehow. If I can defeat them early in the day then we'll have a good class, but otherwise . . ."

Less than ten feet from the Principal's office and from the Quad but utterly separate from both was the teacher's workroom. This was where the ambivalent role of the teacher in the school was most thoroughly expressed.[2] The teachers weren't happy with the administration, but were likewise often frustrated and bewildered by their kids. The workroom was the safe place to voice all of the gloom and cynicism that comes from feeling helpless within a larger system, the same gloom and cynicism they found so unattractive in their students.

Charlene Richmond complained about her trouble in recognizing inappropriate behavior at the school dance she'd chaperoned on

Friday night. "They need to have some code of conduct so that I know what to break up and what not to. It's like they're having sex standing up—it's just disgusting as far as I'm concerned."

Lily Chase entertained us endlessly with stories of her terrible students. "They decided I was a workaholic, because there were a few minutes left in the period and I suggested that we use them productively. And so I said, 'Gee, it's wonderful that I have people who will point out my character faults.' And that got them going. 'Well, you know what your problem is, Mrs. Chase? You just work too hard. You could be like us.'"

She laughed in the retelling. "I said, 'I *could* be like you, couldn't I?' They didn't see any irony in that. It's always the people in the junkiest cars who have the most advice on their cars. Here are these people with zero credits and zero prospects, and they're telling me that I could be like them."

Every day, I knew that if I were in the teacher's workroom during fourth period, I could collect another of Mrs. Chase's condescending moralisms:

> Have they ever been at a party without drinking and without smoking and without pot, and just quietly played a game? Have they ever just had a conversation? Talking to one another doesn't have to mean being vulgar.

> We tell them what to do, and they just won't do it.

> I'd appreciate a civil acknowledgement that I'm the teacher, and that when I tell them to do something that they need to do it in a polite and courteous manner.

> They were tractable. I would tell them, "This is what you have to do to debate," and they would do it.

> She said to me in an arrogant and condescending manner, "All of our other teachers let us talk during the movies." And I said, "Well, you can't do it here." And she said, "You're a witch." I said, "Excuse me?" And she said, "You're a witch." And I said, "You're excused now, you may go home." I'd like her suspended, not for five days but maybe only a couple, for defiance. Because she defied the legitimate authority of a teacher.

This is the same teacher who, while running off one of her innumerable batches of five-sheet busywork sets copied from a sophomore English curriculum book, saw me glancing though one and asked, "Do you know what that's called?"

"No," I replied, expecting some esoteric curricular jargon.

"It's called a 'sponge.' You throw it in when you have some extra time to soak up."

છે.

The year was full of struggles between administrators, teachers, and students, each group seeing the other as opponent. Mrs. DiSalvo, the Drama teacher, battled with the administration (in the form of the assistant principal and the custodial staff) for over a year to have regular access to the multi-purpose room. This room—which abutted the Drama classroom and which held the main stage—had been locked even to her, with the key available only on scheduled request through the assistant principal's office. She finally had to vaguely threaten the school with a discrimination suit ("the male P.E. teachers would never stand for this kind of treatment, not having keys to the gym and training rooms") in order to get keys to the performance room.

Kiki, a tenth-grader, had already talked with me about her experience of being locked out of a room. "We wanted to put our instruments in the band room when we got to school, because it was raining and we weren't about to leave them outside the room. And the custodians wouldn't open the room for us to put our instruments in, because we needed to have an adult in charge. So we had to carry them until fourth period when Mr. Phelps got there."

The year at Curtisville was a year of contract dispute between the teachers and the district. The teacher's association alleged misappropriation of funds and missing records, coverups and embezzlement. They believed that the school and district administration was telling them lies, protecting their positions at the common expense of teachers and students. The administration in turn believed that the teachers were using their classrooms to turn the kids against the district's bargaining position.

The administration believed very strongly that teenagers were in need of continual and unvarying observation and control. The students believed that the administration didn't give a rip about them beyond the financial mathematics of the Average Daily Attendance reimbursement from Sacramento.

The teachers believed that their students were lazy and amoral, best served when quiet, civil, and tractable. The students believed that their teachers were petty tyrants.

It doesn't matter which of these overstated, knee-jerk positions were "right," if any. What matters is that the teachers and the administration and the students were separate enough to foster a constant and mutual mistrust. The strong spatial separation of administrators, students and teachers was only the echo of their organizational and social separation, but it did serve to make those gaps harder to bridge. The three groups each sat in their held spaces and saw the other as adversaries to be kept in check.

Separation allows us to draw caricatures of those "others;" it means that we don't know them well enough to see their dreams and desires, their goals and strategies. They can stay safely "they," adversaries with impure motives that we ourselves have created.

The year I spent in Curtisville coincided with the school's official accreditation review by WASC, the Western Association of Schools and Colleges. Every single teacher in-service day all year was devoted to WASC. I have a copy of the school's final self-report, all 413 pages of it. It describes some school, probably, but not Curtisville High. At least not the one I was in. It describes the school that the administration thought they were running, but not the school the students occupied.

Rosalynd, the student teacher in Biology and Geology, sat in on the science department's WASC meeting when the accreditation team was on campus in March. She later said to me that she noticed that while the Biology room was closed for the lunchtime meeting, a great number of students came and tried to open the door because they actually hung out in the science room at lunch. She hoped that the committee members would take note of that. Of course, they didn't—the report was exclusively written from an administrator's point of view, and talked about "how the school functioned" (as though it were a machine) rather than about how the students or teachers thought things were going. It was a programmatic investigation rather than a human one. And a flawed examination at that, because they primarily looked at what kinds of programs and equipment were in place, not what kinds of outcomes were being achieved. Curtisville High School was at or just below state medians on all the standardized tests, a thoroughly fiftieth-percentile school. That is not grounds for a maximum six-year approval, if in fact we think those test scores are important. The six-year approval is what the school received, because it was functioning well.

Teachers resented spending time all year on WASC, which they saw as a public relations tool and little more. The students—at least those few who knew that WASC even existed, for whom the acronym became "What? Another Stupid Committee?"—made fun of both the process and the product: another exercise by grown-ups for other grown-ups, irrelevant to their lives.

The WASC report only had meaning within one building on campus—but it was the building that mattered.

CHAPTER THIRTEEN

Take Your Seats, Please

First we catalog the artifact: a sheet of plywood, measuring about two feet wide and sixteen inches deep, with a wood-grained plastic laminate top. A fiberglass or thermoplastic seat, swimming-pool blue. Three steel tubes a little less than an inch in diameter, bent so as to make legs and to attach the seat at a fixed relationship to the plywood. A handful of pop rivets and aluminum brackets.

It's an industrial triumph, really, the mass production of school desks from such meager origins. The school desk passes through hundreds of lives during its transition from iron ore and crude oil and timber to its ultimate rest at the salvage furniture outlet. Its story would be the story of specialization and "added value," of capital moving through many hands, all requiring the coordination of extraordinarily diverse laborers by remarkably similar managers. Some talented archaeologist of the future might profitably weave together the social and economic roles of all the people who handle that school desk along its lifeline. My job is considerably more constrained: to talk about this mass-produced artifact as it concerned the citizens of Curtisville High School.

To understand the school desk from the point of view of its owner, consider that it was one of a batch of about twelve hundred. Sturdy, uniform, inexpensive, and easily replaceable, the desk was selected because it would be used for tens of thousands of hours by decades of teenagers, and because it might wind up in any classroom on either campus as the district performed its annual mathematical balancing of teachers, students, and spaces.

The school desk as owned object is a material lesson in Modernist culture, no different except in scale from the uniformity of classrooms, or of schools, or of curriculum packages, or of testing. Educational purchasers and educational merchandisers understand one another; they share a set of beliefs about meeting defined needs, providing cost-effective solutions, promoting standardization and the objective measurement of benefits, acknowledging centralized decisionmakers, pursuing economies of scale.

But the school desk is not simply an owned object; it is also a tool provided to the school's production managers, the teachers. To understand the same desk from the point of view of a teacher, see it as one of a set of thirty or more to be fit into a 960-square-foot classroom with modest walkways to allow access to the open left sides of the chairs.

The arrangement of desks has to support an educational program, but as varied as those programs are thought to be, some pattern of rows and columns is invariably selected. Sometimes it's a simple rectangle, sometimes two facing clusters, sometimes three or four pods, but always the desks aim at the front, ensuring unobstructed views of the teacher and blackboard and overhead projector—of course! what else could students profitably look at?— and minimizing the distractions raised by kids able to look at one another.

Irene, in a fit of frustration, said to me one morning during a break, "I hate this class! We always have to respond to Mr. Jacobs. If someone else says something interesting, you can't respond to that person. We can't just, like, have a discussion. We always have to go through him and talk about what he wants." Irene may believe that this is just a facet of Mr. Jacobs' personality, but it's also a facet of his classroom, and every other. The desks were movable in order to be of use in small group work as well as for lectures, but that was quite frankly an afterthought in most classrooms; if the desks had been nailed to the floor as they had been in decades past, the janitors would have been more inconvenienced than the teachers. If teaching is in fact moving from "the sage on the stage" to "the guide on the side," as pedagogical reform has it, Curtisville's classrooms most certainly were not.[1]

To understand the desk from one final point of view, that of its occupants, see it as a setting for activity. When the kids were assigned to their fixed-position desks, they struggled against their bonds as though they were physically tied, a room full of veal calves deprived of light, movement, and stimulation. They twisted around or over their shoulder to face the person behind them. They sat sideways in the seats, gripping the desktop and seatback in an effort to support themselves. They scooted forward away from the chair's support whenever they had to write or do deskwork, and stuck their legs in the aisle when they needed relief from confinement. And when it became time to do group work, there were the desks, hauled around in front of each person like great pregnant stomachs. The group members sat separated from one another by an uncrossable prairie of plywood, 90 or 180 degrees opposed, and tried in vain to collaborate.

The occupants of the school desks had a different set of criteria for successful seating than did the owners or managers of those desks. They wanted flexibility in orientation and posture. They wanted the ability to move on short notice and to be close to their friends. They wanted to cluster in twos and threes and fours and not in thirties. These must have been the relevant criteria, because they were unfailingly represented in the arrangements that the kids chose freely whenever they could. Over the course of the year, a number of classrooms became particularly strong lunchtime hangouts for one group or another. The Physics and the Art rooms were popular with younger boys who wanted to play cards. The two Biology rooms were filled with girls, mostly, who enjoyed handling the snakes and the rats. Many Cowboys seemed to find the wood shop, the Drama Room was flowing with Geeks, and the Band Room was filled with musicians.

These rooms shared one specific characteristic: they were not based on row-and-column classroom chairs. Kids flocked to rooms where they had control over their spatial organization, where they could crowd together at the end of a lab table or sit on top of one, where they could sit at the edge of the stage and let their legs drape down. They sat far closer together than they could when locked into their cage-desks, hip-to-hip and shoulder-to-shoulder in the physical manifestation of friendship. Up the road at the Arco mini-mart, the Stoners also sat on top of the picnic tables, not in the seats facing one another. By sitting on top, they were able to shift from side to side, to participate in a number of small conversations instead of all facing inward to be a part of a single larger one. They could jump down in instant response to the arrival of food and friends and music, or subtly redefine their allegiances with a turn of their shoulders.

From outside, this often looked inappropriate. Picnic table seats, for example, were covered with puddles of spit and spilled soda after kids left. Inconsiderate behavior, perhaps, but it reflected their use of the table: they sat on top and used the seats as footrests, and spitting on a footrest is no sin. As teenagers learn to do, they had taken an object made for one purpose and reinvented it to serve another.

The school desk is particularly resistant to this kind of reinvention. It was fascinating to watch the difference in the same kids when they met in different places, places which carried clear expectations for proper behavior. Kids who were active and vocal in the halls and during lunch gatherings became quiet and submissive in classrooms, even outside class periods. The Kiwanis International youth group (called Key Club) met every Tuesday at lunch in Mr. Bauer's room, a five-wide-by-six-deep array of desks aimed at a central lectern. Erin, the chapter president, stood behind the podium and led the Club members in the recitation of their oath:

> I pledge on my honor to uphold the objects of Key Club International; to build my home, school and community; to serve my nation and God and combat all forces which tend to undermine these institutions.

Then Erin went through the agenda items, asking for volunteers for specific jobs at the Winter Formal and public service events. The other twenty-two members—all volunteers, all there because they were supposedly interested in the goings-on of the club—sat at their isolated desks, facing the authority figure at the front of the room, not responding at all. They were acting out their spatially proscribed roles as recipients. These kids knew the drill. Whenever they met in a row-and-column classroom for an extracurricular activity, they became teacher and students.

The medium is the message.

CHAPTER FOURTEEN

The Domain of the Geeks

It seems pointless to speculate on what life events might lead one to become a Drama Geek. The big common-sense causes aren't good predictors. Family structure, for instance, doesn't seem to have mattered. Several Geeks have lived through divorces, but several others have had the same two parents for their entire lives. One never lived a day with her father, referring to him as "the sperm donor," and one was officially abandoned (to take care of his fourteen-year-old sister) by his already-absent mother the day he turned eighteen.

There are poor Geeks, living in three-room plywood houses and tumbling mobile homes in the woods, and there are middle-class Geeks who live in comfortable houses with their research scientist and fast-food franchisee parents. There are urban Geeks and suburban Geeks and rural Geeks, male Geeks and female Geeks, athletic Geeks and awkward Geeks, Geeks with perfect grades and Geeks who graduated only through the grace of extra credit in the final week of school.

I bothered with any of this conjecture only because the Geeks were my adopted group over the year, because they were the most like me: quiet among strangers but boisterous among friends, deeply curious about the world but actively skeptical about the ability of school to satisfy that curiosity. I think they recognized me as one of their own and took me in.

The Geeks were infatuated with the world of the imagination. Voracious but selective readers, compulsive moviegoers but not much for watching television, they were kids whose creativity for the most part wasn't well-suited to the classroom. But there was one classroom to which they flocked, their refuge amidst a campus full of Geometry and English and PE and Physics, the room which gave them their collective name.

The Drama Room was unique on the Curtisville campus for several reasons. First, it was held separate from the rest of the academic and vocational classrooms; along with its neighbor the Band Room, it was the only classroom east of the Quad. By virtue of its distance from the mainstream of the school, it allowed the Geeks a self-selected separation from the busywork and popularity contests of the rest of the campus. Second, it contained a small stage, a three-foot-high platform that took up a quarter of the room's floor area. Everyone in the Drama Room was constantly reminded by the presence of the stage that this room was not another anonymous cube of conditioned air assigned at the whim and pleasure of the principal, but rather that it was reserved as a workplace for the imagination.

At the back of the small stage was a rolling metal garage door which led to the full-sized stage of the Multi-Purpose Room, and that was a third distinct difference between this classroom and any other. The Drama Room and the main stage were directly connected, and every student understood that the private work undertaken in the smaller room would be directly transferred to the larger public room beyond.

The fourth difference that characterized the Drama Room was that it was open at almost any time. Mrs. DiSalvo (always and only known as Mrs. D) arrived at school most mornings at about quarter of eight; she unlocked her room, laid down her workbooks and purse at her desk, picked up her coffee cup, and walked off to the teacher's workroom. Most mornings, she was followed into her room by between three and five Geeks who by virtue of unfortunate bus scheduling had to arrive at school well before class. When she left the room—not intending to come back until just before the bell—they stayed behind to talk and play music on her cassette boombox.

Likewise at lunch, she generally kept the room open while she talked with her friends in the workroom. The Drama Room and the hallway and grass just outside were flooded with the constant come-and-go of two dozen Geeks. Nine Inch Nails and Nirvana blasted from the overheated stereo, card games were in full flow, a small hack circle claimed the stage, and three or four conversations were alive with kids sitting on the tops of desks near the door. Walking into the Drama Room at lunch was like walking into a happy day-care center.

Although there were many times when Mrs. D wasn't in the Drama Room, her presence was always with us there. The walls were ringed with posters from the eighteen years of school plays she'd produced, and lined with masks made by students and profes-sional friends. A cardboard box the size of a dishwasher sat under the stage lift and another box was on the side cabinet, both heaped with theater magazines. Her armoire in the corner, bearing a small handwritten sign—"Please Stay Out. Mrs. D"—always stood open but untouched, while the cabinet beneath the sink bearing theatri-cal makeup was opened regularly to sample the promises that await when choosing a new face.

Mrs. D's trust extended far beyond what the school was com-fortable with. Supervision was always deemed necessary at Curtisville High, but there were no supervisors in the Drama Room before school and during lunch. It was no longer a school room. It was a chapel of the imagination, and this congregation of joy would not harm it.

&

The classrooms that worked most completely at Curtisville High—the ones where I repeatedly saw joy in the form of close attention, spontaneous exclamations of insight, fluid relationships aimed at learning, laughter and questioning—were also the ones that had been most completely personalized, the ones that looked least like they might have been someone else's room. Even where there was extraordinary commonality in gross elements like con-struction materials and dimensions (and the ever-present desks), there was a layer of personal history that masked the institutional uniformity.

Dan Jacobs' room, for instance, was almost invisible, buried under a continuous layer of Dan Jacobs. The walls were hidden by posters that could not be bought from a curriculum development company. Posters of the town in Germany where he'd lived and taught for a fellowship year. Reproductions of Renaissance art. Outstanding student posters he had collected over the years, explaining the themes of *Zen and the Art of Motorcycle Maintenance* in concise visual terms. Photos of Einstein and Gandhi, and quotes from both. Under the clock, a gift from a student of years past: a pastel caricature of Mr. Jacobs in high admiral's regalia, standing on a dock in front of a battleship, cannons aimed at the class.

The front right corner of the room was dominated by an armoire that contained his stereo equipment, his VCR and his videotapes; his television, which he used to teach his class "Film and Literature," sat on top, and his speakers were suspended from the ceiling. He needed to have mastery over his equipment so that the magic of discussion or presentation needn't be dissipated while he fumbled with an unfamiliar control panel. Further back in the room was a glass-doored bookcase filled with his reference books. None of this belonged to the Northern Timber Consolidated High School District. It was all part of the personal toolkit of Dan Jacobs, the things that he believed he needed to teach his classes properly.

But it would be a mistake to see it only as a toolkit. Mr. Jacobs' room was also an expression of himself. He surrounded himself with images of his heroes and his high ideals. He told everyone who came into his room that he loved medieval cities and great art, that he loved the German high classical composers, that he loved books and the ideas they contained, that he had the greatest regard for those who held strong principles and could express them simply. He didn't have to use words to tell us those things—words that would have been less convincing simply through being said—because the evidence was all around us.

Just down the hall, Aaron Weimer's biology room was the home to an enormous flock of stuffed local seabirds, the gift of his predecessor in the Science Department. Mr. Weimer had since added seven or eight aquariums that were home to turtles, snakes, and scorpions. Another small cage held a family of rats, interesting in and of themselves as they tumbled on their exercise wheel but ultimately useful as producers of young snake food. A huge wood-and-wire cage became home to a four-foot-long iguana, perched on his tree limb under the sunlamp.

Around the corner from Mr. Weimer, Joe Lyon had a glass case extending the full length of his classroom, containing twenty-five years of rock samples that he and his students had found and identified. Drinking-straw models of the crystal structures of various minerals hung from the light fixtures overhead. A handmade erosion-modeling table gurgled across the room, its trickling river displacing the sand into new channels and deltas.

All over campus, the same scene played itself out in different forms. In those seven or eight rooms where a good teacher had set up shop, the anonymous space became his room or her room, transformed into a deeply personal statement of what was good, what was important, what was worth loving. Those were the rooms where students flocked between classes, where they arrived early and stayed late, where discussions didn't end with the razor-suddenness of the clock.

The school as an organization is concerned with vandalism and theft, and these things do occur. But vandalism and theft were almost unknown in these highly reinvented rooms, because the students recognized the things within them not as "school property" belonging to some unknowable bureaucracy, but as Mr. Jacobs' things, or Mr. Weimer's things, or Mrs. D's things. Curtisville's kids showed a remarkable respect for property as long as that property belonged to a real person. An act against a desk or a drinking fountain was aimed at nobody and everybody, against faceless and unfaceable power; but an act against the personal artifacts in Mr. Jacobs' room would have been very explicitly an act against Mr. Jacobs, and it just didn't happen.

For April Fools', Mr. Jacobs' first-period students covered over every single poster and painting and saying in the room with its pop-culture antithesis. Where once there had been Raphael's "Madonna and Child," there was simply a photo of Madonna. A team photo of the San Francisco 49ers covered his photo of Einstein. The pastel portraying him as a somewhat threatening admiral was covered by a sketch portraying him on a skateboard with baggy jeans and a backward baseball cap, captioned, "Just Do It."

It takes a lot of love to be the focus of such an elaborate practical joke. Nothing was harmed, and the classroom was back to its regular self the following day. Even for those students who had participated in the prank with some degree of malice or frustration, the environment was a palpable symbol of Mr. Jacobs himself. He was performing one of the time-honored roles of the teacher, which is to give his students something to push against. He gave them himself, all over the room, every day.

In those few classrooms where the teachers were willing to say, both in word and in action, that they absolutely loved what they were doing, students were engaged. Not every student, no, of course not. But it was only there that they had a chance, where they were surrounded by enthusiasm. In other rooms, there was nothing to capture them, no spark of visible love to grasp for.

I talked with teachers and students all year about what they loved to do, whether that was photography or surfing or hunting or reading or whatever. When I asked how they got involved in those things, they invariably answered that it was *someone* that got them interested, and not anything intrinsic in the activity itself. They followed someone they respected into an activity that that person loved, and discovered its worth from there.

For the most part, Curtisville's teachers—like most of my own in high school twenty years ago, and even more recently in college and graduate school as well—were embarrassed to death to say that they loved whatever it is that they did. It takes a lot of guts to stand up in front of thirty people who didn't volunteer to be there and say, "Dissecting this pig is going to be the coolest thing I'm going to do all day." It's very revealing, and thus threatening, to let people know that you really take pleasure from poetry, or trigonometry, or theater, or invertebrate biology.

And so they often hid in their uniform rooms behind a curriculum plan, a textbook, and a set of handouts, and said, in effect, "You and I have to do this together because it's what the book says we have to do." They armored themselves in the appearance of not caring, so that they wouldn't be hurt when the kids didn't care either.

Places have an experiential meaning at their core. They have their programmatic function, of course, but there is far more along with it. In a handful of places, we are invited to leave behind the mundane to find the sublime. We are given entry into a new and artificially heightened world. If teaching is the transmission of joy from one person to another, then it's no surprise that in the best classrooms, the manifestations of that joy took all sorts of forms—

posture, tone of voice, creative exercises, and all of the physical surroundings of the cathedral of knowledge.

Mrs. D had been a high-fashion model, got her masters degree in performance, and still longed for a sabbatical year to spend with a theater company. She enjoyed teaching school, but she lived for the theater; that is what made her an extraordinary teacher. This was true of every other great teacher at Curtisville as well: they seemed to enjoy teaching, but not nearly so much as they enjoyed comparative anatomy or Milton or the domestic experience of World War II. When school worked at Curtisville High, it was because some adult who loved what they studied shared that joy with a group of teenagers.

One of Mrs. D's favorite lessons was the neutral mask, a device that covers the face and offers no expression whatsoever so that the emotion has to be portrayed entirely through body movement. She demonstrated for us, putting on the cold white ceramic mask and taking us wordlessly through the slouch of sorrow and stretched heights of joy and rage with only her hands and shoulders and spine to work with, intense in her desire to get theater across to us. Afterward, she reminded us, "You have three masks—your face and your two hands." We won't forget.

Mrs. D filled the classroom easily when she chose, or sat small and let the significance of a student's quiet posture of despair ring from the stage. She was at once tremendously demanding and full of praise for work done well, and the other students followed her example and supported each others' every attempt. She created a room in which the kids could take chances without risk of censure. The only way to lose was to *not* take a chance.

The Geeks had found their cathedral, their monument to bravery and imagination, a place where it was acceptable to dare, where their earnest attempts at explaining the world to themselves and each other were applauded, where they could try on selves and experiment with the most basic facets of their personalities. It was no wonder that they sought it out whenever they could.

CHAPTER FIFTEEN

The Passion Pit

Ethan and I arrived back at school from a cigarette break, a standard drive from the parking lot to the turnaround at Miller Park and back. Ethan took a final drag off the Marlboro and stubbed the last quarter-inch in the ashtray just as we turned off Curtisville Road and into the parking lot; it was the fourth time we'd done this drive in two days, and the cigarettes were as accurate as an egg timer. He'd skipped the last ten minutes or so of Journalism—it was the final Friday of his final school year, breezy and sunny and not academically motivational—but he returned for the start of sixth period and Yearbook. As we walked into the Yearbook classroom, which an hour earlier had been the student store and still smelled of microwaved burritos, Ethan drew me immediately through its rear door and into the darkroom. "Want to watch me do my passion?"

In the darkroom proper, there were six enlargers against the rear wall and a large steel sink at the side. Rectangular plastic bins in the sink were labeled, left to right, "developer," "stop bath," and "water." Each was fed from above through plastic tubes descending from five-gallon tanks.

Ethan flipped on the pale red light overhead, finding the switch immediately in the blackness, and slid a scrap of photographic paper from its drawer, snipping off a six-inch strip to do an exposure test. He fastened his negative, taken from his heavy ring binder filled with several thousand negatives, to the enlarger lens and put a piece of cardboard over the ribbon of photo paper. Then he turned on the projection lamp, slid the cardboard down to expose an inch of the paper, counted two seconds, slid the cardboard down another inch, counted two seconds, slid the cardboard down another inch, and counted two seconds, until the paper was completely exposed. Then he snapped off the lamp, pulled the photo paper out of the enlarger, and tossed it into the developer bath.

A minute of periodic swirling resulted in a banded image of increasing density and contrast. That got moved to the stop bath, where he studied it for the degree of exposure he wanted. Ethan was supremely confident in the darkroom, moving easily around the equipment with the reflexive knowledge that comes from having done it all hundreds of times. I asked, "Which do you like better, the camera part or the darkroom part?"

"I like all of it. I like the anticipation of waiting for a print to come out. Some of it's boring—I've developed six hundred, seven hundred, maybe a thousand rolls of film, and that never gets any more exciting, it's always the same process. But then you get your negatives, and it's like 'Yeah, there's some cool negatives here.' So there's the routine stuff, but if you can get behind that, you can do fun stuff."

Ethan had a really good photo and video class at Nevada Valley, the high school where he'd moved from at the beginning of this senior year. "The guy was real workmanlike about it, and that turned a lot of people off, but it was like the real world. He'd be out in the classroom with all the lights on, and he'd ask you for a piece of photo paper. If people weren't thinking, they'd open their box and start to get a piece out for him, and he'd say, 'Well, there goes that boxful.' I loved it. This is what I'd like to do—I've applied at Photo World, Union Portraits. I've got a pretty good portfolio."

He ran the same negative with a full sheet of photo paper at the exposure time he'd selected, and twelve seconds later put a fresh print into the first bath. Once it was into the stop bath, we opened the door (lightproofed with a thick sheet of cardboard nailed over the air grille) and walked out to see what the rest of the class was doing. Mr. Dover checked on Ethan's progress, and asked him to come in the following day for the group photo of Yearbook, as well as to come back on Monday for some final printing work. Mr. Dover depended on Ethan for basic photo support, letting him manage the entire Yearbook photo process. Mr. Springs was much the same way in Ethan's Journalism class—both teachers were relieved to have a professional to turn the process over to, so that they could count on one thing coming out properly.

We retreated from the commotion and the burrito aroma, back to the darkroom. "Doing photos for Yearbook and Journalism, it's all deadlines and stuff. Gotta do this, need this, do that. I don't like that part as much. It's nice to be able to come in here and not have to deal with people."

"Yeah, it's a peaceful place."

"Sometimes it's boring as hell, but it's nice to be able to be in a place that's mine, even if it is only for a couple of periods." Then he looked at me in the pale red light and said, "It's kind of weird having you follow me. I mean, I don't mind, and I volunteered for it, but I feel like I should be doing more exciting things."

ᷠᷠ

I saw it only a handful of times over the course of the school year, but each time it was so strong that I think I should talk a little about it.

Curtisville High, like most high schools, had a number of ways for students to get academic credit for doing some of the school's necessary work. Office Assistant was worth the same five credits as Biology or U.S. History, and the attendance office would have been swamped without the three or four students who worked each period to do the most basic filing and paper management. Mindi, a junior, was one of the school's most visible administrators as she made her rounds in second, fourth, and sixth periods to collect attendance sheets.

Some teachers had teaching assistants assigned to them, students who weren't responsible for teaching or even knowing their subject, but who typed assignment sheets or ticked off incorrect answers from a test code. Megan had never taken any of the Spanish she graded daily, didn't know a word of Spanish beyond "adios" and "taco;" she just checked student responses on the multiple-choice exam sheets and recorded the numbers in a fresh pale green column of the gradebook.

But every so often, a student was put into a position of trust, given a job that required skill and attention and experience, a job where failure would have been more than personal.[1] To fail would have meant that an entire class's work would have been lost.

It probably happened more frequently and for more students than the four times I saw it—I can only hope—but the four times that I saw it were in two very similar rooms, the darkroom and the theater lighting booth. There, adult work roles took place in adult work spaces—places where expensive and complex machinery was open, not under lock and key; places where resources were quickly and freely accessible; places away from the constant surveillance of a supervisor, where the worker carried out her own strategy on her own accord.

Mara had tried out for the school play as a freshman. She decided halfway through her audition reading that the stage wasn't for her, and put down her script. "Do you need anyone to work backstage?"

This year, as a junior, she was in charge of not only the lighting operation but the lighting design for *Our Town*, as well as for the Native American talent show, the cheerleaders' fashion show, the Advanced Drama performances, a local dance studio recital and my year-end monologue. The computerized sixty-four-channel lighting board presented no challenge to her any longer, nor did the two antique cannon spotlights or the sound system. The challenge was for her to stop obsessing over whether the lights were hung and aimed perfectly, or whether the actors know their stage cues well enough to hit the lights.

It's opening night at 6:50, and Mara has her headset on and is running the programming card into the light board. Mrs. D's husband, Mr. D (the drama teacher at nearby Union High), is the chaperone for the light booth for the evening, as the school requires. He and Mara and Irene all know that his presence is bureaucratic rather than advisorial—they'll do just fine without him, and he sits back away from the workstation, first grading homework and then working the crossword puzzle from the daily paper.

Mrs. D emerges from the frantic dressing room and walks up to tell Mara the 7:15 and 7:30 house-light cues and instructions. Mara complains that the sickly green-tan of the fluorescent backstage lights is seeping below the curtain into the semi-darkness of the theater. Mrs. D laughingly tells Mara to stop nagging, and Mara says, "I know, I know. But just *look* at that, it's horrible."

Mara brings the lights down at 7:32, right on time, and the show's underway. Ryan walks into the small spotlight, wearing his thinning middle-aged hair and small-town brown suit, and tells us a little bit about Grovers Corners. Mara talks quietly along with him, without reading from the script, and pushes the slider for setting number two as Ryan strolls across the front edge of the stage.

Every time a new actor comes onto the stage, Mara intently coaxes him into position like a dog—"Come on, Loren, come up to the center, into the light . . . good boy." The actors can't hear this, of course, but Mara says it as though it makes all the difference, eyes locked on the stage. Irene is equally focused on the sound, but misses one cue when the 5:10 train should go by. She hadn't cued the tape correctly, and no sound appears. Ryan covers it well on-stage, saying, "Must be a little late."

At the end of the first act, the Clear-Com headset system breaks down, so there's no more communication with the backstage manager. This means trouble for the beginnings of the second and third acts, when Mara can't start the new light setting without knowing that the actors are ready to go. "I feel so isolated up here," she moans to Irene at the same time she pulls the slider for setting 23.

In Act Three, during the graveyard scene, Mara anticipates all the lines, quietly urging the actors to hit their timing just right. They've got no body acting to fall back on; they're just stationary in their chairs, and they have to do it all by vocal timing and inflection. Mara shifts the lights from the living to the dead and back again, and says quietly, "You know, Irene, the thing that makes this the most painful is the dispassionate nature of the actors. They're saying the most human things, but they can't behave like people any more."

At 9:40, the show is over. Irene and Mara missed a couple of cues (they say—the only one I noticed was the late train), but calmly and logically improvised their way through the show while their technology was crippled. More importantly, they were able to handle their technical responsibilities in a way that enhanced what the audience saw, without any expectation that they would be acknowledged for it.

Mara had originally volunteered to do backstage work because her dad had already taught her some basic electrical skills. As she was doing lights and set construction that first year, she met Trent, a senior who taught her more about lighting tech and a little about lighting design as well, along with being her first serious boyfriend. That love soon ended, but she's since worked some plays with him at Timber State's theater and has taught *him* a few things about lighting and electronics. One of Mara's final responsibilities for the school is to train someone new on sound and lights so that there's someone to take over when she leaves. The designee is Sarah, a sophomore who'll be taking the helm for the second night under Mara's watch.

Once we get to the theater for night two, we find Sarah, who isn't worried about running the lights—yet. Irene's set to go with the sound (having cued and re-cued the train whistle), Sarah runs an abbreviated light check, and I settle into a chair in the back row to watch the show and catch up on my notebook. The house lights come down and stage lights come up. Mara sits next to me, plugged into the headset. She's cuing Sarah a little bit, reassuring her as well, whispering in the back row. I mostly just get lost in the show, except when Mara is urging Loren to come into the cue spot or telling Sarah to slow her fades down.

At the end of the second act, the show seems to be running fine, but the potential for problems with the Clear-Com is still there, so Mara goes down to talk with Ryan backstage for a minute and gets trapped there when the house lights go down for Act Three.

Without Mara's running commentary, I really get involved in the third act. The off-center acting is extraordinary, especially Julian as Doc Gibbs. He's sitting off to the side of the action, out of the lights, and is still completely in character, drumming his fingers in impatience while waiting for his wife to come home. During the graveyard scene, while the center of attention is on the dead Mother Gibbs and Emily talking about going back to the living, Doc Gibbs stays behind the mourners in the darkness, picks up a flower from Emily's grave, and walks over to his wife's grave with it. (I told Julian that a couple of weeks later that he'd made me cry, and he said, "Do you know what I was thinking right then? 'I never took her to Paris.'") Then the play was over; instead of the standard curtain call, Mrs. D had placed them around the stage in a sort of town portrait, a gorgeous tableau. I can't get over how good these kids can be when we let them.

❧

In Spanish, Senora Poore needs to grade 160 tests, so she puts a Spanish-language melodrama on the video machine and pacifies the room. Benjamin gets permission to go to the darkroom instead in order to work on things for the yearbook. Once we're there, rather than doing the yearbook prints, he pulls out his own notebook of contact sheets and negatives and asks if there are any prints that I'd like to have. I look through them and ask for one of Julian, along with Benjamin's favorite photo of a shaded path in the Union Community Forest. He shows me how to print them, running the enlarger and making a test strip for exposure time, using the various developer and stop baths. He works as quickly and confidently as Ethan, if not as meticulously, cutting and placing paper quickly rather than by measurement. He clearly knows what he's doing and what the outcomes will be, more or less, but he doesn't sweat the details while he's teaching me—he's more interested that I understand the steps along the way. Mr. Dover has him in third period for an independent study in Photography, and also uses him as a teaching assistant for beginning photographers. Benjamin's hoping that he'll be a high school photo teacher one day, if he doesn't (a) win the lottery or (b) do the lights for a Nine Inch Nails tour (Mara's taught him plenty).

Our prints come out pretty well, and we hang them to dry before going back to Spanish with ten minutes left. As we re-enter the room, I see that Senora Poole is still focused on her stack of tests, but that the television three feet from her desk has been changed from the Spanish soap opera to a first-round game in the NCAA basketball tournament (the school has been inundated with betting-pool sheets for two days). Mara's reading *The Grapes of Wrath*, and I ask how long ago they switched to basketball. "About half an hour ago," she sighed, slumping further in her chair, her head coming to rest on her arms.

The re-entry from the stellar space of joy to the dense atmosphere of routine was never as harsh for me as in that moment, in that complete surrender that slackened Mara's face and shoulders. She could overcome any problem in the lighting booth, but was powerless in the face of apathy.

CHAPTER SIXTEEN

Convenience Store Orphans

On the second day of school, I made the seven-minute migration along with about a hundred students to the Arco mini-mart up by the freeway. The group was large because the Arco was one of only two food outlets within walking distance of the school. The other was also an Arco mini-mart, about the same distance in the opposite direction.

The high school had donated five picnic tables to the store over the summer in order to help keep kids from sitting on the curbs and standing in the corners of the lot. Sure enough, there were dozens of kids sitting on the curbs and standing in the corners of the lot, and the picnic tables sat neglected. The tables were on the far edge of the site, on the side farthest from the school and away from the walking path so that kids couldn't sit there and be a natural part of the flow of arrival and departure. The tables were tucked behind some eucalyptus with their backs to the fence along the freeway entry; kids who sat there wouldn't be very visible to the kids in line at the store. The frantic, beer-bellied manager kept trying to keep people from sitting on the curb closer to the stream of their friends—"There's picnic tables over there! Go sit there, that's what we put 'em in for!"

My first thought was that the store had clearly put the picnic tables in the wrong place (the comment in my journal said, "Wrong, wrong, wrong! They might as well have put them on the roof!"), but I was in error, fooled by the temporary diversity and number of customers early in the school year. The Arco knew their core clientele better than I and had planned for the longer term.

There was a sign on the door of the Arco mini-mart (I never saw it, but the woman at the register kept yelling about it, and we could hear her through the door) that there were only six students allowed in the store at a time. We were lined up thirty deep, extending beyond the gasoline canopy and out into the sunshine, with only twenty-five minutes before the bell rang to begin class again. The girl standing next to me said, "You're not a high school student, you can go ahead."

"Really? No way."

Another girl turned around and said, "Yeah, if you're not a student you don't have to wait for the line, you can just go right in."

I said, "I'm in no hurry," and talked to Tami, the one beside me, for the ten minutes it took us to get up to the entry. Kurt, the manager, was standing in the door, holding us back. Tami, worried about getting back on time, asked me, "If I give you some money, will you get me maybe five or six Jo-Jo's [fried potato wedges] and a ninety-nine-cent Doritos, the nacho kind, and a sixteen-ounce anything non-diet?" I decided that I didn't want that level of responsibility, and so I grabbed her arm and said, "Come on in, you're with me."

A claustrophobic would have passed out from the crush of bodies immobilized by wire racks and glass counters and neon signs and other bodies. There were perhaps fifteen people in the store; two-thirds were high school kids. The room was no bigger than a large home living room, and half of its floor space was claimed by racks of snack foods. Glass refrigerator doors lined two walls, and a deli counter pushed its way into the room from the third side. It was efficient enough for twenty-three hours of the day, probably, hours when having two people at the gas pumps at one time would qualify as busy, but it couldn't begin to accommodate a hundred rushed and hungry kids on their second day of school.

The cashier—Roberta, called Bob by last year's students—kept yelling to the closest available teenager that there were too many students in the store, and that somebody had to leave. Nobody did, but it made her feel better, I think. The manager stood in the doorway and hollered at his waiting customers, "Let's make a nice straight line so that people can get in and out past you. Pretty simple, huh?"

The Arco lunch rush is an example of an institution that causes the problems it complains about. The limitation of six students in the store results in a long line outside that probably won't be able to finish their shopping in time to return to school for fifth period. The results look like old films of Soviet citizens lining up to buy their town's weekly meat allotments: crowding in the line, pushing toward the front, everyone trying to get into the store at once. The store manager is angry because the kids can't regulate their behavior better.

One common strategy the students employ in these conditions is to make one person already in line do the work of several who have arrived later. Kids in line are often approached by their friends, who give them a couple of bucks and say, "Get me a Pepsi and a Snickers and a Peanut M&M's." Pretty soon, our agreeable kid has three orders that she has to remember, and six dollars in singles and small change in her hand. Once she gets into the store, she has to try to remember everything, often making several tours of the place in order to get it all. Then, after standing in line, she gets to the one register and has to fumble around with more money, not having as good an idea of what all this stuff is going to cost. Paying with a stack of coins is not efficient, and also not unusual if several of her friends each gave her three or four quarters to get them something. Then, because she's got so much stuff, the cashier has to bag it, taking even more time away from those outside.

At both Arcos, students in line with me invariably said, with what seemed to be real generosity, "You don't have to wait. You're not a student, you can go on in." They seemed to accept that the store was justified in keeping them outside while letting adults, even adults like me who had the same amount of time and were buying one thing like a cookie or a pack of cigarettes, go in without waiting. Oddly enough, though, once inside, adults wait in the same line as teenagers. No privilege there. So why the six-student rule? Not because adults are special, because then that status would extend to all lines. No, it's because if the store were full of teenagers, it would be more easy for them to steal things without being seen. If there were seven or eight people in the store, adults could still go in—the rule isn't six people in the store, it's six students—and we could steal things more easily too. If the store were really busy, I could go in there and stand a much better chance of pocketing a candy bar without being noticed. In fact, I'd stand a better chance than the kids because I wouldn't be watched as closely, if at all. But kids steal things and adults don't, so their numbers are limited and the management keeps close watch on them. What the Arcos have done is to create an artificially constrained resource—time available to buy lunch—under the belief that they have to maintain order in the face of potential hooligans and criminals.

Just in front of me in line a week later at the other Arco, two girls were having a conversation. It was increasingly clear that we weren't going to get into the store in time to buy lunch and get back to school in time for fifth period, much less eat any of it. One girl said, "That math teacher—he looks like Al Bundy, you know, his eyes?—he's gonna ask us why we're late."

Her friend replied, "Just say, 'I dunno.' "

Resignation and inarticulateness can sometimes be a strategy for conflict resolution. If a kid knows she's in a situation she can't control and an argument she can't win, why play at all? Why not roll up like a bowling ball bug and say, "I dunno?" It minimizes the conflict by giving the teacher no chance to cut you twice. It keeps you from getting embarrassed further in front of your friends.

Within a month, the freeway Arco only got three dozen students a day. Others had given up and turned to the student store, some had started to catch rides to restaurants and grocery stores that lie farther away, and a few skipped lunch altogether and drove down to the old railroad bridge to get high. Those who remained at the Arco were gathered under the big pines and eucalyptus trees by the freeway ramp, clustered together on and around the previously shunned picnic tables while a speed-metal band boomed from the open hatchback of a car ten feet away.

The freeway Arco had become the land of the Stoners.

Other kids ("freshmen who don't know any better," in the words of one Prep senior) still bought their lunches there, but they stayed on the school and foot-traffic side of the store. The picnic tables on the opposite side, which I had thought were grossly misplaced, were adequately serving their intended clientele. The tables provided a place for the Stoners to watch the world with backs protected, to smoke cigarettes at the legal minimum distance from the tobacco-free campus, to greet their older friends who drove in to see them. The tables were raised up on a slight berm from the parking lot; for someone to leave the pavement and climb that berm could not be an accident, could only be a clear social act to be welcomed or repelled. The Arco had been right about the tables after all.

Only some of the Stoners were Curtisville students. At least a third of them were recent graduates (or nongraduates who had reached eighteen and bailed out) who came back to visit with their friends at the Arco, the only environment in which they were successful. They had cars, which the student Stoners were sorely lacking, and thus possessed music and mobility and status. They had survived the ordeal of high school and were thus heroes of a minor sort to their younger peers who hoped only for survival themselves.

There's a difference, hard to identify and harder to describe, between Stoners and high school students who smoke pot. Smoking marijuana was not an accurate identifier of membership in any particular group, especially in Timber County—dozens of athletes and musicians and actors and straight-A scholars weren't immune. The Stoners probably didn't smoke any more pot as a group than the Preps, especially since they didn't have as much money, but there didn't seem to be much else to talk about. Love had been tried and found wanting; sex was nothing but a health hazard, family offered little comfort and typically much pain. There was no classroom, sport or hobby that had captured them, and no joyous adult who excited or inspired them. The Stoners were more deeply cynical than any other group of kids, assured that schools and government at every level were wholly corrupt ("drug busts for the users, but the rich Republicans who import cocaine and heroin never get busted," as Tami put it). They were young and weary, left with no resources but one another. They clung tightly to their group, without much to offer each other except the occasional cigarette or quarter and a sense that they weren't alone.

Every group found their own lunch spot. The Cowboys went to McDonald's just over the White River at the edge of Union, and the Preps went to Edie's Hamburgers or the Main Street Deli in the middle of Curtisville's town strip. They all had their cars and trucks or friends to ride with, and enough money to spend four or five dollars on lunch. Back on campus, the artists went to the Art Room, and the animal lovers went to the Biology Room to visit with the snakes and the rats and Mr. Weimer and Mr. Lyon. The Drama Geeks went to the Drama Room and the musicians to the Band Room. The freshman boys went to the Physics Lab to play cards around the lab tables, and the freshman girls sat around the Quad near the office.

The Stoners chose a refuge that was within walking distance of the school but beyond its official orbit, a store that offered filling food for forty or fifty cents and cigarettes to be bought or borrowed. It was near the woods if someone was fortunate enough to have a joint to share. It welcomed their older friends, allowed for their music, and provided seating that required little care and carried little hassle.

When cultures collided on claimed territory, fights weren't surprising. The year saw one big fight at McDonald's between a few Curtisville Cowboys and a bunch of Union kids, and three or four smaller fights at the Arco between the Stoners and interloping Cowboys. The morning after the McDonald's fight, Principal Dawson and Assistant Principal Phillips paid a visit to every first period class and warned all the students that the school was in danger of having the campus closed if they couldn't curtail their proclivity to violence. Several teachers told me that there had been periodic pressure put on the school and school board to close the campus anyway, mostly from parents and neighbors who felt that the kids should be under the watchful eyes of authority at all times without a forty-minute anarchy break in the middle. Senora Poole, the gregarious (former Prep) Spanish teacher, said at the beginning of the school year, "I'd like to see a closed campus, at least at Union High but here too. I think kids get to know one another better, get more involved in school stuff. This way, they all just scatter."

After lunch period was over, I was headed home. Jason was hitchhiking along the freeway edge near the bottom of the on-ramp, and I stopped and picked him up. Jason was about sixteen, at five-feet-six just taller than me, and his black and white parents had both contributed to his skin tone, hair, and facial structure. He wore a black leather jacket and small oval wire-framed glasses, and talked with the archetypal Stoner intonation, with vowels drawn out to full length, maaan. No rush, no hurry, just takin' things as they come, maaan, like his friends at the Arco.

He told me he lived in Sunriver, which is about seven miles inland, a compact community of about 1500. As I drove him out there, we talked about how he liked Sunriver (not very much, nothing to do) and how he'd moved there last year from Curtisville and the year before that had lived in River Bend, and liked that town best because he could go out in the country and go to the river and go rock sliding down the cliffs. I know Jason didn't do much in school; he wasn't dumb, he just didn't see any reason to go after it. That's why he hitchhiked home every day: he took the school bus to come in, but he ditched school in the afternoons after he saw his friends at the Arco for lunch.

By the end of the school year, that's what I was doing, too, which is why I happened along to pick him up.[1]

Anyway, we got off the highway at Sunriver, and as we were driving along Levee Road toward town, I asked, "Where we headed?" Jason replied, "The Arco." I drove to the Arco in Sunriver, a familiar building in new surroundings, where he got out of his car and thanked me for the ride. He walked to meet another boy standing next to the newspaper rack by the door.

Jason found his sense of belonging by moving around from one mini-mart to another, banding together with a decentralized but interrelated group that had found its ecological niche. Home and school were both secondary; he had become a convenience-store orphan.

PART THREE

At Home

CHAPTER SEVENTEEN

Negotiations and Boundaries

Every day at lunch between October and mid-December, I would set two desks at a ninety-degree angle to one another in Al Lawton's History room. I'd put out my notebook and tape recorder on one desk and a can of chocolate chip cookies on the other. About five minutes after lunch period started, someone would come through the door into the quiet, empty room—someone who typically didn't know me very well, knew me only as that guy who wanted to know about kids—and I would spend the next half-hour asking them about the places in their lives.

After two long research projects, I know one thing about myself: I am not a good interviewer. I've met some good interviewers, watched them work, seen the skill with which they probe and the way their subjects respond. I'm far too self-conscious to impose an uncomfortable question or to push for an elaboration with someone I don't know well, sitting in that echoing room with its thirty-four other empty desks all around, and I'm usually too locked to my interview questions to be alert to promising side roads that answers bring up. I've read a dozen social science manuals on interviewing, and I know the strategies. I just can't quite do them.

Nevertheless, there are some topics that are so important, so charged, that even the most inept conversant will discover them. Everything I learned from my fifty or so interviews I learned in spite of my technique, and the idea of home brought many of them to the surface.

Quentin:

> (At school) I express myself more, just . . . feelings, all my feelings more than I do at home, because at home I just kind of . . . just, I don't really talk that much, and at school I talk a lot, humor other people a lot. I don't know, at home I just feel a lot calmer, I don't really say much . . . And also that there's friends here, after they get here, someone to talk to and someone to do something with.

Mindi:

> I hate having to go home when they're all there. 'Cause me and my dad just argue all the time. Mom says it's 'cause we're so much alike that we can't stand it, and he sees me and he sees himself in me, and he has to yell at me so I don't do what he did, and . . . it's just crazy at home. I like have no feelings for him whatsoever, he's just like a person that's there. 'Cause we've had some really bad times, and I don't like being around him. He's just ornery.

(How long has it been that way?)

> Since my sister was born. We were like really close, I was like the baby, and you know, I was like daddy's little girl, and Stacy came along, and he used to drink really bad, and you know when she came along, he slowed down on the drinking, but it just like went downhill for us. You know, we just like argued—the past eight years have only been of arguing—and bickered with each other.

Kathleen:

(When you think of your home right now, it really came to mind as a least favorite?)

> Yeah. 'Cause of the atmosphere in the house. Well, like you know, parents and all of that, and tension, it's like walking on eggshells. School has like, more of a family atmosphere, you know, everyone, you talk and you know, they don't like

rag on you all the time for . . . and you can be what you want to be, you know, you can wear whatever and nobody says anything, you know? But then you're like at home, and your parents will say, "You went to school looking like that?" you know, and you're like, "Um, yeah. Nobody else said anything." (laughs)

Parent/child relationships, like all human relationships, are carried out in a particular place. There would be no unions without factories, no zoning codes without cities, no principals without schools. These places help define the roles of everyone within them, and home is no different.

Part of the parent's role is to provide and manage the home. It is "under their roof" where the family is protected. As the provider and homeowner or rent-payer, the parent develops the home's rules of engagement: the scheduling, allocation, and uses of space. The teenager's role within the home is much more ambiguous. They don't contribute economically to the maintenance of the household, and in our culture, that means that they have far less input over its administration. They don't get to choose their home, or the city their home is in.[1] They typically don't get to choose which room they want, nor do they have complete and total control over that room, its contents and its behaviors.

The adult role at home is even stronger than the competent and empowered role they play with others in their work and community environments. They exercise control and choice more thoroughly, without the variety of constant negotiations they conduct with co-workers, clients, and schedules. The teenage role at home is closer to the role they play in their own work environment, the classroom: subservient, provided for, given a space that is nominally their own but which is tightly bound to the wishes of their superiors. Thus home is a particularly favored environment among adults, the place where they go to regain some control over their lives, to live at their own pace with their own belongings around them. Teenagers in their homes are surrounded by things they didn't buy, organized in a way that they didn't design, tied together by a schedule that they didn't determine. It's no surprise that for so many kids, home is an ambivalent place, a tangle of love and powerlessness, the intersection of the child they were and the adult they want to be. Of the eleven kids I watched in their houses, all but a couple took every opportunity to be out of the flow of life in the house—to their bedroom or the computer room, or out of the house altogether. The house was first and foremost their parents' domain.

Irene:

> I'm the person in my household that does everything outside, and I repair the fences and barn and everything that needs to be done, you know. If I need a bigger fence post or do anything like that, I do it. It's my territory. And the house is like my mom's territory. My mom like makes sure everything is clean and makes sure, you know, the food is being cooked and stuff. She *wants* me to cook and everything, and I try to cook, but I'm more like, okay, outside is where I'm . . . I am in control. And when I go inside, it's more like, my mom tells me what to do.

Roger:

> If I want to use the phone, I have to go out to the kitchen. Which is, I mean, I can't express myself out in the kitchen, because . . . my parents are right there. And then, you know, I will definitely admit that I like to watch MTV and Beavis and Butt-Head. And I can't do that out there . . . I'm generally in a good mood when I'm not at home. And I get along with my family when I'm not there, too. Because I have my own personality and they have theirs, and . . . and they clash often. But I'm not going to stop who I am just for them. And I guess when I'm out, people have accepted the way, who I am, and so it's like then the pressure's off.

So what were these houses like, these eleven game boards that I got to watch? Eight of them were built since 1965 in the rectangular one-story "ranch" style most typical of middle-to-low-priced development in America. The climate of coastal Timber County being as it is, there is no frost line to build below, and the houses rest on concrete slabs at grade. I come from the cold Midwest where full basements were a structural necessity as well as a comfortable

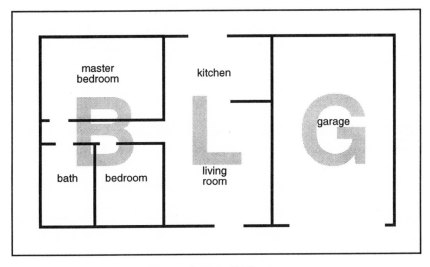

Fig. 3. A B-L-G House

place to get away from summer heat and winter winds, and I never lost the sense that these Curtisville houses were simply set whole onto their lots like the refrigerator boxes we made clubhouses of when I was a child, that they could be picked up and moved with ease.

These one-story houses were mostly of the style shown in Figure 3, a configuration we might call the B-L-G house: a long rectangle divided neatly into thirds, with one outer third as bedrooms, the central third as living area (including the kitchen and television), and the opposing outer third for the garage.[2] Architects refer to these divisions as private and public spaces, or as service and served spaces, and they draw lines between them on the floor plans to divide them one from another. When those lines are extruded up into the third dimension, they become two-by-four stud walls on twenty-four-inch centers covered with Sheetrock and hollow-core doors, affording visual privacy but not much else. It's never far out of mind in the negotiated house that the north wall of the living room is the south wall of someone's bedroom.[3]

The bedroom wing is centered around a hall that leaves the living room as the perpendicular central bar of a T lying on its side. The hall might be an awfully short hall, more a cultural hint rather than a real passage, but the bedroom doors will always be as far down that hall away from the living room as possible. To one side are either two bedrooms or one bedroom and a bathroom. To the other side will be the "master bedroom," defined by the real estate industry as the bedroom which is slightly larger and adjoins a bathroom that can only be accessed via that bedroom. If the opposite side of the hall has two bedrooms, the master's side will also hold the "public" bathroom—tucked into the niche between living room, master bedroom and master bath, sharing the plumbing with the master bath for the sake of simplicity and economy.

The bedroom wing can bring the negotiations over privacy and autonomy to their hottest disagreements. Both parents and teenagers are escaping to their most protected and private spaces, the part of the house in which they can be most completely themselves, and those sanctuaries are jammed together into a tight auditory adjacency. There were only three houses in which the kids and adults were separated by more than a single wall; Kirk's house in Sandy Cove was the most striking example. A late '70s design inspired both by Sea Ranch to the south and by suburbia everywhere, Kirk's house was a triple split-level on an acre-plus lot in the redwoods. The family spaces—kitchen, dining room, living room, stereo room, deck, and yard—were on the central level. Half a level upstairs were Kirk's folks as well as the two grade-school children. Half a level down was Kirk's and his sister Paula's rooms, their joint bathroom, and a family room which had become their own living room. The lower level was their domain, and both parents and even the younger children knew it.

But two of the least expensive ranch houses managed this kind of generational separation by putting the master suite on the opposite side of the living room from the rest of the bedrooms, nested behind the kitchen. I have no firm evidence as to whether this distancing was a peacekeeping influence within the family, though in those particular three cases, both the kids and the parents appreciated the distance. I did talk to a couple of kids whose situations carried this configuration to its extreme.

Holly:

(What came to mind as a favorite place?)

My old room [in another city] . . . Umm, it was really big, and it was away from the house, I lived in a different house than my parents, it was really private . . .

(Really, literally, you lived in a different building?)

Yeah, so it was really nice that way, and . . . it was just . . . I don't know, I didn't like the room very much, I just liked everything that could happen there . . . (laughs) That sounded bad, but . . . just talking and laughing . . . what we used to do, just sit around and do nothing, you know (laughs). It had windows everywhere, except for one wall, so it was like, all pink curtains everywhere (laughs), and a big bed in the corner and a TV, and my stereo in the other corner, and a lot of empty space on one side, so it was too big for me . . . I don't know, I really didn't like *the room*, I just liked being free. It was my place.

Matt:

I have my own little trailer away from my parents. They have their place and I have my place. I like being there because . . . I know when I'm looking out there, I can walk anywhere I want, miles and miles or days and days, whatever. . . . they like it and I like it and we're all happy. (laughs)

(What do you like most about it, what's the best thing about not being in the house?)

Freedom. My parents aren't saying, "Don't do that under my roof." They don't keep track of me really.

There are some other architectural forms that seem to have affected communication between family members in these homes. Compare the two house plans in Figure 4: the front doors of some homes (often those that were less expensive) opened right into the living room, a circumstance that ensured at least a minimum of family contact. These were the homes of families at the two ends of the emotional scale, both those that were the most positive and the

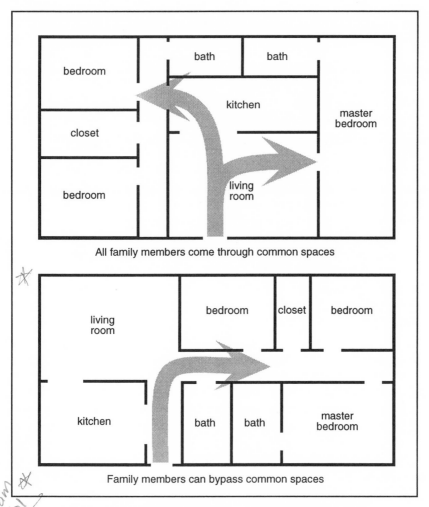

Fig. 4. Two traffic patterns of Curtisville's homes

most tense. Other (typically "nicer") houses had an entry hall that allowed kids to bypass the family on the way to their own rooms. Where that bypass option was available, both kids and adults generally used it, and the families seemed looser, cooler. Another chicken-and-egg question: did the kids living in the bypass houses learn to avoid family contact because they were taught that behavior by their houses, or were those the sorts of houses chosen by families with relatively loose bonds?

Another architectural feature of communication was the dinner table. Six of the eleven families who adopted me during the spring had dinner as a family on a regular basis. This status—family dinners vs. eating on separate schedules—couldn't be predicted according to whether the kids were male or female, whether the families lived in town or away, whether the kids had jobs or not, whether they had cars or not, or whether they were living with both birth parents or a single parent or a parent and step-parent. The mode of dinner was more likely predictable by whether the family resided in a family house or a bypass house:

Mode of Dining	*Family-Core House*	*Bypass House*
Family Dinner Together	5	1
Family Dinner Rare/No Dinners	1	4

Perching at the breakfast counter or watching TV with the balanced plate on the knee were the most common dining modes I encountered all year in people's homes. But the most common overall was eating something in a car, stopping at the supermarket deli counter or the fast-food drive-through, and continuing on with an open bag on the center console.

Architectural scholar Amos Rapoport notes that one reason houses look so different in different parts of the world is that they enclose different functions.[4] Laundering clothes is done inside the home in some societies and outside the home in others; so is storage, or keeping animals, and all of those patterns of action have a bearing on the form of the house. Eating may be that way for us in the near future, a part of life that takes place somewhere other than the house. The dining table may become a vestigial organ in most American homes, tucked off to the side as a quaint reminder of earlier times, available for theme parties in the bygone Martha Stewart fashion. We may be recalled in history as the generation that lost dinner.

Generations before us, though, had already lost the integration of home and work. In her book *The Death and Life of Great American Cities*, Jane Jacobs notes that one of the great voids in our segregated-use communities is that children cannot in the normal course of things see adults at their work, and thus cannot learn what, if anything, about adults' lives is worth being interested in.[5] In Curtisville, a modern community which has learned modern planning, it is rare indeed to have an adult working at or near home. Those that do tend to be employed at independent work (going to graduate school, for example, or driving a logging truck). In those few cases, kids seem to have a relative respect for not just their parents' jobs but for adult work in general. Irene's brothers and mother were all attending college at Timber State at the same time she was in grade school, and she was deeply affected by having them all around her hard at work. "Ben used to read to me, he was reading me Tolkein when I was six or seven. He used to say, "I can't wait until she's a couple of years older, and then I can read *this* to her!" And he used to sit down to read, he'd be all serious, and I would pick up *my* book and sit down next to him and read, too. I was all proud."

Mara's house is a happy clutter. There's a computer in the breakfast nook, with books and software and games all around it. The magazine bin is stacked to overflowing, with more on the couch and on the kitchen table. Mara's room is likewise buried in paper—books, magazines, catalogues. The house is descriptive of the family; Mara said:

> My mother and father still take college classes, just learning about things they're interested in. I want to know everything there is to know about everything . . . They're both computer programmers, my mother is an architect and a geographer. They're both incredibly well-read, and my father is so eloquent, uses his words precisely. I'd like to be like my father in his intellect, and like my mother in her emotional stability, her practicality. He's completely irrational, comes up with all of these impractical schemes, and she's the one who says, "Well, that's a good idea, and now this is the way that you can do it." I think that without each other they wouldn't be anything, I really do.

Both Irene and Mara have been in the center of their family's work and intellectual life right from the start. Their parents didn't simply come home from distant work and plunk down across from the television, didn't try to lose the frustrations of the day in recreation, and didn't shove the kids away when they talked about work or money or "grown-up" ideas. Mara said once in passing that she spent all her time around grownups when she was a kid; that more than anything is probably what made her impatient with so much of her teenage role in society, made her ready to move on and take more responsibility. Most often, we place kids outside adult spaces; they spend a lot of time with other kids, and there's no place for them to go to learn how adults actually live. At home, most kids just see their parents collapse in front of the TV or do home chores. Nothing's wrong with those things, but they aren't the sum total of adult life. If that's the only view the kids get, they'll never see potential for more.

This sharp division of home and work is another modern ideal that doesn't work well for kids. We recognize this, since we institute meager gestures like "Take Our Daughters to Work Day" to try to fill the void. Teenagers are trying to figure out exactly what their mission in the world should be—for parents to say to them that work, a potentially central aspect of life, can and should be left in some other building rather than be a consuming interest, suggests exactly what we often say in words to one another but would hate to communicate to our children: work is for money. We don't like it much, we often find it absurd, but we do it begrudgingly because there are bills to be paid. Leaving work exclusively at work, hiding or escaping or denying our way of making a living, is an admission of defeat; one that teenagers can read and believe.

CHAPTER EIGHTEEN

Twelve Rooms

You've already visited Kirk's room, one of two on the ground floor of his family's massive, shingled split-level up in the Sandy Cove redwoods. He and his sister share a bathroom and a family room ("This is my living room," he said when he showed it to me). Kirk's room has jeans and t-shirts all over the floor and the couch—"I don't have a closet." An unmade futon lies on the floor along the back wall, under the small high window looking out at grass level into the back yard. On the shelves, there were a stereo, books, and a few plants.

His varsity letter from soccer and his summer soccer camp certificates are tacked haphazardly to the walls. His grandmother paints watercolors, and a few of her nature sketches and paintings sit on a ledge in the poured concrete wall that separates the bedrooms and supports the upper level of the house.

There's a small alcove in Matthew's bedroom where his dad had built him an inset desk. The wall above that is covered with track ribbons and his old race numbers. The rest of the room is full of books and photocopied cartoons, and he's tacked a big Toxic Fart Zone poster to the outside of his door.

But that room doesn't get a lot of use since the divorce. Matthew spends more and more time living with his dad a couple of miles away in a mobile home parked in a forest meadow near Flat Lake. He has a room there, too, about seventy percent filled with his bed. In the alcove in that room is a dresser, on top of which are three cassette decks, an equalizer/booster, and a big 1970s Marantz 110-watt receiver. Two of the five dresser drawers are full of cassettes. Matthew turns on the Bob Marley tape he'd left in the deck the last time he played it. "Bob rules!" he says, grinning.

Laurie's room was the first you saw, the shrine to Marilyn Monroe. Both times I saw it, the floor was strewn with clothes and magazines and books and shoes and hangers, but the closet still looked full. "It's just typical for a teenage girl—that's what I tell myself." On the nightstand at the side of the bed was a Bible, a new *Cosmopolitan*, and the TV remote control.

The first time I was at Duane's house out across from the airport, the Timber Cable guy was there installing cable TV in Duane's bedroom. The room was about ten feet square, and the walls were covered with posters of motorcycles, sports cars, bikini chicks, bikini chicks on motorcycles, bikini chicks on sports cars, and a couple of country music/movie posters. Some of the chick posters had been signed by the chicks themselves, at one of those "meet the Bud Girls live" events. Duane's small knickknack shelf on the wall held a few of the dozens of models he'd made—cars, trucks, motorcycles. A "drug-free campus" sign stolen from some schoolyard leaned against one wall, and a real estate "For Sale" sign stolen from a nearby yard was propped behind the door.

A tropical fish tank stood on top of his dresser and a shotgun lay under his bed, loaded. Three other rifles in their cases leaned against the back of his closet. Clothes were scattered all over the floor. As the cable installer left, his mother said, "Now that he's got cable in there, he'll never come out except to use the bathroom and *maybe* stop in here to grab some food."

Maggie, the Irish exchange student, explains her host family's ranch house to me as though I hadn't been in hundreds just like it. *She* hasn't, and she still hasn't figured it out. "Back home, the living

room would be a room, with a door. I really miss having some privacy (pronounced "privvacy"). This is why I never get any homework
done, it's just crazy here all the time." She shares a very small bedroom with the two girls in her host family, ages ten and about four.

Maggie sleeps in the bottom bunk, and the ten-year-old in the
top bunk. The youngest one is in a large crib against the opposite
wall. The walls are still covered with football and monster truck
images, remnants of the two eleven- and fourteen-year-old brothers
who had lived in this room until Maggie arrived eight months ago.
Above the top bunk, the older girl has three or four photos of cute (or
"tidy," as Maggie would say back home) guys from *Tiger Beat*.
Maggie's entire personalization of the room is a small Japanese calendar, about four inches wide and a foot tall, hung just inside the
door above the light switch. Right now, three days' clothes are
heaped on the bed. She swears it isn't usually that way.

Benjamin keeps his bedroom door closed at all times, whether
he's in the room or not. The floor in his room is scattered with
clothes and photographs and cassettes, and the walls are decorated
with drawings of knights and skeletons created by his friends. He
dives onto and off his top-bunk bed to grab clothes and get dressed
for the day.

The top drawer of the dresser has half a dozen *Playboys* in it,
as well as one that's a little racier, one of those liquor-store specials.
There's another year's worth of *Playboy* in the closet, along with
Scrabble and Pictionary.

Benjamin was the only one to invite me to sleep over while I
was trailing him, which I did on Friday night. I took the bottom
"bunk," which was a mattress on a piece of plywood on the floor
under his loft-bed. I woke up at 7:30, showered, dressed, and wrote
at the kitchen table. Benjamin slept until quarter of ten. "Damn
dogs woke me up," he muttered, shuffling down the hallway to the
bathroom.

Tami takes me up to her new room. Her six-year-old brother
Tyler was given the huge bedroom on the second floor "because he's

going to be here for another thirteen years, and I'm not." Fair enough. And after eighteen years of mobile home life, even this smallish room seems palatial to her (though she's more impressed by the enormous new bathroom).

She apologizes for the messiness of her room, but everything is more or less in its place, a few clothes on the chair. The furniture is one twin bed, an armoire, a set of shelves, a desk, and a lounge chair. There's almost nothing on the walls, which are too new, too perfect, to modify. Besides, Tami says she's "grown out of that." She had had rock band posters and cute guy photos on her walls in the trailer. She shows me instead a set of male nude porno playing cards that her friend Maria got for her—"No girl I know wants a guy that big, because you know that's gonna hurt." When we leave her room, she closes the door behind us.

ะ

Mara's room is a scatter of paper—books, magazines, college catalogues. She says, "It's messy right now . . ." She's got her bird Dusty in its cage, and her saddle and blankets on a rack. She's left all of her brother Peter's wrestling and soccer photos and certificates on the wall, partly because she just moved into his room when he left home six months earlier, and partly because she likes him and is preparing to lose him completely for a few years to the Marine Corps.

ะ

Just before we leave, Irene says, "Do you want to see my room?" She goes upstairs to ask her mom, and she comes back down to get me: "She doesn't usually let *anyone* upstairs." We walk back up the stairs together, and turn left away from Mom's room. Irene's walls are covered with horse posters and horse calendar photos, maybe twenty-five or so, with a couple of wolves tossed in for good measure. Between the photos and the bookshelves, no actual wall surface is visible anywhere. Her saddle is on a stand in the corner.

It's a small room—maybe eight by eight with sloped ceiling areas under the roofline, almost an attic corner—with a bright east-facing window in the gable. A real hideaway. She likes being sick and staying home from school, she tells me, because then she can just lie in this room and read.

ะ

Ivy gives me a quick tour of the house, closing the door rapidly on her room. "This is my room, and that's enough of *that* . . ." I persuade her to open it back up for two minutes—it's not all that bad, just clothes strewn all over the bed and the floor. Her sliding closet door is mirrored on both panels, and has tiny photos of herself and her friends wedged between the glass and the aluminum frame all around it. Most of the photos are professional—class portraits, prom photos—but about a third are snapshots. There's not a lot of stuff on her walls, although there are some oil portrait reproductions of Native American figures that her mom has hung in other rooms as well.

ॐ

At the end of dinner at Ethan's house, Damien calls and wants to play hoops later, so Ethan and I go to his room to hang out for a while before we leave. Ethan's large room is pretty spare—there's a futon on the floor, a waist-high dresser, and a desk. A Yamaha synthesizer sits on the floor at the foot of the bed, and a guitar stands next to it. He can't really play either one but fools with them when the urge strikes. There's one small chair in the corner, his grandfather's chair, upholstered in a spruce green fabric from the late 1960s. "I can still remember him in it, sitting up straight." He demonstrates for me, then slouches back down again.

On the walls, it's Grateful Dead, Jim Morrison, Jimi Hendrix, Iron Maiden, Motley Crue, a couple of his own photos, and a Harley poster. Next to his desk a sign reads, "Everyone is born right-handed— only the greatest overcome it."

ॐ

Mara takes me on a Saturday to meet her friend Giselle. Giselle's bedroom is cluttered with costumes and fabric and accessories, and two dresser drawers are full of theatrical makeup. Dozens of little pieces of shattered mirror have been glued artfully back into a composition next to the dresser. Giselle has an elevated bed and keeps her paperwork and books in the space below it.

She and her friend Kelli are making a video for the local cable-access channel; Kelli is wearing a bride's dress, thick white makeup, and a trickle of theater blood from each tear duct. She lies on the floor, practicing being dead, while the rest of us decorate her face and head with plastic flies. Kelli and Giselle are both wearing leotards under their filmy long skirts; Giselle's mom has about a third of the house taken up by her custom sewing shop, and she made all of Giselle's considerable costume department.

If you wanted to do a photo shoot about avant-garde teenagers, you'd come to Giselle's room to do it. She's taken the room over completely—there's nothing about it that suggests you're in a suburban tract home. Mara, in her t-shirt and jeans and no makeup, is the same age as Giselle and Kelli but looks about twelve years old, sitting fascinated in the big girls' room.

Twelve rooms. Twelve lives written in temporary collections and arrangements of inexpensive things. These are the kinds of data that can make ethnographers feel impotent: I spent a year for these scraps, these broken fragments? Where is the meaning in this harvest?

Meaning lies in how they showed me their rooms as well as in the artifacts themselves. I spent less than fifteen minutes in eight of the twelve rooms—in six of those eight, the kids conducted the brief and official tour in less than two minutes and quickly closed the door behind us as we left. So many of the kids, especially the girls, apologized for the conditions of their rooms when they brought me there. It's as though they'd opened themselves too far, and were trying to regain some of their privacy. Very few people got to see these places, and the honesty was sometimes more than they cared to share with a relative newcomer.

I wrote and performed a stage monologue at the end of the year as my final report to the kids, parents, and teachers of Curtisville. About two months before presentation, I auditioned some of the things I thought I'd learned in front of some of the kids I'd befriended. They stopped me after every segment to argue with my ideas or to amplify my examples with things they'd seen as well. But one comment struck a particularly truthful tone for them: I was talking about what I'd seen in their rooms, and who else got to see those rooms, and I said, "You can almost divide the people you know into three groups—the people you know at school and work and church, the people that come over to your house, and the people you sit around in your room with."

And before I could inhale to start the next sentence, Julian had leapt out of his chair and onto his knees and was bowing to me. "You are a GOD!" he cried, followed instantly by a mass kneeling and bowing and burst of talk and laughter by all seven others.

"That is so true!" Irene said to Mara. "There are so many people that come over all the time, and you're the only one who ever comes in my room. Oh, my God!" The sudden shock of recognition overcame them briefly, and the monologue was lost for the next fifteen minutes in favor of conversations about the intense privacy of their rooms.

This is no surprise, really, although my putting it into words surprised them. Because what other place did they have that was theirs? Where else could they tell themselves who they were? The rest of the house was their parents' possession. The yard and neighborhood were irrelevant to them. School was impersonal and supervised, a tool only briefly borrowed and then turned over to others. Their hangouts were temporary and immaterial, formed out of three parked cars or a bonfire or a circle of bodies focused around the hyperbolic arcs of a Hacky Sack. The larger material displays of identity their parents took for granted—choices about home decoration and landscaping and painting and pictures on the desk at work—were closed to them. That doesn't mean that the kids had no desire for these expressions; it means that those impulses were incredibly compressed into one private room, forming a dense code of self-messages that could be too revealing in the wrong hands.

Only two of the kids I followed had me spend much time at all in their rooms. Ethan and Benjamin were both deeply involved in searching for themselves, in coming to peace with who they were, and I think they wanted my assistance. Benjamin mostly wanted to know about marriage, and about whether having once had sex with another boy meant that he was gay. Ethan had a larger past to work with. As we sat in his room, he told me about his brother.

We were living in a cabin, I guess is what you'd call it, behind Glenn's (his stepfather) parents' house down by a river. We came home one day with some friends, which was a major no-no. We were never supposed to have friends in the house when nobody was home. But I'd borrowed a new Nintendo game and I went into the house to play it. They all went down to the stream. After a while, one of them runs into the house and says, "Your brother's in the water and he's not moving!" And I'm all, like, "Yeah, right, he's pulling your leg." But I go down there, and there he is in the water, and his face is all blue, his lips are blue. And I go, "Oh, shit!" So I run back to the house and call 911, and leave another guy there to give directions, and I go back down to see if I can help him. And as soon as I get in the water, I can feel the electricity running up my legs. What happened is that somebody's irrigation pump kicked on and sent all this electricity into the water. It was just lucky, because he was in the water when it happened and the other two guys weren't in yet, or all three of them would have been killed and it would have been a real tragedy.

And then, after the police came and took my statement and the medics took my brother away, the police took the other two guys home and I was there by myself for four hours. The phone rang and my stepdad's dad answered it up in the house, and I listened in on our phone. And it was Glenn, and all he said was, "He's gone." And his dad just said, "Oh, shit." And I don't remember much of anything after that.

My social development sort of stopped there. I'd be a totally different person if my brother was still alive. But he died, and then we moved up here, which we had already planned on doing, and I was all alone.

My first friend was just great when it was just the two of us. I used to go to his house all the time, he would never come over to mine. But if it was him and another friend, they would just totally make fun of me. So for about five years, I thought there was something really wrong with me, or else why would these guys be saying this stuff? It wasn't until later that I realized that it was just because they thought it was fun and that they were insecure. I thought it was something wrong with me.

On Saturday night, we left Ethan's house at about eight to have a look for a party. I drove, in case we found something interesting and he overindulged. We tried the beach. We tried Damien's brother's house. We tried a guy who lived out at the end of Fuller Road and had a party last year once. We went to the beach again. Nothing was happening anywhere, and we got back to Ethan's at about ten-thirty. "Watch this," he said. We walked in, and his mom was right there next to the doorway. She wouldn't go to bed until he was home. We said goodnight to her, went back into his room, closed the door, talked quietly. After half an hour, Ethan said, "I feel bad, because you're just doing sort of counseling. I mean, you're supposed to be observing me in my environments."

"And I am. I mean, do you spend a lot of time in here, being quiet, thinking, having conversations?"

"Yeah."

"I'd have been amazed if you said no. This room seems sparse, open, meditative. There's not many things on the walls, not like some other rooms I've been in where you can't even see the walls. There's lots of open floor space. It's a thinking room."

We had exchanged positions from the first time we were there—he sat in the chair in the corner, and I sat cross-legged on the bed. We talked about the purpose of life: Ethan thought it was to learn, to gather experience; I said I thought it was to help others. He talked about wanting a real friend, maybe a girlfriend, who could help him out of his shell. I tried to prompt him on what kind of a person that would be, and said, "And you're looking for someone who. . . .?"

He laughed. "Yeah, that's interesting, that's right. I'm looking for someone who. I'm looking for someone who . . . blank."

≈❧

In the two rooms where the resident kids had attached almost nothing to the walls, there was an overwhelming sense of distance, of non-ownership. In Tami's case, the house was six months old and very expensive, the plastering still unmarred. The public rooms held tastefully casual assemblies of Southwestern artifacts (Tami's mother ran a tourist gallery in Sandy Cove), spaces not unfamiliar to readers of *Architectural Digest*. The home hadn't yet lost the material preciousness of a new possession, and hadn't acquired the emotional preciousness signaled by a layer of visible history. For

Maggie, the room was a way station in a year abroad, shared with two young host sisters she had almost nothing in common with. Nothing about it was hers alone. Nothing about it was even familiar, compared with spaces in her home in Dublin. Her important places were hidden away in her luggage—copies of her yearbook from her previous year in high school, a postcard album of Dublin, images that she shared with a very few friends and with me but not with her host family.

Later, an adult friend told me of her childhood bedroom in a household in which cleanliness and organization were more highly prized than privacy or self-expression. She said, "I never put up anything personal on my walls, because *they weren't my walls!* They were my parents' walls." Clearly there are cases in which the literal ownership of the teen bedroom by adults becomes a more important kind of ownership, one that resists honest expression.

In the other eight rooms, the ones that were thoroughly decorated but in which we didn't sit for long periods, there were no real surprises. Duane, the aspiring trucker/rancher and avid hunter, covered his room with symbols of working-class humor and aspiration: photos of fancy vehicles and the fancy women that come with them, a poster of blonde jokes, his treasured guns. Irene, the contemplative horsewoman, filled her room with novels and with photos of horses, and her saddle sat in the corner. Ivy, the girl who lived in brief but intense love affairs, had several years worth of prom and dance photos on her mirror, each with a different dress and a different boy. In every case, the material collection was consistent with the person I knew, but it was still too personal to offer to me freely. The public persona could be laughed off with a self-depreciating comment if it became uncomfortable, but the slow accretion of placed objects in their rooms was a clear and conscious embrace of a deeper personality. The bedroom was testimony that couldn't be disavowed, a statement too clear to deny.

CHAPTER NINETEEN

The Irrelevant Neighborhood

Over the course of almost five hundred hours I spent following my volunteers on their Thursdays, Fridays, and Saturdays, I witnessed exactly two instances of kids being involved with their neighbors. The first was when Irene had to collect pledges for her twenty-four-hour walk-a-thon, and spent about fifteen minutes across the street at her five neighbors' houses asking for donations. In only one house, that of a retired couple, did the occupants recognize her immediately (as "Betsy's girl"). At the others, they didn't call her by any name, even though she was vaguely familiar from riding her horse down the street over the course of the thirteen years she'd lived there.

The second instance was at Benjamin's house. It was a Thursday, and we'd just gotten off the bus after school. After shedding his jacket and having a look at the laser-printed chore list on the refrigerator door, he walked onto the back patio to take the trash out and to pick up the can and the prior trash that the neighbor's cat had overturned. The patio, a word that must have sounded good in a real estate listing, was actually a six-foot wide strip of concrete bounded on one edge by the back of the house and on the opposite edge by the neighbor's wooden-slat fence. His family used it for outdoor storage.

Benjamin introduced me to the neighbor's dog, King, who lived on the other side of the wooden fence. He said, "Watch this," and then called the dog. "Here, King, c'mere, boy." King obligingly trotted over to the fence, looked at Benjamin, poked his muzzle through the slats and sniffed for a moment, and then lifted his leg and peed on the base of the fence. Benjamin gloated at the accuracy of his prediction. "He always does that. One time I peed into a bottle and saved it until I had a whole bottle of it, and then I poured it onto the fence. The dog was really confused, and he peed on the fence for hours."

That was the full extent of social interaction I saw among Curtisville's teenagers and their neighbors.

છે.

Neighbor is a word with two distinct meanings, one about proximity and one about friendship. My dictionary has one definition of neighbor as "a person who lives near another," and a second as "a person who shows kindliness and helpfulness toward his or her fellow humans."

This dual meaning was borne out in research conducted in England by Terence Lee during the 1950s.[1] He had an elegantly simple method: he and his wife walked from door to door in Cambridge, asking the housewives they met to talk about their neighborhoods and to draw perceived boundaries around them on fairly detailed maps.

What he found was striking both in its consistency and in its contrast to urban planning beliefs of the day. While planners were creating "neighborhood planning units" with a population near 10,000 in a housing-only zone around a centralized school, recreation, and shopping core, Lee's housewives drew their boundaries around neighborhoods that were most commonly only about 90 acres—what in an American city would be about five blocks by five blocks. The most common number of dwelling units contained in that area were about three hundred, which would correspond to a neighborhood population of fewer than 1500. Their drawn neighborhoods included an average of five or six community buildings such as clubs, recreation halls, and churches, and an average of fifteen to twenty small shops.

Equally striking was the relationship between the mapped neighborhood and the mapper's social life. The availability of local shops and local amenities was reflected in increased local shopping and membership in local organizations. This intense use of neighborhood facilities translated into strong local friendship ties; three-quarters of the respondents had friends within their neighborhoods.

Move this behavior data to 1990s Curtisville, and the contrasts are clear. There are no businesses whatsoever in residential areas, no recreation centers or social clubs, and only a smattering of churches. The two encounters between kids and their neighbors was exactly two more than the number of encounters I saw between their parents and their neighbors. There are plenty of developments, but few neighborhoods.

I was invited to a meeting of the visioning group of the community center subcommittee of the Curtisville Action Committee. Their job was to make Curtisville's upcoming General Plan revisions more thoughtful, and to help new development in Curtisville be friendlier. I drove out to the meeting, following the directions I had been given over the phone, and at some length arrived at a large home on a spacious lot nestled into the forest. The property was bounded on both sides and along the road's edge by a dense palisade of fifteen-foot poplar trees, so that the house and yard were invisible to all other residents and passers-by. Inside that house, five professional, well-educated, high-income adults who had bought their way out of neighborhood contact sat around a zoning map and tried to imagine ways in which downtown Curtisville could be made more welcoming and friendly.

One thing they were adamant about is that through streets were bad and that local neighborhood stores were worse. When I suggested the idea that perhaps not all of the community's businesses ought to be strung along one street and that purely residential neighborhoods can be boring and less social, one committee member immediately corrected me and said that zoning out businesses made neighborhoods "quiet." But the point was moot anyway, she said; there were only two non-Main Street parcels in the entire twenty square miles of the map that were zoned for commercial activity.

These, like the house that Jack built, are the cultural attitudes that lead to the institutional codes that lead to the physical characteristics that lead to a lack of neighborliness. There are no neighborhood-based shops or social clubs that would allow people to run into one another locally. With all of Curtisville's businesses on five-lane, thirty-five mile-an-hour Main Street, driving was one of the primary household activities, and pedestrians over the age of fourteen were a rare sight. The car-intensity of this configuration was compounded by the fact that most of Curtisville's developments are drawn around culs-de-sac, our polite planning term for dead-end roads and blind alleys. In a cul-de-sac development (in French, literally "bottom of the bag" or something that can only be left the way one came in), large branches of through roads sprout small stems of street that in turn end with pods of homes that have no through paths to any other pod. This, in most developers' eyes, has the great advantage of eliminating through-traffic, making the street quieter and safer for children to play in. It also has a less mentioned but equally popular effect of enhancing the social division of the development by greatly reducing the possibilities of outsiders driving or walking through it.[2]

Marjorie Stone worked at a clerical job and raised two daughters by herself, but had been able to afford a small mid-1960s ranch house in one of Curtisville's dirt-road working-class neighborhoods. One daughter, Ivy, was a good friend of Rick. Rick's parents, local businesspeople who opened the local McDonald's franchise the year I was there, had bought a large new two-story home in the nearby (but security-walled) Pleasant Meadow subdivision. Both Ivy's and Rick's neighborhoods were based around dead-end planning, as you can see in Figure 5; Ivy once told me that she could throw a rock and hit Rick's house, but that she couldn't walk there. I doubt if that's quite true—I've seen her throw—but I'm sure that a good center fielder could have thrown out a baserunner in Rick's back yard from Ivy's driveway. It would have taken Ivy less than three minutes to walk to Rick's if the developers had allowed it; instead, as close as their houses were, the walking or driving distance from one front door to the other was almost a mile and a quarter.

When there are no through streets and no common neighborhood destinations, it becomes more difficult to interact with people who are nearby. People enter their cars more often and have no reason to walk anywhere. The ranch houses, with their attached-entry garages or deep carports, encouraged this lack of interaction. People didn't even have to go to the curb to get out of their neighborhoods— they could enclose themselves in the car directly from their kitchens, without ever having to go outdoors.

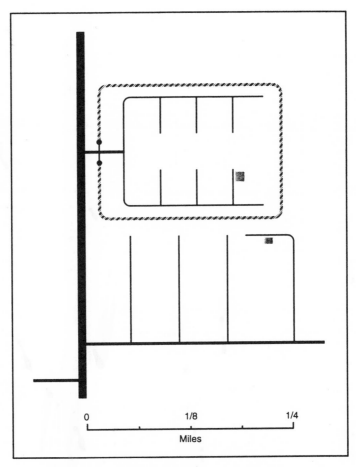

Fig. 5. Ivy's division from Rick

Some kids tried to circumvent what the planners had made for them. When Mara wanted to go up to the deli on Main Street, she had two choices: walk an eighth of a mile west on Knoll Court, a tenth south on Madison, a quarter mile east on Ocean View, and another quarter mile north on Main; or she could hop the fence and walk five minutes to the deli across the vacant lot behind the Paulsen Farms nursery.

Shortcuts like Mara's in Figure 6 were common in Curtisville—I saw them near the school on the way to convenience stores, and between neighborhoods wherever the fences weren't too

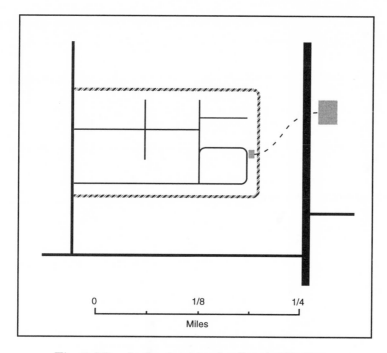

Fig. 6. Mara's shortcut to the Curtisville Deli

tall or the woods too thick. But using any of these shortcuts meant trespassing; moving sensibly through Curtisville involved breaking the law. This "disrespect for private property" wasn't vandalism, wasn't malicious, but it wasn't the "right" way to use their community.

All of these things—the cul-de-sac planning and the resulting disconnection, the direct and immediate linkage between kitchen and driver's seat, the centralization of business and community functions miles away from most residents, and the degree to which Curtisville's residents fought to maintain the isolation that increased their feelings of ruralness and class security—made pedestrian travel out of the question for both adults and teenagers. It kept the streets quiet. It kept potential neighbors apart.

Social networks can be formed via institutions, interstate highways or the Internet as easily as they can be through physical proximity. But real neighborhoods offer sociability for those who are less mobile than our auto-centered norm: seniors, small children, younger teenagers, stay-at-home parents.[3] Neighborhoods introduce us to people we haven't chosen on the basis of work or hobby relations but who are like us nonetheless; they clearly share a part of our cultural reading of the good life, by virtue of selecting a location that we too have selected. That small, locational connection may allow us to see them more clearly, doing more things, and ultimately help us to understand each other.

Neighborhood life has values beyond personal satisfaction as well. Planning critic Jane Jacobs has called the smallest-scale, street-based neighborhood a unit of local self-governance which, at its best, allows residents "to weave webs of public surveillance and thus to protect strangers as well as themselves; to grow networks of small-scale, everyday public life and thus of trust and social control; and to help assimilate children into reasonably responsible and tolerant city life."[4] Good neighborhoods might help us reclaim the habits of citizenship.

Adolescence seems to be the time when the physical dimensions of life expand.[5] High school pulls kids away from neighborhood friends; the onset of car mobility pulls kids away from neighborhood friends; and the larger mobility of their parents moving from town to town pulls kids away from neighborhood friends. The trend toward increasing the scheduling of kids' lives through private lessons and organized youth activities drives teenagers out of their neighborhoods and into centralized baseball fields or dance studios or karate dojos.

All of these forces would strain the holding power of even the most lively neighborhoods upon the lives of their teenagers. But Curtisville's neighborhoods exerted almost no gravitational pull at all that might counter those forces. They were seen as neither good nor bad by their teenage residents; they were irrelevant.

CHAPTER TWENTY

Other People's Houses I: Dad's House

Of my eleven volunteers, ten came from divorced families. I didn't select them on this basis; I didn't even see it until eight months later.

Of those ten kids, five had a non-custody parent who lived nearby. Laurie's mother lived with her boyfriend about fifteen miles south in Port City; Ivy's father lived about twenty-five miles north in Cramer Beach; Tami's father lived about fifteen miles from her house, right in Curtisville. All three girls had a relatively distant relationship with their absent parent, visiting periodically but always seemingly happier to be at home.

The two boys had closer contact with their absent fathers. Kirk lived comfortably with his mother, a social counselor, and his stepfather, a television engineer, in a rambling luxury house up in the redwoods on the Sandy Cove bluffs. But he regularly drove the twenty miles to roll in unannounced and visit his dad, the resident landlord of a shantytown at the edge of the tidal marsh on the north spit of Timber Bay.

Kirk's father Tom, a macrobiotic hippie with a long gray beard and no visible body fat anywhere, had been building himself a new house for about ten years. It appeared he had another eight years to go at the rate things were progressing: the framing and sheathing were complete, but the windows were only framed-out holes, and the interior was an undefined box. Tom lived fifty yards away in a 1958 mobile home, full of books and records and papers and a Frisbee and old shoes and stereo components stacked every which way. A valley large enough for his recliner had been carved out of the clutter, hewn by the erosion of thousands of trips between the chair and the big TV in the corner. The sink faucet was dripping, the kitchen light was a bare bulb shielded with a Payless brown paper bag, and the refrigerator was outside in a plywood and fiberglass panel lean-to. It all seemed more or less clean, but looked as though several trips to the dump might be in order. "A real bachelor pad," Tom called from the back as he undressed to take a bath after a day of working with drywall board while wearing only running shorts, "but only temporary. I've only been here ten or twelve years."

Kirk seemed perfectly at home at Tom's, standing in the mud and feeding the ducks with bread from the fridge. It would be wrong to say that Kirk was a different person in this house than he was in his fancy home in Sandy Cove, but the two places did show up as different aspects of that one person. Kirk was the active and satisfied member of a family, doting on his little half-brother and half-sister, cooking dinner and playing with his dog Dog and holding some responsibility for gardening and maintenance, with a space that he decorated and claimed as his own. But Kirk was also the laid back hippie-surfer, taking no stock in the social status of his home and property, comfortable alone, living with all of his senses wide open in the midst of chaos.

We are not our places, not entirely. We do, however, choose places because they're us.

ॐ

Matthew had two home lives as well. His parents were recently separated, and his mother lived in their custom home in a grassy clearing halfway between Curtisville and Flat Lake, just short of a mile up a rutted dirt road. The family had lived on this property ever since Matthew was six months old, the first ten years or so in a trailer about where the chicken coop is now. His dad Carl, a general contractor, built the two-story white house six years ago, when Matthew was eleven.

After track practice on an early May Thursday, I followed Matthew up to the house, where he'd come by to do some chores— feeding and watering the chickens, spraying down and oiling the lawnmower. He brought me into the house, and started out by being a tour guide—"This is the kitchen, this is the pantry, this is the pool room . . . " But his talk soon turned to having been lonely, being an only child this far out in the country. He used to bicycle a lot to visit friends, and sleeping over was common because people lived so far off that "we just made a day of it."

After only a few minutes in the house, we headed back out and spent most of our time playing with his old dog Bud and walking in the woods. We visited all the creeks and crevasses, clambered up the stream banks to his old treehouse (completely covered with redwood duff and advanced in plywood rot), walked down the driveway to the pond. Matthew hopped lightly from log to rock, easily traversing the slick, mossy boards and branches while I cautiously followed, yards behind. At the bottom, he pointed to a small pet graveyard up on the side hill. "That's where I buried all of my pets. I used to make little crosses for them."

The divorce wasn't final yet, but the house was for sale. It had become a maintenance problem: the solar collectors on the roof and the huge living room, the wood stove and the chickens all demanded attention, and not only had Carl moved away, Matthew wouldn't be around to help his mother with it for much longer. I met his mother only once, two days later on a Saturday evening. We had gone there again to feed chickens and to see if the grass was dry enough to cut. She arrived home shortly after we got there, and greeted him by saying, "The assessor was supposed to be out to look at the house, but it's going to be hard with the grass four feet tall."

"Well, it's been raining, I can't cut it until it dries." He tried to change the topic to his impending graduation. "I got my senior schedule, I'll make you a copy."

"*That* would be nice, maybe I'll have some idea what's going on. I haven't seen anything, I have to call Roger's mother to find out what's happening."

"I came up to invite you to brunch tomorrow for Mother's Day, and find out what time you wanted to go."

"I suppose you invited your grandmother, too."

"Yeah, we were just there."

"You could have told me first."

"I *did* say that, earlier this week, that I was going to take you and Grandma out to brunch."

As we walked out into the yard, Matthew told her about the afternoon's track meet in which he had set a personal record (or a PR, in runners' jargon) in the mile, a noble effort that his father and I both watched from the bleachers at the university track. "I ran really well today, and I got a PR in the mile."

She snapped, "I don't know what a PR is." This from the mother of a boy whose bedroom walls were covered with racing mementos, a boy who runs thirty miles a week, a boy who has been on the track and cross-country teams all through high school. She had his track schedule, and was angry to learn that he had just finished the last meet of his high school track career—she had apparently been planning to come to one of the two which remained on the schedule, but they were both regional tournament meets that he and the Curtisville team didn't qualify for.

She never acknowledged me, never asked the polite questions I heard over and over during my first introductions to parents. Matthew and I fed scraps to the chickens, got them penned up, and drove away. "She was in kind of a bad mood today," Matthew said quietly. I didn't respond, and after twenty long seconds of silence, my car bouncing over the potholes on the narrow dirt road, he started telling me about her ovarian cancer four years earlier, the operation she almost didn't recover from, and the fact that the risk of recurrence kept her from starting hormone replacement therapy. "I can't even remember the person my father married. I have a picture of them when they were first married—you should see it, she was really pretty. And he had hair."

Matthew's dad's place was even farther out in the country past Flat Lake. Carl Brunner lived in a clearing in the woods as well; his rented mobile home sat in the midst of a small ranch, surrounded by cows in the meadow and towering redwoods beyond. Matthew lived with one parent "until I pretty much can't stand it, and then I go stay with the other one." He's been with his dad since mid-March, an arrangement about to become permanent.

Carl had no hair. Or rather, no hair on top of his head, but a vigorous beard. Matthew said, "It looks like there's a hinge at his sideburns, and what used to be on top just swung down onto his chin." When we walked into the trailer on Thursday afternoon, Carl was boiling potatoes and cooking chicken livers, having already finished making a bean salad. We had a quiet, friendly conversation for a few moments, and then Matthew and I retreated to his room at the end of the house. He turned on the Bob Marley tape, pulled out his Econ book, and lay across the bed for half an hour's reading.

Carl had extended the mobile home with wooden eaves and a deck in the back. Inside, Carl's bedroom and bathroom were enclosed on one end, Matthew's bedroom and bathroom were enclosed on the other end, and thirty feet of unbroken kitchen/dining room/living room lay in between. We went to the kitchen end to dish up, and then sat in the living room end and balanced our plates on our laps, talking and watching *Jeopardy* on the little twelve-inch black-and-white.

After dinner, Matthew wanted to show me around the mountain. Carl gave us the combination to the lower gate, and we took Matthew's small pickup 2½ miles up the steep dirt road to the ridge. Once we got to the upper American West Forest Products gate (after having already passed three AWFP "No Trespassing" signs), we left the truck and walked over some rocks to get around the gate and up onto the ridge road. "I hope you don't mind trespassing," he said while sliding through the gap in the fence.

We walked out the logging road for about forty minutes, looking out at the view. Matthew ran from the trailer up this hill about once a week as a sort of fitness check/time trial, and he knew his landmarks, picking out Rocky Head and Manoa. He also knew his plants and trees—it was clear that he'd spent some time in the woods in his life.

As we walked farther out the dusty road, Matthew asked what high school was like for me: was I social, did I have any good classes, that kind of stuff. His favorite classes had been Mr. Fischer's auto shop—"Mr. Fischer really taught me how to think, to hook things together and be logical"—and Mr. Jacobs' English this year. He's a shy person, didn't really have a "best friend" or a girlfriend, and he was troubled by this a little—"But at least I recognize it and I can work on it." He'd decided he wasn't going to Coastal College right away; he was having an interesting time working as an aide at a senior day care center, and was looking forward to more hours once graduation came. He didn't know what he wanted for a career yet, but he seemed content to wait and find out as it came.

We headed back downhill; the cloudy evening turned to drizzle, then to rain. We ran back through the fence and into the pickup; Matthew backed downhill until we got to a wide spot to turn around in. Once we were pointed forward, he drove toward home neither fast nor slow, just doing the job competently, the way he did most things.

About halfway down, we encountered Carl driving uphill in the Big F to rescue us. Once he'd spotted us, he turned around and led the way back, getting home a few minutes ahead of us as we stopped to lock up the lower gate. As we walked in the trailer door, he was already in his chair. He said, "I figured you guys were just talking or hiking around, but it was just the parental instincts coming in. It's getting a little dark, and I could imagine you guys backing off the road and getting stuck. The American West security guy comes through here every so often, and he usually stops and talks to me to ask if there's been any traffic up the hill. He's seen black bears and a couple of mountain lions up there, so I figured I'd come up and check on you."

Once inside, Matthew challenged me to arm-wrestle on the living-room floor. He beat me after about two minutes with the left arm, I beat him quickly right-handed. Then he and his dad arm-wrestled to a draw for over three minutes; the draw suddenly ended when Carl chose to wrestle for real, pinning Matthew's shoulders to the plywood floor, both of them laughing.

Matthew had received a whole box of Jelly Belly beans as an early graduation present, and the three of us ate our way through a plateful of them while talking about all the oddball flavors— Buttered popcorn?? Caramello bars?? Watermelon??—and listening to more Bob Marley from Matthew's room. Finally, I left for home at about ten o'clock. Matthew says he went to bed at about ten-thirty, as did I.

About a week later, I received a letter from Matthew's mother. She explained that she had felt awkward at our meeting because Matthew had not been attending to his chores until the weekend I was with him. She said that she had asked him a few weeks before that to "please come home and be responsible." She said that he had replied, 'There's more to life than responsibility.'"

Matthew was torn not only between two homes and between two parents, but between two Matthews as well. At his dad's home, he was a peer: two bachelors sharing a trailer, cooking and working on their cars together. At his mom's home, he was a child, with a list of chores and a designated room within a fancy large house. By choosing to live with Carl, he was really choosing which Matthew he was—the competent, trusted household partner. I'm not surprised by his choice.

CHAPTER TWENTY-ONE

Other People's Houses II: Tami's Weekend

Thursday, 6 P.M.

As Tami and I drive north past the Murphy Road exit on 420, we spot three people hitchhiking. "Slow down, I gotta see who this is . . . " says Tami. "Wait, stop!!" Jason, Shawn and Aurora all run to the car and pile into the back seat. We pull back onto the freeway just as the rain starts again. Aurora and Tami haven't seen one another for a few weeks (Aurora has moved four times in the past three months), and they fill each other in on current affairs.

Everyone in the car will be at the beach party on Saturday, and they learn that I'll be there because it's my weekend to follow Tami. Aurora doesn't know me very well, but she's seen me around the Arco a lot, so it's okay with her. Jason knows me from the Arco, too, as well as from the mosh pit at Manoa and from my giving him a ride home to Sunriver, and he thinks it's cool that I'm coming. Shawn, the birthday boy for whom the party is being given, doesn't know me at all, and he's clearly nervous—there's been $110 collected at school over the past couple of days to buy pot and LSD for this party. He doesn't know that I know this. Jason reassures him that I'm okay, but Shawn doesn't quite believe it.

I drop all three of them at Shawn's mobile home in the Big Timber Trailer Park across from the Honda Point State Park, where the big party will be. Then we return down Coast Trail Road to Tami's new house, well back off the road into the woods.

The house is new within the past few months, and quite large. It's done in Southwestern flavor, with deep reveals in the stucco walls to suggest earth construction. Exposed four-by-four beams under the dining room ceiling are stained dark and hung to the walls with black iron brackets. The rugs and furniture fabrics are Southwestern as well, but the furniture placement is contemporary, the living room chairs and couch floating in the middle of the large room rather than against the walls.

Tami's mom Lenore and little brother Tyler are talking in the living room with an aunt visiting from San Diego. Her stepdad Terry sits in the doorway to the next room, in the dark, eavesdropping, though I don't know that yet. I explain my presence to a clearly surprised group—Tami hadn't told them anything about me at all, much less that I was following her this week. She's eighteen now, and was able to sign her participation forms without taking any of them home, but I'd have expected that she might have told her folks *something*. Mom and aunt seem interested and friendly when I explain myself, but Terry won't have any part of it. He scares the hell out of me when he says "hi" from his seat in the shadows behind me in the next room; it's the only word he says while I'm there.

Lenore calls Tami by her middle name, Eve. Tami freely says that she was late for dinner because we'd just spent a couple of hours at Planned Parenthood in Port City, but tells her mom only that she's going to spend the night at Aurora's house on Saturday instead of filling her in on the details of a party on the beach with drugs and thirty kids.

After Tami gives me a quick tour of her room, Lenore says that she'd be glad to have me to dinner if she'd known I was coming, but . . . No problem. Tyler eats, Tami picks at her dinner. It's about eight o'clock, and I'm flagging a little. Besides, it's tense around the table. So I make an appointment to interview Lenore at her shop on Saturday morning, and I excuse myself, knowing that Tami wasn't going anywhere for the rest of the evening anyway. She tells me the next morning that Lenore and Terry were (understandably) mad at her for springing me on them. "What if we'd been doing something we shouldn't have?" Terry said. "I don't want that guy around here."

❧

Friday, 3:30 P.M.

We go into Mr. Barry's room to take a make-up math test, but by this time on a Friday Mr. Barry has split for the weekend; he was expecting Tami right after school at 3:05. It shouldn't be a surprise that he's left, but Tami's surprised anyway. So we walk back out onto the lawn and talk with Shawn and Jason again. Mr. Dawson and Mr. Phillips both come out onto the sidewalk and spot Jason. He's not a Curtisville student any longer, having enrolled in Union High's continuation school instead, and the principal and assistant principal tell him he has to stay "at least 1000 feet away from the school property." That's an interesting and grossly abstract number. I'll bet Mr. Dawson couldn't tell you how far 1000 feet from school was, much less Jason.

Anyway, Shawn and Jason walk down to the picnic tables at the Arco (1490 feet away) so that we can pick them up and give them a ride home. As we walk around the the back parking lot to get my car, Tami meets another friend who quit school just before he would have been suspended for yet another smoking violation. Right about this time, I start to wonder just how persecuted these guys are. Sure, they shouldn't lose their educations for a cigarette violation, but it seems as though they're taunting the school, *trying* to get tossed.

We pick up Shawn and Jason at the Arco and drive to Tami's house, but we're not taking Shawn and Jason home—they're all going swimming at the Union Community Pool instead. She asks me to wait out at the foot of the driveway as she walks to the house. Within a minute, she returns with the bottle of tequila that she'd bought in Mexico for her dad, and swimsuits for herself and the two guys.

As we drive to her dad's house out in the Curtisville ranchlands, she's not giving me any directions at all until we're right at the intersections, pointing suddenly and saying "Turn!" rather than saying "go left" or "right" or "your side" or any such thing. When we get to her dad's tiny, rundown house, all the blinds are pulled. Tami says, "It looks like he's not in the mood for any company." She runs in with the bottle, and she's back out with us in two minutes.

Then we're off to Port City again, first to the same house we had tried to visit after school yesterday, with the same results— Lori's not home; but we stop a block away at another friend Ron's house. Ron is there on a couch, along with Lori (the girl we were trying to visit) and another girl to whom I'm never introduced, all three smoking like crazy. A blue fog hangs in the dark living room, and all the shades are pulled. They find out that I'm working on a book, but that doesn't deter them at all from talking about "getting tweaked" (speed? coke? Ron sold his friend's pager for forty dollars, and when the owner complained, Ron told him, "Hey, you got a line out of it . . . "), or about more or less indiscriminate sex (during one conversation, Lori corrected the third girl: "If I remember correctly, I was kissing him while his penis was in *your* mouth"). The girl whose name I don't know says quietly, more to herself than to any of us, "I haven't done any drugs at all, all day." They're quiet when Ron's mom or dad are in the house, but they couldn't give a rip about me.

For all of their yakking about drugs and sex, though, we're all bored stiff. If drugs and sex are all you can look forward to, then that leaves a lot of free time. Ron polishes his leather high-top Doc Martens, they take turns playing with someone's Zippo lighter, they show off new tattoos. The phone rings well over twenty times in the hour and a half that we're there, a lot of them from one friend that Lori keeps telling, "We're leaving right now to come pick you up." But they make no move to leave.

There's a cat with runny eyes and matted fur hanging around in the living room. Ron teases Lori about borrowing his bedroom for screwing her boyfriend—"I charged them like five bucks a time, and the tenth time was free." Lori turns eighteen in eleven days, and her mom is giving her $100 because she said she would if Lori made it that far without getting pregnant. "Not that there weren't a few scares in there, though . . ." Ron puts on some Metallica, but nobody's really listening. Seven people, no ideas.

Swimming at the Union Community Pool starts at seven o'clock, so we finally leave at about 6:35. When we arrive at the pool,

I give them five bucks for admission—they don't have any money with them because Tami invested her cash in the weekend party's drug fund earlier that afternoon—and drop them there, leaving for a couple of hours at home.

At 8:45, I go back to the pool. They're all there, wet-haired, and we stand on the curb and talk to other Curtisville students, including Ray. Poor Ray—he's got a big-time crush on Tami, and she can't tell him plainly enough to go away. She's been very direct with him, tried everything she can think of, but he's completely stuck on her.

Tami wants to visit her friend Cheri back in Curtisville since I'm driving and she can't usually get there on her own. We arrive at about 9:20; her stepdad answers the door and says Cheri's already asleep, so we drive back north to take Shawn and Jason home.

Once we get onto the highway, Tami's sleeping in the back seat, and Jason is almost asleep as well. Shawn is up front with me. I ask him, "Big Timber, same as yesterday?"

"Sure, if you don't mind."

"No problem."

Shawn pauses for a second, and says, "I like you, you're a nice guy." I'm surprised, and pleased of course. But it just shows me how much these guys need some nice adults in their lives, because they're surrounded by nobody but their bored and disengaged friends all the time.

We drop Jason and Shawn at the Big Timber Trailer Park, and then go to Tami's house in the woods, where I drop her off in the black night at the end of the driveway at about 9:50. The closest streetlight is two miles away. I wait until I see a house light come on, and then I pull back out onto the road. As I drive away, I occasionally turn off the headlights for five seconds at a time and relish the feeling of driving into nothing.

I stop at Oyster Beach to check the party scene, dying to be around active kids. But the dunes are deserted, and I go on home.

Saturday, 10:45 A.M.

I drive to Tami's after interviewing her mom at the tourist shop she owns in Sandy Cove. Tami walks out as soon as I ring the door-bell, and we're off. It's her day, but she asks, "Where do you want to go?"

"Anywhere you want."

She wants to visit her friend Maria who used to live near her in the trailer park but now lives about ten miles up past Roosevelt. Okay, fine, let's go. I comment on a couple of things we see along the way—the herd of elk, the forest cover over the road—but she's not interested.

We get to Maria's at about 11:30, and find her sitting out at the picnic table reading a book. She and her family (father, older sister twenty-four, two younger brothers fourteen and thirteen) live in a motor home—not a mobile home, but a motor home—parked in a roadside strip of ten concrete pads with electric and water hook-ups. Maria's house has curtains across the windshield; a small corrugat-ed steel storage shed stands beside it. I'm introduced around, and Tami decides we should play poker along with Maria's little brother Pete.

We start out with chips and betting, but I win everything, which isn't any fun, so we scrap that and play without chips for a few hands. Tami's bored—she missed her friend, but has no idea what they should do. (In retrospect, I obviously should have left them alone for an hour, but my brain was on idle like everyone else's that weekend, dumbly repeating the mantra, "stay close to research subject . . .") Instead, I teach them how to play a simpler three-card rummy game, and we all seem to win about evenly.

When it's about one o'clock and time for me to get home and take my wife to work, Tami asks Maria if she wants to come along to visit Cheri. "We have to come up to Curtisville anyway, so it won't be any hardship to come up here and bring you back," Tami says. Maria *does* live almost fifty miles north of Curtisville, but Tami doesn't have a great sense of what that means. Maria gets the go-ahead from her older sister, and we zoom back south. When we get to Curtisville, I have to stop for gas. I've driven 285 miles since Thursday morning, with probably a lot more to go the rest of today and tonight.

We pick up my wife and go into Port City, getting her to the post office five minutes before her shift begins. I'm hungry and need lunch, and it wouldn't be polite to eat without getting them something too. So we go to Larry's Deli, where I get a half-sandwich. Tami gets a whole sandwich and a soda; Maria doesn't want anything. We eat in the car for a few minutes, and then return to Curtisville and Cheri's house at 2:45.

Cheri greets us at the door and brings us into the living room. Clothes and old food and dirty dishes are strewn throughout the kitchen and living room. There are clothes on hangers suspended from the chain of a Tiffany lamp above the dining table. Cardboard boxes piled full of Harlequin romance novels line the entry hall.

Cheri is alone for the day while her mom and mom's boyfriend are off at grandma's, and she's watching *Scooby-Doo* cartoons in the dark living room with all the curtains closed. There are years-old stains on the walls and the ceilings. Her mom has an MFA in photography, and there are some funky double-exposure abstract prints hanging on the walls, along with some gaudy ceramics.

We spend four hours watching TV—first *Scooby-Doo*, then the last hour or so of the movie *Free Willy*, then a 1990s version of *Animal House* called *P.C.U. (Politically Correct University)*. We sit numb and inert in a dark, musty room. I have no energy at all; it's been a long, long time since I was this bored, and I really would prefer to be going to Benjamin's light show at TSU tonight, to be a part of something that was being done on purpose.

Tami asks Maria if she'd like to go to the beach party. She would, but we don't know if her dad will let her, so I don't know if I'll be driving to Roosevelt at seven o'clock or at ten o'clock or not at all.

Cheri goes off to the bathroom, and Tami tells Maria, "I really like this house. It's not like spotless clean, and nobody cares. Well, I mean, they *care*, but they don't insist that everything is perfectly neat all the time." A slight understatement. It would take a gang of cleaners two weeks to get it all straightened and repaired and washed down. Cheri's family could never possibly sell it—the trim boards are falling off the walls, and there are fist holes punched in the drywall and the veneer of the bedroom doors. The carpet seems to be composed mostly of tufts of dog hair. The outside of the house is bright Crayola orange, painted this color "just to piss off the bitch that lives next door," according to Tami. The aluminum window screen frames are broken and peeling up from the corners of the windows. We are in a postcard from Oklahoma by the Sea.

It's 5:30. The party is supposed to start at six o'clock, and we know we have to ask Maria's dad or older sister if it's okay that she goes, and we know they don't have a phone, so we know we have to drive the fifty miles back up past Roosevelt to ask them and then the forty miles back south to the park. We hang around at Cheri's. "Nobody *ever* goes to a party right when it's supposed to start," Tami explains when I mention the time. Cheri pulls a chicken out of the fridge to start dinner for her family before they come back home. Tami borrows a piece of stationery and scrawls a birthday card for Shawn for tonight.

Tami's not supposed to hang around with Cheri (for reasons she never tells me), so when she calls to ask her mom if she can stay all night, she shushes Cheri and Maria and says "I'm at Aurora's, can I stay the night?" It works fine, she reports after she hangs up. "I've gotten really good at lying to my mom. Too bad I can't just snag a bottle of liquor from my parents' cabinet, but I think they'd miss it."

Tami needs a birthday present for tonight, and so Cheri takes her into her brother's bedroom and goes through his dresser, pulling out two pairs of jeans and a couple of t-shirts for Tami to give Shawn.

Cheri makes some microwave popcorn. Tami says, "I hate popcorn," and eats most of it. It looks as though we're never going to leave, but Cheri's mom and the boyfriend come home, seemingly not at all surprised that there is a thirty-six-year-old man they've never met in their house with three high school girls. They all chat for a few minutes, and we leave at 6:25. Along the way, we make another detour back to Tami's; I stop at the foot of the driveway again, and she goes in to change into warm clothes and pick up a blanket.

It takes about forty minutes to drive the rest of the way up to Maria's, and it's a quiet drive. We get to their park at quarter after seven. Maria's older sister Juanita, the mom of the family, gives Maria the okay to stay at Tami's house until about noon tomorrow.

The motor home is small and tight, of course, but it's all pretty neat. It has to be—there's no way that five people could live in that small a space if it were cluttered. Five cats, all black and white and interrelated, roam around us. The driving area is open to the inside, and it looks as though you could pull down the windshield curtains and go driving tomorrow if you wanted to. (Two months later, they did.) In a cabinet above the passenger's seat is a TV with a Nintendo box hooked up to it. In the map pocket on the back of the driver's seat are magazines: *Woman's Day* and *Good Housekeeping*. Seems funny to have *Good Housekeeping* in a motor home, but there it is. A picture of Jesus laminated onto a sawn burl hangs on the closet door, and a rubber skull with long silver hair hangs from a string over the couch.

Clothes are stored in the kitchen cupboards, along with food and medicine-chest stuff. Juanita makes Maria eat a bowl of clam chowder, since she hasn't really had anything to eat since breakfast, and she makes a cup of tea for each of us. For all of Tami's interest in this party all week long, we don't seem to be in any hurry to get to it. One of the neighbors comes over, wearing a flowered house dress. She's going to take her kids bowling (I presume she's going twenty-five miles north to Coastline rather than sixty miles south to Union), and wants to know if Pete and Juanita would like to go too. Pretty soon, everyone has some plans for the evening—older brother Tim is going to stay home and play video games while everyone else is out.

At almost 7:45, we put it back onto the road for Honda Point State Park. We arrive at the Big Timber Trailer Park at about 8:20, and of course there's no big crowd of teenagers waiting for us. Tami doesn't know which trailer Shawn lives in, and I don't know either since I didn't see which one he entered after we'd dropped him off, so we can't ask at the trailer park where we should go to find the party. But we go across to the state park anyway, where we proceed to drive around for the better part of an hour, cruising every section of the park with no success. We drive back over to Big Timber, and of course there's still no one there, and still no way to tell at which trailer to ask.

Tami is furious at her friends for not telling her where the party would be. She thinks she knows a couple of people she could call who might know something, so we drive off in search of a pay phone. Being out in the country, it takes us about a half an hour to do that, Tami getting angrier the whole time. When we find a phone booth, I give her two dimes for a call—she drops them both in the grass and says, "Shit! Gimme two more." I do—no answer. We drive to another person's house on Coast Trail Road who might know where they're all at, but nobody's home. While driving, I see a skunk plain as day walking down the side of the road. I point it out and

Tami says, "Oh, joy . . ." in a go-to-hell voice.

We end up at the Ocean View Market phone in Sandy Cove, where Tami finally connects with someone who claims to know where the party will be. She gives the phone to me to take directions—a bored girl on the line tells me, "About a hundred, maybe two hundred yards into the park, turn left, and then you'll come to a bunch of trailers, and it's the second to last one on the right. There's a white truck parked in front of it." I'm elated to finally have something specific to do beside dispensing dimes. We drive back to Honda Point. I check the park map posted at the front gate; sure enough, there's only one road that goes left, and it's a couple of hundred yards in from the highway entrance. We take that left, and find nothing whatsoever—an empty parking lot, no trailers, no trucks, no people, no clues. Tami's really pissed, talking about torturing and maiming all of her so-called friends who left for the party without her. "I've been thinking all week long about Saturday, that's the only thing that's kept me going all week long."

We drive through the park one last time. I stop to use an outhouse, and Tami and Maria meet a guy who says he saw about twenty kids down on Stony Beach earlier. So we drive to the Stony Beach section of the park, and there's a nice wide groomed trail with stairs that wind down the bluffs to the beach. The problem, though, is that we're hundreds of yards from the nearest light, it's after ten o'clock at night, and it's *dark* out there. We decide to go down the trail anyway, lit by the crescent moon. We poke our way downhill for about ten minutes, more or less able to see the next five feet of trail. But before long, the path switches back into the woods, no longer open to the sky, and it just turns black. I know my job is to let my victims do whatever they want, but this is too much, and I really do feel some responsibility for them, so I pull rank and turn us around. They both feel relieved, I think; at any rate, Tami doesn't complain.

We walk back up the hill. Maria and I stop on a footbridge and look at the stars, an unbelievable smear of lights. I'm not used to so much darkness, and it's just beautiful. May as well get some pleasure out of the evening, and this is the perfect spot. Tami's not interested in the sky, but she waits quietly for us. After a couple of minutes, we continue up the hill.

Once we get to the car, Tami says to Maria, "You can't stay over at my house, because I don't want to deal with asking my mom if it's okay. Can I stay at your house?" Maria thinks probably so, and off we go to Roosevelt one last time. It's a really quiet trip this time, just Maria and I who talk, and not very much of that. A little after eleven o'clock, we get to Maria's. She goes into the motor home and comes back out to give us the news: her dad said that most nights it would be okay, but Juanita has to get up really early the next day to do laundry before church, so no. I think frankly Maria's a little relieved at that. She gives Tami a hug, and says to me, "It was nice to meet you. You're very patient."

Tami and I drive back to Sandy Cove. I'd been irritated earlier, but now it was just late and dark and pretty, and we were quiet, and I enjoyed the drive back. The blackness of the forest around the corridor of freeway was different from the blackness of the near-midnight sky only by the forest's absence of stars. As we got close to Sandy Cove, Tami complained one last time, "What kind of a party is it where they don't give you any directions about how to get there or what to look for?" I replied quietly, "Well, it would have been easier to find at six o'clock." Tami seemed surprised that I said anything, and said, "I'm sorry."

We got back to her house, and stopped one final time at the foot of the driveway. She took her coat and blanket and the bag of gift clothes from the car, and asked if I'd take Cheri's sleeping bag and other blanket back to her tomorrow. Sure, fine, whatever. Then she was gone into the night.

I drove on home, occasionally turning off the headlights, driving into nothing.

CHAPTER TWENTY-TWO

Other People's Houses III: Julian's House

"I'll see you, and raise you this Burger King pop-up puppet."

I could barely hear Julian's bet over the music and the eight other people talking in the living room/dining room/kitchen of his tumbling plywood house. Becky glanced briefly at her hand, more interested in the *Dirty Dancing* soundtrack on the CD player than in poker. Besides, she always brought junk to bet with—her mom was a dental hygienist, and Becky had once again showed up with a bag of Colgate samples and old magazines. "I'll match with a dental floss, and raise you a Hot Wheels and a condom."

"So it's three to me, huh?" I grabbed a handful of pretzels and considered my three queens. "Well . . . I'll call that. Here's a flamingo swizzle stick, a pair of rubber Vulcan ears, and a poem." I tossed my bet onto the pile in the middle of the table.

Julian threw in a postcard and a rubber stamp to call, and we showed our cards. My three queens would have been okay except for all the wild cards, which gave Julian four sixes. "All right! I got the Hot Wheels *and* the poem!" he shouted as he raked the pot over to the growing heap at his elbow. "My deal."

"Benny and Joon poker" was only one of the events featured at Julian's house. We went through trends about once a month. Stephen would come over with his video equipment and a script, and they'd spend a weekend making a movie. Or we'd play endless games of Assassin, in which every player draws the name of another player and then has to lure that person into a trap and kill them.

Nobody knows who might be trying to kill them, and mistrust runs deep. When we taught the game to Rosalynd, a student teacher who had befriended Julian and Ivy, we put our names into a box and drew victims—Ivy, Benjamin, Rosalynd, Julian, Stephen, and myself. I didn't look at whose name I had drawn until everyone else had picked and started plotting against their respective victims, and I discovered that I'd drawn my own name. The behavioral observer stands outside again. Of course, I didn't tell anyone else, so they all suspected me anyway. Once the game started, Rosalynd discovered that she really couldn't do anything without worrying about it—starting her car (there might be a bomb in it), putting her car in gear (or, as Julian suggested helpfully, "It might be like *Speed*, where once you get out on the highway, you can't slow down again"), accepting possibly poisoned chocolate from me. "I hate this fucking game already!" she said, laughing. She held her breath, started her car, and drove cautiously away.

Over the summer, the primary game was Benny and Joon poker, drawn from the movie *Benny and Joon* in which Benny, his disabled sister Joon, and their friend play poker using things like baseball cards and sunglasses for their bets. The crowd at Julian's house was Geek-heavy and movie-literate. Their new CDs were likely to be soundtracks. They almost never watched TV, but the trip to the ninety-nine-cent matinees and the midnight movies in Union were weekly rituals.

Julian's mother didn't mind that the house was full at all hours, because Julian's mother had left him. She had recently moved in with her current boyfriend. Julian and his sister didn't like this new guy and refused to go, so Mom simply gave them a check once a month for rent and food (a stipend that would end on the day that Julian graduated from high school), and left them on their own in a crumbling three-room house on a dirt road: another image that might come to mind of the Curtisville that most of Curtisville had disavowed, another snapshot from Oklahoma by the Sea.

My trips to Julian's were frequent and routine. I would make a U-turn and park on the dirt-and-weed margins of the gravel road in front of Julian's broken picket fence, reading the other cars to see if I knew who to expect inside. The front door didn't work at Julian's, and I had to walk around to the back to come in. The royal-blue door was splintered and had holes gouged out of it, and was unlocked most of the time. I always knocked, which I think was unexpected, and Julian or Stephen or Larry or Lauren or whoever was living there at the time would get up and let me in. I don't think I ever came to Julian's house and found just Julian. He gathered people around him, loved to be the center of attention, loved to have other people depend on him and need him.

The house, as shabby as it was, was one thing that Julian's friends depended on him for. For some like Becky, it was as simple as knowing that they had a place where the music would always be on and they and their friends could relax. For others like Stephen, it was a refuge from their families, a place to live for a few months. For all of us, it was where we went when we couldn't think of any place else to go.

A lot of kids had an older friend, always male, just a year or so out of high school, who'd moved away from home and gotten an apartment. These guys never had much money, and so they almost always shared an apartment with someone in one of Union's dozens of college-student warrens. I visited any number of these apartments, but they came to seem always the same.

The door opened inward immediately off the sidewalk, with no porch or overhang outside, and placed the visitor immediately into the living room with no hallway or foyer.

Outside. Inside. Nothing in between.

The living room was as sparsely furnished as the rooms in architectural photographs: a couch against a wall, an ashtray full of cigarette butts balanced on one arm, and a television on the opposing wall. Probably a stereo by or on top of the television. Probably a weightlifting bench, rarely used, and one or two mismatched dumbbells or iron plates lying around it.

These apartments were always dark. There were windows, of course, but they were apathetic windows; it seemed as though they had simply surrendered their duty to bring sunlight into the room. The outside disappeared as soon as the door was closed, even on the brightest day, and the only light came from a seventy-five watt lamp off in a corner. The air was Marlboro blue, almost luminous, a light source in itself.

We were never invited into the other rooms of the apartment, except perhaps the breakfast nook. The privacy of the bedrooms was inviolate, and the negotiated public space of the living room and kitchen was left to mere function. Neither roommate claimed the living room, neither dared to place his stamp on it. There was rarely anything on the walls. No paintings, no posters, no centerfolds, nothing. Just a box with four off-white walls, an off-white ceiling, and dark landlord carpet, filled with smoke.

Here was freedom, the swinging bachelor life. Unchecked hedonism, all-night parties, heaping bowls of marijuana, the refrigerator full of beer, girls girls girls.

Well . . . no.

Here was boredom. You could have all the beer you could afford, but that wasn't very interesting on a regular basis. You could have girls come over any time, but they rarely did. You could watch whatever was on cable without having to argue with your sister or your stepdad, but there was never anything interesting on. You could play the new Green Day CD as much as you wanted, but you only bought it because of that one song on the radio, and the CD isn't really all that good. You could have the weight bench out all the time and never be nagged about putting it away, but there it sat, reminding you that lifting weights is hard work and not especially interesting, and that it'll be several years before you look like the guy in the Soloflex ad.

All this freedom, all of this autonomy and self-regulation and control, came down to being able to smoke more cigarettes.

When Curtisville's kids, male or female, took me to their friends' apartments, it was with a sense of envious anticipation: "I can't wait 'til I get a place of my own." They wanted to show me this place, this great friend, this idealized future that they aspired to. And we'd get there, and be offered the couch, and maybe listen to a song off a new CD; and then sit around and say, "So, what do you want to do?"

ટ્રે

Julian was a needy kid, starved for attention after having gotten precious little from his family over the years. He was unsure about his sexual orientation, attracted equally (and voraciously) to boys and girls, but bisexuality was less the issue than that he simply wanted everyone to love him and was always fearful that they wouldn't. He opened himself to everyone—you always knew what Julian wanted, what he felt.

His walls were covered with himself. He was absolutely unafraid to put his dreams on display. His bedroom wall was a shrine to Hugh Grant, who Julian thought was simply the most beautiful man in the history of movies. He read his poems to anybody who'd sit still, and played his soundtracks and not only sang but acted along. And because he was open, because he was daring, so were we. Non-dancers became stars of the dance floor at Julian's, non-singers crooned along with everyone from Alan Jackson to Janet Jackson. You could be dumb and childish at Julian's, which is why we all loved to go there. You could be honest about wanting to have fun, or about telling your friend they were your friend, or even about being bored if that was true.

Just kids at play, you might say. Wasted time. It's nice they're having fun, but so what?

Here's what. Irene and Mara and I left school on a Wednesday and stopped at Julian's house at about 3:30. We'd intended to drop off his script for our upcoming performance and just take off; but we went in and sat down for a minute, and that became ten minutes, and that became five hours. And during that five hours, we discussed which soliloquy from Hamlet was our favorite. All three of them were actually passionate about their choices, interrupting one another to finish a passage in unison, as though discussing a favorite song from the radio. We talked about thirty or forty movies, both current and historical; and about another dozen or so books; and about going out dancing at the Run Club in Port City; and about possible careers; and why Julian was confused about whether or not to keep on going toward being an elementary school teacher. We talked about friends and lovers; talked about why it's so hard to have a really affectionate relationship between men; talked about the difference between friends and best friends. We talked about ideal educations and how we aren't really close to them yet. In short (and it can only be in short, because I can't possibly do it justice, can't report it verbatim because it was unplanned and because I was participating instead of recording) we had a five-hour-long, erudite, skilled conversation; the sort of wide-ranging and fearless talk that can only occur among people who trust one another, in settings not broken by someone else's schedule, surrounded by visible proof of aspiration and desires.

Julian's house, like his hero Mrs. D's classroom, encouraged honesty and activity, rewarded citizenship. It was a place to be unafraid.

PART FOUR

After the Fact

CHAPTER TWENTY-THREE

The Hidden Program of the High School (or Six Metaphors in Search of a Box)

Very often, folk knowledge tells us things that a more rigorous study leaves behind. Regular people talking have fewer constraints upon them than experts, and tend less to cut the world into distinct subject areas. In this way, they can often speak a deeper truth. To this end, here are two brief stories.

One. A friend who owned a furniture store told me once that he'd looked at renting a storefront in the mall. He'd decided against it. "They tell you what hours you have to be open. The bell rings, and you open the store. Another bell rings, and you close the store. No, thanks. I've been to high school once already."

Two. Curtisville High English teacher George Springs returned to school from his day of jury duty, from which he'd been excused. He told his class about his discomfort and indecision, about both wanting to do his service to his community and also not wanting to be away from his classes so near the end of the semester. But he was clearly fascinated by the experience of being a potential juror. "It was a terrible way to spend a day—cooped up in a little chair, waiting around for something to happen, being told where to go and when you could leave and when you could go to the bathroom." He smiled broadly. "We were treated just like students."

It is worth trying to figure out why most of us can smile in recognition of these stories, and why, once we recognize their truth, we go ahead and replicate that meager and uncomfortable experience of high school anyway. The fact is that our physical construction of high schools reflects important but unspoken beliefs, and that both the beliefs and the construction make the ensuing experience almost inevitable.

If I were to ask you to name the physical components of a high school—not your high school, not any particular high school, but just "a high school"—what would they be? Surely there would be classrooms, and hallways. Lockers. A principal's office. A teachers' lounge. A gym. Bathrooms. Wood shop, auto shop, home-ec room. Labs for chemistry and biology, for computers nowadays. A library. Possibly an auditorium, probably a band room and a cafeteria. Storage for tables and chairs. The janitor's room, maybe as part of the boiler room. A place for buses and station wagons to unload their kids, some parking for the older kids, some parking for the teachers. A football field surrounded by a track and bleachers, a baseball field, a soccer field, tennis courts.

This is all so innocent. This is the inventory of the American High School, from Riverdale High in the Archie comics to Muskegon Catholic Central, where I graduated almost twenty-five years ago. It is, however, an inventory that tells us quite a bit about what we think a high school ought to be. That we take it utterly for granted tells us quite a bit about how powerful those beliefs are.

This list, once we know how many kids are going to be at a particular school, can then have numbers applied to it: How many classrooms? How many lockers? How many toilets? How many parking stalls? Multiply those answers by their individual sizes, gotten from *Architectural Graphic Standards* or state guidelines, and you have what architects commonly call "the program" of the building, the annotated list of what ought to be included in the designed product. Sometimes the program also includes some vague introductory text about "sense of community" or "promoting interaction," but that's far less important than budget limits. The list of spaces and its associated geometric and financial arithmetic is what the design is based upon, what the school district expects and the architects provide. It can be done in its most basic form in half a day—we just did most of it already in the last three paragraphs.

When I first arrived at Curtisville High School in July of 1994, I met the principal, Jeff Dawson, for our first appointment. Mr. Dawson is a friendly sort, a former athlete and former football coach and former girls' basketball coach who moved up from history teacher to assistant principal to principal.

He asked some about my work; I'd sent him six copies of my research proposal, but they were in an untouched stack in a cabinet next to his desk, and he told me he hadn't had time to look at one. He was, justifiably, more interested in *his* major project for the year, which was to get the school shepherded through its six-year accreditation review coming up in the spring. He was honest about what he saw as the school's successes and its shortcomings—the accreditation visit wasn't likely to tell him much that he didn't already know.

After about ten minutes of small talk, he gave me a tour of the campus, completely quiet except for a handful of student workers who were painting the spruce-green trim all around. Jeff had been spending some of his summer on moving teachers into different classrooms so that all of the faculty in individual departments would be closer together—there was now an "English wing" and a "Math wing" and a "languages wing." The science and vocational wings had long been established, since the lab-based rooms were about the only ones on campus that were unique to their purposes. I saw the new computer lab full of high-performance machines, and the two-year-old "multi-purpose room" which was partly auditorium and partly big unallocated space depending on whether the telescoping bleachers were pulled out.

He spent the greatest amount of our tour on the Main Gym and South Gym, then beyond to the new infield on the softball diamond, the just-installed bleachers on the baseball field. We finished the trip at the entry to the football field, where we stood and surveyed the newly donated scoreboard (courtesy of Riteway Trucking, who had painted their logo on it). "I used to love coming here on the night of a game," Jeff said, leaning on the rail of the track. "I really looked forward to it, it was the highlight of the week. We had some great teams when I was coaching. I always tell people that it wasn't great coaching, we just had the horses. This year . . . I'll be honest with you, we'll be doing good if we win a game all season."

But the wistful former coach faded quickly and the administrator returned. "Now that I'm not coaching, I'd just as soon never come here again. I have a headache all day on the day of a home game. Last year, we had a really ugly crowd at the Port City game, some of their kids wanted to mix it up. I've started hiring security for the games now, because a few teachers just aren't enough any more. If it happens again, we're going to move the games to Saturday afternoons."

We walked back to his office and shook hands. "If you need anything at all, don't hesitate to come and see me. My door is always open." As he walked through the door of the administration building, it closed behind him.

I spent the next two days measuring hallways and classrooms, walking off the distance between the soccer field and the baseball diamond in order to draw a campus plan and a larger site plan. I didn't know it then, but between my tour and the drawing, I had seen not only the physical school but also the ideas behind it.

Curtisville High is a collection of eleven single-story buildings connected by covered walkways as shown in Figure 7. Each class-

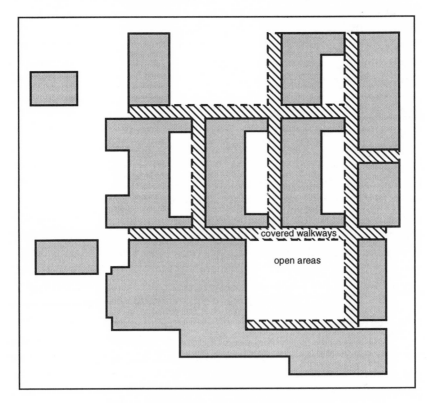

Fig. 7. Curtisville High School plan

room building is between five thousand and eight thousand square feet, with the main gym and multi-purpose building much larger. In the late 1950s, when Curtisville High was planned, the California Department of Education contributed a certain amount of building construction money for each student. A great number of school districts decided to maximize their classroom space and not spend any of this money on enclosed hallways, so passage from room to room was designed with less expensive courts and arcades. There is an entire generation of outdoor schools in California, an interesting idea in San Diego but not so great in Timber County where the kids mill around before class in the thirty-five degree December rain.

The buildings at Curtisville are rectangular, mostly with one or two sides exposed to the weather and the others facing one of these covered arcades. The weather walls are made of concrete block; the arcade-facing walls are made of plaster-composition panels with batten boards at the joints, with windows that open into the classrooms at ceiling height. All of the exterior walls are painted a calm, pale green, with doors, cornice boards, and lockers in a darker woodsy green.

Within those buildings are thirty-two non-athletic classrooms, four athletic rooms, administrative offices, a library, the office for Native American education programs, a kitchen, a theater, four student bathrooms, and three teacher bathrooms. This collection of school buildings sits on about seven acres, surrounded by two acres of parking and about thirty acres of athletic fields on a quarter-mile-square plot at the outskirts of town.

In light of nationwide stories of school buildings which are literally crumbling while still occupied, Curtisville appears to be a tremendously well-maintained campus.[1] There are few luxuries but room enough for all, weatherproof and adequately heated. The program has been fulfilled. The list of spaces has become three-dimensional and material, and everyone and everything has its place.

𝔞

The program of a building succinctly expresses our beliefs about its job and about the people who inhabit it. Architects Murray Silverstein and Max Jacobson help us to read those beliefs in the building.[2] First, they say, we have our basic definition of the building type, the image not only of the building but of the enclosed behavior that comes to mind when we say "office tower" or "shopping mall" or "high school." As their example, Silverstein and Jacobson offered an architectural definition of a supermarket: a single building of at least 70,000 square feet that offers not only food but "all needed household goods" to a population of several thousand.

Each building type has a specific arrangement of spaces that make the building type recognizable, the sort of inventory we created a few pages ago. To continue their supermarket example, Silverstein and Jacobson identified four characteristics that are always part of our understanding of a supermarket: a site which is more than half parking, located near a major traffic artery; a building which offers all merchandise in self-service displays, but which holds back-stock off the sales floor; a layout with the most basic food items at the perimeter and impulse items closest to the central paying area; and an environment which is controlled in every way—sound, lighting, temperature, and organization of products. These are the characteristics that give a supermarket its "supermarketness." Without any one of these internal patterns, the supermarket would cease to be a supermarket and would become something else.

These shared characteristics have larger causes, cultural patterns that mold both our spaces and our expectations. For the supermarket, Silverstein and Jacobson have identified three underlying cultural roots: the factory farm and the industrial model of food production; government policies that support agri-business over small producers; and an economic system based on large corporate ownership of supermarket chains (and their associated house-brand packagers). I think they've left some out—brand-naming that offers broad but meaningless choices, the sale of shelf space to wholesalers, the increasing gulf between farmed food and processed food—but their point remains valid: a different system of food production and distribution would result in an entirely different building type to fulfill the same functions.

Larger social patterns like these are inherently brought into the creation of any new building. The basic cultural ideas of a building type make the same basic program inevitable; beliefs and context are, as Silverstein and Jacobson put it, the hidden program. The places that result then act as metaphors for ideas that we normally don't express in words but say plainly through our actions and our creations.[3]

☙

The first metaphor that guides school construction and administration is the *separation of kids and adults,* removing teenagers from the community and placing them into the hands of appointed experts. The school building and grounds are both the evidence of adult desire for separation from children and teenagers and the means of separating them.

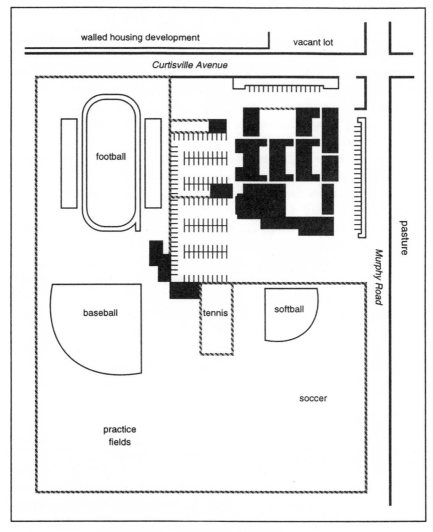

Fig. 8. Curtisville High School site plan

Except for the oldest schools in the most urban areas, high schools are generally constructed on huge parcels and set far away from the community they serve. Curtisville High was built on a forty-acre lot shown in Figure 8, located over a mile away from downtown. When it was opened in the early 1960s, it was extraordinarily isolated, set onto ranchland at the far north end of town. The town has grown out toward the school in the thirty-five years since its construction, but a couple of dozen placid Black Angus still graze on the lot across the street.

The school sits out at the corner of Murphy Road and Curtisville Avenue, as far away on its site as it can get from the few houses that are nearby. The school has no kitchen or lunchroom, but the "open campus" rule has been repeatedly challenged by both parents and nearby property owners who view loose kids as a breach of their security. Early in the year, the lunchtime exodus from school included fifty or so kids who walked across the soccer field to a broken piece of fence at the end of Rasnor Road. Leaving via this gap in the perimeter allowed these kids to get to the convenience store about five minutes faster, no small consideration in a forty-minute lunch period. But within the first two weeks of school, this announcement appeared in the morning bulletin: "ALL STUDENTS—WHEN LEAVING CAMPUS, please respect the rights of citizens and their property. Dispose of trash properly and stay off private property. The fence by Rasnor Road is <u>NOT</u> an exit—please use Murphy Road when leaving campus." That announcement (and the posting of the assistant principal next to the hole in the fence that noon) reduced the flow of kids from fifty to about five.

The request to the school had come from the manager of the apartment complex through which the students flowed on their shortcut to the Arco mini-mart. My own examination didn't turn up much trash or worn grooves in the lawns, and the kids didn't break anything or threaten anyone when I made the trek with them about twenty times over the course of the year. The perceived threat was greater than the actual events.

This supervised distance between teens and community ensures that teenagers only rarely come into contact with adults engaged in their work. Kids get to see teachers at work, and janitors; they get to watch the lady who makes their sandwiches at the Deli; they see the guy who fries potato wedges in the convenience store and the woman who runs the cash register. But they're held apart from the real economic doings of their town and the human aspects of that working life. If one of the jobs of school is to enculturate teenagers, we act counter to that if we separate them from the most basic elements of that culture: the ways in which we make our livings. (Of course, they might only learn how bored many adults are with their work, which would itself be an important—and tragic—lesson.)

Even on campus, though, kids are held separate from the adults around them. Teachers have separate bathrooms, a separate lounge and work room, a separate parking lot. Within the classrooms, there are two zones set aside for the teacher: the front wall of the classroom, an area often marked off by a desk or a lectern and an overhead projector, and behind which students are clearly out of place; and the desk in the rear corner of the room where the teacher does his or her grading and sits while supervising tests, watching the backs of heads for undue variation from stillness. Physical proximity between teacher and students is very rare at Curtisville—and it was, over the year, to become a reliable sign of a good classroom.

The administration of the school is also sharply divided from the students, both in function and in building. Students play very little role in the planning of their school or their education, planning which takes place on the site but in buildings that are never entered by students except for punishment. At Curtisville High School, like most others, being called into the principal's office isn't usually an invitation to help the school develop a more responsive curriculum.

To return to the classroom, we find much evidence of the second guiding metaphor of schools: *teaching is active, and learning is passive*. The students sit in their regularly-claimed seats (which may or may not be assigned but which must be consistent in order that the teacher might take attendance more quickly), seats which are permanently constructed as part of the desks so that kids cannot even choose a favorite distance from their writing surface. Occasionally, the desks are turned to make small groups, but the individual desk (and associated private learning) is the norm, and the kids know it; after all, that's how the payback is determined at test time.

The teacher stands, head higher than those of the students; the students sit, looking upward. The teacher moves; the students do not. The teacher is the performer, using blackboard, overhead projector, desk and podium as tools and props; the students are the audience, who (ideally) view and take notes on the performance. The audience may be set in rows and columns facing the blackboard, or in three angled sets of rows and columns making a sort of level amphitheater, or in two facing sets of rows and columns like the parted Red Sea with the teacher working the resulting central aisle. Regardless, there is one person who transmits, and thirty-five who receive.

The teacher begins class and ends it. The teacher opens discussion and closes it. Educational literature is full of terms like "time on task" and "disruption" and "interruption" and "inappropriate responses," all of which are definitional ways of establishing the norm of audience silence and passive compliance. The teacher knows "where the class should be" at the end of the period, and is responsible for taking them there. This is highly unlike most adult-adult interchanges, in which even if one person is responsible for the outcome of many, the others all at least know the destination.

We have constructed a model of learning that is inherently boring and alienating exactly because it encourages this passivity, because it removes the linkage between curiosity and active, self-guided exploration. In order to see this more clearly, imagine a white-collar worker with a set of tasks to accomplish, a set of people to supervise, and a set of supervisors of her own to satisfy. More or less, she's left on her own to do her work. But once a week, there's a staff meeting in which the division manager talks for an hour. Staff participation in these meetings, while nominally requested, is neither encouraged nor necessary; the agenda comes first. Meetings like this—tedious, agonizing, eternal—are the low point in the week.

High school is nothing but staff meetings.

This passive-audience metaphor is made more literal whenever the TV and the VCR come out, which is surprisingly often. Curtisville High has spent tens of thousands of dollars in television and videotape equipment and video curricular materials over the past few years; eleven of the thirty full-time classrooms have a television and VCR as permanent equipment, with several more units available from the library on portable carts. In a minority of class-rooms, television is an integral part of the course, as for example in Dan Jacobs' English classes that examine first the novel and then the film version of, for instance, *Pygmalion.* In many classrooms, though, television is a "preferred activity," a Friday treat for having been more or less orderly through the rest of the week, as when Mr. Peterson gave his Individual in Society class two periods to watch Olivia Newton-John and John Travolta in "Grease."

Video can convey information straight from some curriculum development company or the California Department of Education, which combine to put out an extraordinary number of videotapes every year. Television can be a pacifier that allows a teacher to grade papers, or helps a substitute teacher to keep from being taken for a ride by students who recognize and exploit indecision. Regardless of its use, though, the widespread classroom employ-ment of television is a recognition and acceptance of the conception of passivity in learning, an exploitation of our shared convention that students are an audience.

This expectation of passivity extends to all school-related activ-ities. The adult conception of "going to a football game" is to sit in one position and move only for functional purposes like bathroom and concession stand trips. When I sat in the stands and counted, I was passed by five and six times as many kids as adults in a crowd that was nearly evenly split in age. Those kids were far more likely to be in pairs and threes than the adults, who were often on solo trips to the john or the hot dog stand. The teenage conception of attending a football game is fluid: the stands and the grounds are places to meet people, have roving conversations, and only now and again to turn their attention to the remote but nominal "event." The real event is to be with friends, and that entails movement. This is a source of constant frustration to Mr. Dawson and the rest of the administration, who wish that the kids would just sit down and watch the game like their parents and the Booster Club members. Teachers and rented security guards alike are instructed before the game to keep kids in their seats and out of the aisles, a futile task diligently pursued.

Mr. Dawson passed me in the halls one afternoon at two o'clock and said, "There's nothing better than walking the halls and there's no students in it—everybody's in place." Students know that they must ask their teacher for a hall pass in order to use the bathroom during class periods; they know that they must ask the attendance office for an off-campus pass in order to see a doctor or dentist. The management of students is paramount to the success of the school in the terms that it has established, and management is always easier when those to be managed see themselves as inevitably passive.

ॐ

School leaders, like those of many of our institutions, consider one of their greatest successes to be the fact that the school treats everyone the same regardless of their differences. One of the most central metaphors of education, the third in our list, is *the celebration of abstraction and the avoidance of the unique.* Students are allocated to classrooms mathematically, as are their teachers. The classrooms themselves are seen as interchangeable, one box the same as the next—in the architectural world, this is known as the "egg-crate school." And the day is divided into six egg-crate periods of equal length, with morning nominally the same as afternoon.

The human facts of these decisions are rarely discussed, although they're central to any learning that goes on. I saw students and teachers who quite simply never got along all year, to the enormous frustration of both; I saw students and teachers alike struggle to stay awake every day immediately after lunch, or consistently lose their concentration during fourth period. But counselors are charged not to let students change classes for these messy human reasons. Principal Dawson assured his teachers before the school year began that "we aren't doing drops to let kids avoid teachers or get a certain period free or get sixth-period gym."

Curtisville's teachers are officially differentiated by their position on what's called the "down-and-over" chart. The District's pay scale for teachers is based both on years of employment—a scale which maxes out at twelve years, even though ten or more teachers have been at Curtisville for over twenty years—and on the number of college credits completed beyond the bachelor's degree, to a limit of sixty. Thus a teacher is monetarily rewarded by moving either down (more years) or over (through continuing education) on the chart. In the abstract terms used by the school, Dan Jacobs and Lily Chase are the same teacher, and a student assigned to either one of them for English 3 would get an equivalent experience. This is, in the experiential world, clear nonsense; it is also a belief that guides school planning.

The belief that rooms are all the same allows the administration to shunt teachers all around the school. New teachers find that they have classes in two or even three different rooms over the course of the day, and veterans can come back in the fall to a room far removed from that of the previous year. While this is recognized as unfortunate, the misfortune is expressed in terms of inefficiency and inconvenience to the teacher, and not in terms of the inability to create a stable home from which to work and to welcome.

During my initial tour of the campus, Jeff was clearly pleased that he'd been able to bring his teacher and room assignments together by departments, so that all of his English teachers were in one building, all of his language teachers in another, all of his social

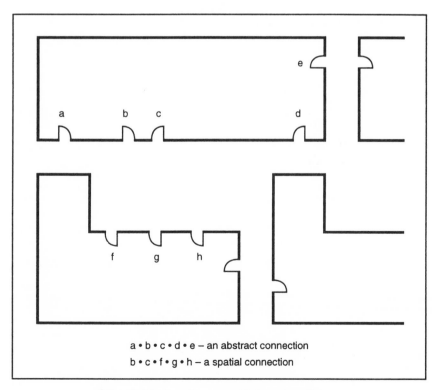

a • b • c • d • e – an abstract connection

b • c • f • g • h – a spatial connection

Fig. 9. Abstract vs. spatial connections

science teachers in a third, and so on. The facts, though, are that the teachers in these departments almost always have different prep periods and thus aren't able to collaborate during their off-times; that students can hardly "major" in a subject and thus spend most of their time in a certain region of the school, as they might on a college campus; and that the space that would have mattered for collaboration in the English department was certainly not common possession of the 500 Building (which put Mr. Springs' classroom over two hundred feet from Mr. Bauer's, and arranged them in a linear and thus not-social pattern) but common possession of the courtyard between the 500 and 600 Buildings, which could have brought all five teachers within a sixty-foot radius and in an inward-facing and thus more interactive pattern. The administrative achievement was entirely abstract and had no effect on real behavior.

The abstract, however, is easily measurable, while the actual is often impossible to enumerate clearly. Achievement is defined as a test score, for example, allowing sharp divisions to be defined (between a "B" and a "C," for instance) where none in fact exist. I picked up a scrap of paper on the hallway one afternoon; it turned out to be a computer printout of a grade report for a student in Bio 1. To that point, there had been three tests and two labs included in the grade. Her test scores were 100, 100, and 93. Her lab scores were 0 and 0. Her combined grade was printed at the bottom: 293/400 = C. Whatever this set of numbers might mean, it distinctly does not mean that she was an "average" student. It might mean that doing the labs was irrelevant to understanding the material—after all, she got three superior scores on her tests without doing the labs. Conversely, it might mean that the tests were far too simple, and that I could have walked in from the Quad and done just as well. It might mean that she had a terrible environment at home in which to do homework, and often couldn't get it done. It might mean that she was lazy, doing only what was supervised and enforced, blowing off all her other work. It might mean a lot of things, but it goes into the book as an unambiguous "293/400 = C."

The fact of Curtisville's cold, windy, and wet outdoor corridors appears nowhere on the balance sheet of maximizing educational square footage; the fact that Mara at age sixteen was accepted into Stanford's advanced program for a combined senior year of high school and freshman year of college was not taken into account by

Curtisville's administration, who insisted that she take four credits of Phys Ed in her very expensive year at college in order to meet California's high school graduation requirements. Our insistence on treating everyone equally and "fairly" ensures that we treat almost no one sensibly.[4]

The linkage of so many schools to mandated curriculum frameworks has led to a massive industry that creates and sells teaching aids in careful compliance with the California Department of Education guidelines. Teacher mailboxes overflow with catalogues from curriculum development companies offering videos, workbooks, software and CD-ROMs, and "curriculum modules" on everything from the Civil War to tobacco abuse. For the less materially-minded, there are courses, seminars, and conferences on classroom management, multi-modal learning, and integrated curriculum strategies.

Teachers are caught in the middle of this struggle, attempting to deal both with administrative abstractions and with the realities of classroom and personality and interaction. Some teachers align themselves closely to the state curriculum, using it to outline their classes over the year; they are the ones found in front of the photocopy machine, running off pages sixty-four and sixty-five of a packaged, state-approved "study unit." (The California Department of Education encourages this, of course; their standardized achievement tests are the stick that they use to punish non-compliant teachers and schools, and the phrase "teaching to the test" is heard across the land.) Others use the frameworks as a broad outline, filling in the details with personally chosen—often personally created—classroom work. Still others treat guidelines and uniformity as the enemy: Dan Jacobs, a twenty-five-year veteran, told me early in the year that "you've got to break the rules if you're going to get anything accomplished in the classroom."

Tom Fischer, an eighteen-year teacher of Auto Shop, dreaded the day that the state issued a mandated curriculum for automotive technology. "We've been lucky so far to avoid that—the other subjects got theirs a long time ago. I hate all this stuff about tests and reports and frameworks. The way I teach Auto Shop is that it's a performance-based course. Can they disassemble, rebuild, and repair an engine by the end of the school year? Can they think diagnostically and analytically? Can they go through a process and figure out what might be possible causes for a particular problem? That's what I want my students to leave with at the end of the year, a respect and an ability for analytical thinking. But the state is going to want them to pass a test on pistons and compression, and a test on lubrication, and all that junk." I asked Tom to tell me his favorite thing about teaching. He paused, then smiled. "Seeing in a students' eyes that they've already figured out something I'm explaining just before I've finished saying it."

Four months after that explanation, Tom Fischer, along with thousands of other auto shop teachers, got his three-inch-thick binder containing the Automotive Technology curriculum from the California Department of Education.

Given the model of schooling we have pursued—a standardized mass curriculum delivered to a passive audience and evaluated through measurable test outcomes reported mainly in the aggregate—it makes some sense to pursue our fourth metaphor, *economies of scale.* We strive to eliminate redundancies, to provide equivalent or greater services to greater numbers for the same expense.

When the Northern Timber Unified High School District was created in the 1950s, it was following a nationwide trend of school consolidation; in the two Wisconsin townships I'd studied earlier, the 1950s brought a state-mandated reduction from twenty-two school districts to three. The idea was to bring students into a smaller number of modern, well-equipped schools—they'd have used the term "state of the art" if it had been trendy then—in order to accomplish both an improvement in educational quality and an economic savings at the same time.

Derek Drummond, Director of the School of Architecture at McGill University in Montreal, has written recently on people he calls "institutional entrepreneurs," school administrators and hospital boards and church councils who have been driven by the same sort of "aggressive, 'bottom-line' thinking" as Wal-Mart and Microsoft. "In the belief that great efficiencies can be realized by eliminating local or community-based and supported hospitals and providing the equivalent of 'one-stop shopping' for health care in a mega- or super-hospital," he writes, "the authorities are once again disregarding the critical impact of such an initiative on the urban environment. . . . hurt[ing] many citizens whose associations with these institutions are as profound as life and death."[5]

If we replace his concern over hospital mergers with a concern for high schools (a concern which Drummond has abandoned, believing probably correctly that there are few truly local high schools remaining in North America), his message is pertinent in Curtisville as well. Curtisville High School is the home to kids who, forty years ago, would have been in different schools all around the northern third of Timber County. Curtisville draws kids from Flat Lake (five miles east); Sandy Cove (eleven miles north); Cramer Beach (twenty-seven miles north); Roosevelt (forty miles north); and all of the ranches and forest houses in between. About a quarter of Curtisville' students are from widespread communities and homes spreading over several hundred square miles.

Clearly, if the fifty or so kids who lived in Flat Lake went to an imaginary Flat Lake High School, they wouldn't have the level of material support that we take for granted in a modern high school. They wouldn't have the weight room with its full complement of Universal machines, free weights, stationary bicycles, stereo, and mirrored wall. They wouldn't have as many televisions per student, nor as many tools and specimens in the Biology, Physics, Chemistry, and Geology labs. They wouldn't have rooms full of fast new computers, and might not be linked to the Internet. They wouldn't have as much administrative support: secretaries, outreach specialists, special-needs counselors, home-study coordinators, and a continuation school.

Those are, of course, abstract ways to measure the effectiveness of high schools, measurements that obscure and preclude some others. One thing these economies of scale hide is the loss of local culture and environment. This is most clear in the communities that don't have their own high schools. Curtisville's kids and teachers alike used quick catchphrases to note the observable and acknowledged differences between kids from different communities—the Roosevelt Cowboys, for example; the Moonstone Hippies. Had the Cowboys been educated in a Roosevelt school, they might have had more contact with their at-hand environment, might have learned new ways to understand the matrix of ranching, timbering, and tourism that formed the facts of life in Roosevelt.

We might say that integration is all to the good, that we are able to bring kids out of the fairly narrow world views that characterize their small towns, that we open their vision to a new and more tolerant way of living. This is a wonderful theory, but one which is not at all put into practice because the school's official policy is that these local culture differences don't exist. Diversity is a buzzword in educational theory right now, but the diversity that's talked about at Curtisville High is packaged in the language of the mostly urban places that make up so much of the state's population. Textbooks and videos all have their obligatory white and Black and Hispanic and Asian faces, but they're all white and Black and Hispanic and Asian yuppie children. There aren't any curriculum materials that show teenagers with cowboy hats and lifted pickups and Skoal circles worn into their hip pockets; there aren't any materials that show teenagers in tie-dye and dreadlocks, carrying surfboards and playing Hacky Sack; there aren't any materials showing teenagers who shave their heads and wear white makeup and velvet cloaks and paint their fingernails black. Curtisville High School brings together as diverse a set of kids as exist anywhere in any school—though the diversity is not on the ethnic grounds that distant urban analysts believe are the important ones—and then refuses to address those contrasts as an object of study. They offer up canned "We Are The World" platitudes, delivered in shrink-wrap from Sacramento, and dismiss the differences between the Punk and the Prep, between the Cowboy and the Stoner. They might as well have left the kids at home.

But the loss of the local high school in small towns is only the most visible effect of consolidation and standardization. The larger and less often considered loss is that there is no room for the local anywhere in the state curriculum. Curtisville's campus, made for an imaginary California with no driving winter rainstorms and no cold fog, is the architectural counterpart of its curriculum, made for an imaginary student who has no environment around her, a student who is merely being prepared for entry into the national labor pool. Curtisville has a government which makes no appearance in Government class; it has an economy which isn't discussed in Economics class.[6] Curtisville has a history with no place in the History books, and a literature with no means of entry into the

English curriculum. There is an amazing range of biology and geology in northern Timber County, most of which goes unmentioned in the science labs. There is a tennis team, though few kids play and no one plays well or seriously, but there are no surfing or rodeo teams because the regional school insurance pools consider those sports too dangerous. The local languages of social importance are Native American, not Spanish and French. There are Agriculture classes memorizing 1961 cotton-yield data from their thirty-five-year-old textbooks, from which most students go home and tend to their cattle and horses and sheep.

The community holds the school at a distance, both physically and socially, but the school holds the town away as well. The community-school interchange is minimal because that's the way we've designed it. The local environment is a superb resource for teaching, especially in light of the immediacy and experiential focus of teenagers, but it is entirely wasted. Curtisville didn't just appear by the hand of God; it was built by developers and speculators in response to some of the great pressures of twentieth century economics and culture. To have these teaching tools—these roads and highways, neighborhoods and small towns, the bluffs, the creeks, and the ocean—literally right outside the window and then to ignore them in favor of a curriculum designed hundreds of miles away is an incredibly telling decision.

Kristy, a girl in the junior class, was working on a college application and had her most recent report card on the desk. She seemed puzzled, and came over to ask Mara a question. "It says my GPA is 3.57, and that my class rank is 27 out of 173. But the application wants to know if I'm in the top tenth of my class, or the top fifth, or the top third. Where do I find that?"

Our fifth metaphor of *objective evaluation* has become one of the central driving beliefs of the school, and our most common form of evaluation is competition. Our schools are centered around competition, from the notion of "grading on the curve" to the constant array of state and national tests—ASVAB, PSAT, SAT, ACT, CLAS, Golden State. The results, learned weeks and months after the fact, are expressed in incomprehensible sets of incompatible abstractions. 460 verbal, 520 math, on the recentered scales. 73rd percentile. Combined score 17 out of 36. Second quartile. So many precise values linked to the inherently imprecise business of knowing.

And of course, there is the more overt competition of interscholastic sports. Curtisville High School fields girls' teams in volleyball, soccer, tennis, basketball, track, and softball, and boys' teams in football, soccer, tennis, wrestling, basketball, baseball, golf, cross country, and track. Three quarters of the school's site is given over to athletic fields; within the fraction that's left over, the two gymnasia take up an area equivalent to all of the classrooms in four buildings.

Curtisville fields its share of lousy teams, teams which have seasons of 0-9 or 2-14, but they have some winners as well: moving to sectional and regional competition in baseball, taking the girls' state basketball championship in the mid-'80s. Those, of course, are the teams that are remembered, with photos and trophies filling two cases along the entry to the gym. The collection tells us that school sports exist not so much to be loved and to fill our lives with intensity as to prove our worth against others.

Sport is the model that we use in other realms of education as well. An acquaintance of mine coaches junior-high kids in competitive math, calling them "mathletes" and bragging that three of them went to the state finals. Competitions abound in the arts, in music, in clubs and hobbies, as a way to make firm evaluations even in the absence of numerical criteria. It seems to be impossible to know whether or not you're good at anything unless you beat someone else doing it. Even the school's Christmas rituals of decorating classroom doors and gathering canned food for the poor are arranged as competitions.

Unfortunately, the mindset of the sports world (which is the mindset of the larger business world we expect our children to enter) bleeds into all other fields as well. Irene, who played clarinet in the school band, said, "Mr. Phelps puts all of his energy on winning superior ratings at Sectionals. It doesn't matter whether we really grow or learn anything about music, and it's not about bringing a piece of music to life that doesn't exist unless we play it. It's all about doing everything to get that unanimous superior rating. He's a really good teacher if you're a really good player, but he's not a good teacher if you're just okay."

This single-minded focus on testing brought about bizarre distortions of priorities: an English teacher who spent eight months out of the school year making sure her class could pass the State's year-end exam; a football coach who tried to recruit a star soccer player to do place-kicking on the football team instead; a band director who decided that students should play a new instrument. Amy, a senior, had played the flute since fourth grade. In her junior year, Mr. Phelps told her that the band needed a bigger sound, and switched her to the alto sax because she was a good musician and could make the change. In a convincing demonstration of the Peter Principle, Amy struggled with the new instrument for both semesters and quit the band altogether at the end of the year. She owned the flute metaphorically in knowing its feel and nuances of sound and fingering, in understanding her abilities and limitations; she owned the flute literally as well. She had no possession over the saxophone, again both metaphorically (its unfamiliarity of fingering and mouthpiece, its weight and center of gravity, the sound and shape of the notes) and literally (she was given a "disgusting school saxophone, old and beat-up, it even had mold inside it"). She now plays neither instrument, and only occasionally plays the piano.

Amy has been lost to the world of group music because of an abstract decision made in favor of a predetermined musical repertoire, a predetermined "right sound," a predetermined conception of what high school music should be about and a belief that quality can only be reliably told through ribbons won at regional competitions. The school was full of forbidden personal stereos, smuggled under sweaters and jackets at the potential cost of confiscation. They played Clint Black and Nine Inch Nails and En Vogue and Too Short, AC/DC and Nirvana and Bob Marley—music which is easy for us to dismiss but which has at least as much technical and cultural merit as "I've Got a Gal in Kalamazoo." Music was central to the experience of so many kids who could never express it through high school band, just as the desire for physical expression found outlets in non-competitive (and unauthorized) forms like surfing, skateboarding, Hacky Sack, and the mosh pit. When we look for a balance of instruments that will win us awards, the people behind those instruments have disappeared.

Perhaps most importantly, these sorts of objective evaluations are self-defeating because they serve to *limit* what we attempt to do rather than to expand it. Any time we try to offer a definitive description of what we want, we leave out essential things in our rush to be objective. Jobs with careful and precise job descriptions are deadly boring, and tend to be precarious exactly because they're so inflexibly defined; education that pursues numerical criteria of some sort or another faces irrelevance, because the criteria miss most of what makes people successful.

❧

Teachers often noted with some frustration that they couldn't get their kids to see beyond Timber County. "There's an incredible xenophobia here," said one teacher who spent considerable time traveling through the U.S. and Europe. "We had scholarships all set for twenty-two students last year, to good schools like Wheaton. One applied." He shook his head. "If it's out of the county, they just won't go. These kids are as good as anywhere, but they think, 'Well, I think I'll go to CC [Coastal College, a community college just south of Port City], I'll go to Timber State.' "

We have in modern America an extraordinary assumption, one that would not have been shared by many of our grandparents. We believe in our sixth metaphor, *personal mobility*. We believe that we might live almost any place in America, and that we'll probably live in several places. The curriculum shares and encourages that expectation. Educational reforms are focused on "statewide performance standards that reflect the needs of a competitive world-class economy."[7]

Such a seemingly common sense statement is fascinating in the assumptions it hints at. It's important to note, for example, that the conference from which that goal was drawn was sponsored by the U.S. Department of Labor, and that it took the form of a focus group for the purpose of clarifying consumer desire for a product. In this case, the consumers are nationwide "business leaders" or major employers, the producers are educators and politicians, and the products are students being prepared to compete in the future world economy.[8]

The whole notion of statewide standards is an interesting one. Why is it particularly important that we make it clear how our students rank on some statewide or national scale? Because our large employers and major universities demand it. Uniform rankings make it easier to draw recruits from a large geographic area. Our mobility makes us easier prey for huge institutions, because people are willing to move extraordinary distances and to uproot themselves in order to pursue a career. Local people are competing against everyone in the larger region, even perhaps more than that, for the same jobs. What will happen as we continue to move into our highly touted world economy? Will we in fact require international grading of students so that we know that someone from Indonesia would be better suited to a particular San Francisco job than someone from Toledo? Who benefits from this grading and sorting technique? Clearly not the students being tested and evaluated (literally, "given a value").

It's no surprise that the curriculum, just like the campus, avoids that which is local and concrete. The local is of no worth in a national or global economy.[9] Understanding local watersheds is a negligible skill in a society that expects us to move whenever and wherever we're transferred. Local government is a futile preoccupation when zoning and building rules come from the county and state, who copy one another's rules on a national scale anyway. And the local timber and fishing economy is waning—it's far more profitable to study the stock market, that abstract and global speculative machine that drives the failure of local economies. The school district's office sign was carved out of a redwood burl, and that's as local as they felt the need to be.

These six metaphors are almost completely intertwined, all part of a single and coherent master narrative; it's hard to imagine that any of them could exist separately from the others. But take them all together and put them into a single paragraph:

> The school building and its associated program are based around placing passive kids into an isolated and homogeneous environment for mass-produced training. This training will be delivered by rule-bound experts who prepare youth at the least cost for a life of mobility and participation in the global economy. Continued participation is always contingent upon periodic competition and evaluation.

We don't say things this baldly in our mission statements, but our landscapes often let the truth slip.

Most industries have taken considerable steps toward a management strategy known as "total quality management," one of the central tenets of which is that the business exists to do exactly what the customer wants, only better. The casual observer might be surprised to see the degree to which this mindset does not exist in the high school, but that surprise is based on the illusion that the students—or perhaps the parents—are the customers.

Let us be both clear and honest about this: the student is not the customer. The student is the product. The customer is the labor market, through the proxy of the California Department of Education. If California hopes to attract new businesses and hold its existing ones, and if it hopes to decrease spending on unemployment and welfare and incarceration, then it must create an attractive business climate. In our modern economic terrain in which the desperation of labor is a resource available worldwide—whether from a manufacturing plant in Ciudad Juarez or a worldwide bookkeeping company in Seoul—an attractive business climate must include a labor force which is relatively passive, unattached to the local, willing to be continually evaluated and occasionally to lose, whether through personal fault or through accident. Those are the products that Curtisville High School is set up to manufacture.

CHAPTER TWENTY-FOUR

A Teenage Acre

Part of what attracted me to Curtisville to do my research was that a new community recreation center was under construction. I was curious how it would be seen and used by the kids, how it would be administered. After a year among the kids and another year of writing about them and continued conversations with my volunteers, I never saw the inside of the rec center except for my tour during its construction, and never talked to a single kid who'd been in it.

In 1991, the voters of the Curtisville Community Services District passed Measure R, a district amendment that brought recreation under the control of the community services district to join services such as street lighting and waste-water disposal. It also imposed a $30-a-year parcel tax for twenty years to be allocated to recreation needs.[1]

Over the next four years, the District board spent much of that accumulated (and anticipated) tax revenue on the Curtisville Recreation Center, a building located at the southern edge of Founder's Park. The Community Services District newsletter dated July 1993 described the project:

> The 7,500 square foot multi-use room would accommodate roller skating, a wide variety of indoor sports (basketball, volleyball, indoor soccer, etc.), exercise classes, youth activities, dances, and parties. The room would be big enough for a competition basketball tournament or two full court games.

237

A roller skating rental booth and games arcade would be located in the lobby adjacent to the multi-use room.[2]

As the building left paper and became steel, the planned activities came into sharper focus. The Union *Post* of January 20, 1994 reported that:

> The district plans to hire a part-time facility coordinator. . . . The coordinator, however, would not actually run specific programs—a task that would be carried out by private vendors. . . . Monday through Friday, the center would have aerobics and fitness programs from 6 A.M. to 1 P.M. and gymnastics programs from 2 P.M. to 5 P.M. On weeknights, there would be a variety of youth and adult basketball leagues using the facility. Roller skating would be offered on Friday and Saturday nights and Sunday afternoons. On Sunday evenings, the facility would be available for rent and community events. . . . Curtisville residents could rent the facility for $29 an hour for parties and wedding receptions.

At the end of 1994, the district hired that coordinator, a recent TSU graduate with a degree in physical education. She and the district's Recreation Advisory Committee reviewed proposals from a number of recreation vendors, and together they suggested that Health World Inc. offer gymnastics and health and fitness classes on Monday, Wednesday, Friday, and Saturday mornings; that the Curtisville Area Human Services Center use the recreation center on Monday, Tuesday, Wednesday, and Thursday evenings for "sport-related programs" and in the summer for "a proposed Summer Youth Program;" and that Timber Tumblers, a private rhythmic gymnastics school, use the recreation center on Monday, Wednesday and Friday afternoons. The District Board approved the proposed schedule without dissent.

Dissent, however, arrived.

> An organization that had proposed running several youth programs at Curtisville's new community and recreation centers has dropped its plans, saying the rules set for the facilities are "hostile to kids."

Diane Crowell, president of the Curtisville Area Human Services Center, said rules prohibiting video games and loud music have forced the non-profit organization to seek another venue. . . . The group previously griped about scheduling problems and decided to look elsewhere for a site after the Curtisville Community Services District Recreation Advisory Committee narrowly decided to not allow video games at the facilities.

"It's supposed to be a place for kids and it's not. It's very hostile for kids," said Crowell, who did not appeal the committee's recommendation to the CCSD Board of Directors, which has the final say on such policies.

CCSD Manager Richard MacDonald said the district wanted youth to participate in programs at the facility and not use them just for a hangout.

—Union *Post*, March 16, 1995

The sharp contrast between "programs" and "hangout," and the obvious moral superiority of the former over the latter, summarizes the entire history of the American park. Sociologist Galen Cranz has traced a 150-year development of the American concept of public recreation, in which the nineteenth-century idea of the park as a slice of undisturbed (or more properly, reconstructed and perfected) nature within a city was gradually replaced by an increasing emphasis on structured and scheduled activities for groups segregated by sex and age. This conceptual move was pushed along, she believes, by an increasing need to see all problems as essentially quantitative in nature: able to be carefully defined, neutrally measured, statistically analyzed, and professionally administered.[3]

Recreational facilities are increasingly available for use only under scheduled and administered conditions. A local sportswriter observed:

There might not be a regulation-sized baseball diamond in Timber County where some kids could hop a fence and play ball. There isn't a diamond in Port City available for youngsters who might still have some desire to pitch or hit or shag fly balls.

> Youth leagues and others who maintain baseball fields here are just a bit too protective of their turf. Why is it treated like a breach of national security if a kid dares sneak on a field to play some before teams are drafted, uniforms are handed out, and adults are on hand?
>
> For good or bad, we've turned baseball into something the best players "work" at or "practice" rather than a game they "play." Recalling my years as a player back in the Dead Ball Era, it seems my baseball buddies and I'd ride bicycles to the nearest decent field and choose teams. Then, before we knew it, we'd be playing baseball.
>
> Now, my kids and hundreds of others drag out a batting tee and hit balls into a net. Maybe, if the kid's lucky, he can get a buddy and hit plastic balls. If he's lucky and has some cash, he can go hit at a batting cage. No one, believe me, will tingle at the memory of hitting plastic baseballs off a batting tee or bashing balls tossed by a pitching machine. It will make them better players, sure, but who's going to recall the day for his children that he spent $8 at the batting cage?
>
> The big leaguers have taken the game from us, but we've taken our national pastime away from our kids.
>
> —Staff Sportswriter Tom Randall,
> Port City *Patriot*, Sunday, March 5, 1995

Considerable "parks and rec" bureaucracies have grown up at all levels of government to administer these supervised recreation facilities, accompanied by concerns over permits and legal liabilities. This increased professionalism has led to more purchasing of standardized recreation equipment from the handful of play vendors sophisticated enough to meet ever more stringent and esoteric codes: for example, the string of safety warning signs in the Founder's Park playground, shown in Figure 10, are off-the-shelf products of Quality Industries, Inc. Included among their thirty-seven distinct warning statements are such recreational oxymorons as "play carefully" and "no running."[4]

Cranz summarizes this crazed professionalism by saying that parks administrators have always been dually motivated by a con-

RULES OF THE PLAYGROUND:
FOLLOW THE RULES — PLAY CAREFULLY

CLIMBING:
DO NOT CLIMB DOWN UNLESS AREA IS CLEAR
WATCH CAREFULLY TO AVOID OTHER CLIMBERS
DO NOT CLIMB WITHOUT USING BOTH HANDS
USE CORRECT GRIP, FINGERS AND THUMBS FOR HOLDING
DO NOT PUSH, SHOVE OR CROWD
WAIT YOUR TURN

HORIZONTAL LADDER:
DO NOT START AT OPPOSITE ENDS
EVERYONE START AT THE SAME END AND MOVE IN THE SAME DIRECTION
DO NOT STAND ON TOP OF LADDER
STAY WELL BEHIND PERSON IN FRONT
AVOID SWINGING FEET
DO NOT USE WHEN RUNGS ARE WET
USE ONLY WHEN DRY

SLIDES:
DO NOT CLIMB UP SLIDING SURFACE
USE THE LADDER
HOLD ON WITH BOTH HANDS
TAKE ONE STEP AT A TIME
DO NOT SLIDE DOWN IMPROPERLY
SLIDE SITTING UP
FEET FIRST, ONE AT A TIME
NO PUSHING OR SHOVING, WAIT YOUR TURN
WAIT UNTIL THE SLIDE IS EMPTY BEFORE SLIDING DOWN

SWING:
DO NOT TWIST SWING CHAINS, OR SWING EMPTY SWINGS
USE SWINGS PROPERLY
DO NOT STAND ON SWINGS
SIT AND HOLD ON WITH BOTH HANDS
ONE PERSON AT A TIME
DO NOT STAND CLOSE TO A MOVING SWING
WALK AROUND SWING

RULES OF THE PLAYGROUND:
FOLLOW THE RULES — PLAY CAREFULLY
DO NOT USE EQUIPMENT WHEN WET
NO RUNNING, PUSHING OR SHOVING
DO NOT USE PLAY EQUIPMENT IMPROPERLY
NO BARE FEET
WEAR PROPER FOOTWEAR
DO NOT USE EQUIPMENT IN THIS PLAYGROUND WITHOUT ADULT SUPERVISION
DO NOT USE EQUIPMENT UNLESS DESIGNED FOR YOUR AGE GROUP

Fig. 10. Founder's Park playground guidelines

cern for "the problem of finding something to do for every person to whom idleness is an irksome and deadening problem" and by an attempt to "control by diversion" those social groups who are seen as potentially dangerous. This is borne out in modern accounts, such as the news article accompanying the opening of the Curtisville Recreation Center:

> About 100 wide-eyed kids and relieved-looking parents attended ribbon-cutting ceremonies for the 'CRC,' Curtisville's new Recreation Center. Now kids from the area will have a place to rollerskate, shoot hoops, play indoor soccer and co-ed volleyball, among a plethora of other activities—undoubtedly leaving many a parent at ease with the long summer vacation just beginning.

> —Port City *Patriot*, June 11, 1995

The professionalization of American recreation has led to a common pattern: one group defines acceptable actions, and another group is defined as the target of programs. The definition of leisure time as "an irksome and deadening problem" casts recreation management into a sort of medical model, providing a restorative and wholesome prescription for a patient who has unsuccessfully managed his or her own condition. Another historian, Roy Rosenzweig, has captured the inevitable conflict between definers and defined in his history of the parks of Worcester, Massachusetts at the turn of the twentieth century.[5] Every use of the parks by Worcester's working-class Irish and Eastern European immigrants horrified the Yankee community managers. Loafing, loitering, and drinking were one class of offense; but the opposite and equal offense was "rowdyism," "vandalism" and "disorder." Baseball playing was called a "dreary amusement" by local officials, sporadically and ineffectively outlawed. Recreation planners worked with police to ensure correct park behavior ("peaceful," "inoffensive," and "quiet") and to eliminate incorrect behavior ("rude and boorish," "disorderly and obscene"); they continue to do so, not only in New York's Central Park and San Francisco's Golden Gate Park, but also in Curtisville's Founder's Park. The newspaper reports that:

Ex-Marine MP Brings Law and Order to Founder's Park

The Curtisville Community Services District has completed the caretaker's residence at Founder's Park.

The manufactured home is located next to the tot lot/restrooms and it has an excellent view of the park. Colin Franklin started on April 22 and will live in the unit and provide surveillance for the park.

Colin recently completed a tour of duty as an MP for the U.S. Marine Corps and has extensive training in private security. Park users who need help dealing with anti-social behavior or observe vandalism should consult with Colin at the residence.

—Timber *Democrat*, April 25, 1996

The nineteenth-century term "rude and boorish" is the analog of our twentieth-century term "anti-social," of course, and both come from a particular cultural narrative that has never been shared by all park users. In our own time, the urban design analyst Paul Groth reports that, whereas the middle-class park visitor expects supremely framed specimens of preserved wilderness that he or she might contemplate in quiet, the working-class or "vernacular" park user anticipates something quite different:

> Automobiles, trucks, loud radios, or a motorboat (in the case of water) were usually considered essential. . . . The easy juxtaposition of everyday activities with a naturalistic background reveals an attitude among those users that does not separate culture from nature—at least not nearly so much as do the people who design official parks. . . . In their own minds, vernacular users are not desacralizing the park. For them, it was never particularly sacred in the first place.[6]

These conflicts are played out in Curtisville over driving trucks on the dunes, riding horses on timber company property, and "hanging out" at the rec center. In every case, any definition of correct recreation behavior ensures conflict when the definers are socially isolated from the defined. Laura Hall's study of teenagers in

Rohnert Park, California included an interview with the Director of Parks and Recreation:

> The Director of the Park and Recreation Department expressed his belief that the "heart" of Rohnert Park lies in its athletic facilities. However, even though the Department offers teenagers a wide variety of athletic and social activities through its community center, these programs are not fully subscribed. The director was unable to give an explanation for the poor turnouts. . . . When asked if there was an access problem in getting to the community center, he replied that "there are plenty of bicycle trails in Rohnert Park but today's teenagers are just lazy."[7]

In no other industry would it be possible to create a product with poor demand and then blame the prospective customers.

❧

I came to Curtisville expecting to find a few public, downtown teen hangouts. I had done an earlier study of teenagers and their places in a little town called Oostburg, Wisconsin. Oostburg was a picture-postcard of a town, with a two-block business district that closed every night at seven and four churches of the same basic denomination. When I asked what I might need to know if I were going to move to Oostburg, one savvy high school senior said, "Well, you shouldn't mow your lawn on Sundays."

One of the businesses that occupied the primary intersection in downtown Oostburg was Pippert Tires. Pippert, formerly a gas station, had a gravel lot in front at the street corner. Every night all year round, that lot was the living room for somewhere between half a dozen and thirty teenagers who gathered for conversation augmented with a few clandestine beers and cigarettes. The residents came and went repeatedly; Pippert was just one stopping point in the course of a larger evening of entertainment that might include a trip to Hardee's or Taco Bell in Sheboygan, a race down Highway 57, or a visit to a girlfriend's house in the nearby village of Hingham.

When I asked the owner how long kids had gathered at his garage, he replied, "I bought the place twelve years ago, and the kids came with it." And there were some obvious physical characteristics that had made the Pippert lot a popular spot for a generation of Oostburg's kids, the same physical characteristics that had made the Quad so important at Curtisville High. It was right at the four-way stop sign, under a street lamp. It was small and easy to see into, and thus to know who was there. It was enclosed on two sides by buildings and on the other two sides by the sidewalk, so there was a room-like feel about it that allowed the occupants to claim it and visitors to know that they were entering someone's space. And there was an occupying group of regulars; the kids of Oostburg High knew who was likely to be at Pippert, and were strong in their loyalty to that group or their discomfort with it.

Pippert, ranked on its visual attributes, was plain. But it was a place where meetings took place without scheduling. It was a place where a particular social group came together in a domain that none of them individually owned. It was a place where the school's rankings of grades and class level were minimized, where social status was assigned by the group on the basis of skills that the group themselves valued. It was a place based around playful conversation and serious belonging.

In short, it was a hangout.[8]

There are no hangouts in downtown Curtisville, at least not any with the level of predictability and regularity of the Pippert lot. The new businesses stay open until nine, or midnight, or even twenty-four hours; but there isn't any street life. Why not?

The 10 P.M. teen curfew is an obvious reason, making any nighttime gathering clearly illegal rather than negotiable. But there aren't any public hangouts in Curtisville in part because of the nature of Main Street itself. It's too wide to easily see across and be able to identify who might be standing in a parking lot. There are few places where people have to stop; the width of the street, the amount of traffic and the thirty-five mile-an-hour speed limit all make it difficult to casually turn into or out of side lots. The parks and parking lots themselves are too large to serve as enclosed rooms for a small group at any rate; claiming any portion of one of them would be an arbitrary act, and the boundaries would be too soft for groups to feel protected and in control. And the clear shift toward distant ownership and corporate control of Main Street makes local negotiation impossible—institutional rules on private property are pretty hard and firm, and the benevolent local tire store owner is nowhere on the scene.

But these things, as much as they make hanging out difficult, are only part of Curtisville's larger absence of hangouts for any age group. There is one bar in Curtisville; the cafes have given way to take-outs and drive-thrus; there are no neighborhood grocers or beauty salons. Curtisville, it seems, is built for a new model of community: intensely private, filled with highly mobile newcomers and short-timers, defined by services provided and services consumed. Its youth center—scheduled, supervised, focused inward, hidden away—fits right in.

ₑ❧

I got a request from a student of a friend back in Milwaukee. This fellow's architectural studio class had been charged with designing a teen center.[9] There's a good rule of thumb for knowing when some kind of place is trendy: it becomes the basis for assignments in architectural design courses. When I was in design school in the late '80s, we designed a winery and visitors' wine-tasting center, a "mixed-use" row house with a single-family home above a retail store, and a tourist retail center next to an abandoned factory that had been renovated into a faux-historical den of gift shops. Now it's teen centers.

This student asked me if I could steer him toward any ideas on the teen center topic. As part of his request, he e-mailed me the class' program statement for this project:

> The Youth Center would serve the town's teen-age community as a social, recreational, and cultural center. The center would sponsor organized activities such as: theater performances, concerts, dances, movies, art & craft classes, lectures, clubs, and a teen-ager run local radio and cable station.
>
> The center would serve the town's teen-age community at large but would also compliment the town's School System by providing a series of centralized facilities and courses that individual schools cannot afford or have sufficient interest to sustain.
>
> Young people in the teen years have a great deal of energy and vitality which is often seen as disruptive and undesir-

able to "Nice Communities". Frequently, institutions and businesses shun persons in this age bracket. However, some urban areas suffering from "semi-comatose quietness" can use a healthy dose of teenage noise and bustle. Such a center should be designed to encourage and project this energy and activity.

The proposed design should include the following:

An auditorium (6000SF)—as a multi-use space
Entrance (1500SF)—to include reception, information, lounge/TV room, cafe/snack bar, kitchen
Game room (2300SF)—10 pool tables, 3 ping pong, video games
Gallery (1100SF)—display area
Music (2400SF)—5 practice rooms, instrument storage, recording studio/mixing lab
Radio Station (1500SF)—2 broadcast studios, support rooms
Video/cable (1500SF)—recording studio, editing lab, support
Photography (1100SF)—studio, darkroom, mounting
Computers (600SF)
Arts (3600SF)—painting, printing, ceramics, sculpture
Crafts (4700SF)—carpentry, metal, mechanics, electronics
Reading/Library (1000SF)
Lecture hall (1000SF)
Meeting rooms (1100SF)
Various offices for clubs, etc.
Total Gross Area 43,512 square feet.

That's the raw version of the program. Let's cook it a little, starting again at the beginning:

The Youth Center would serve the town's teen-age community as a social, recreational, and cultural center. The center would sponsor organized activities such as: theater performances, concerts, dances, movies, art & craft classes, lectures, clubs, and a teen-ager run local radio and cable station.

There are some important words to catch there, beginning with "The," implying one. This is, of course, the general model of modern recreation, provided in a centrally located and centrally planned space. "Youth" tells us that the Center serves one specific population base defined by age. The word "serve" itself is an interesting choice; much as politicians serve their constituents or hospitals serve their patients, the youth center serves youth by deciding what will be best for them and by letting them choose from among tightly constrained options. "Teen-age community" assumes a singular entity which thinks and desires like things. And always, the word "organized;" there will be no dropping in to work on your painting when the urge strikes, or to just hang out with friends at work on their paintings.

This program is not for the design of a hangout, a place to go and converse and belong. This program is for a temple of youth improvement. And why should those services take place separately from the adult facilities that this imaginary town almost certainly has for theater and concerts and movies and classes? Because we insist, again and always, on segregating teenagers into "their own" places, not for their comfort but for ours.

But let us continue:

> The center would serve the town's teen-age community at large but would also complement the town's School System by providing a series of centralized facilities and courses that individual schools cannot afford or have sufficient interest to sustain.

There's that "teen-age community at large" again, an enormous number of people even in a small town. Over a thousand kids attend the middle and high school grades in Curtisville, and they don't all like one another or do the same sorts of things. A "centralized facility" for a town of any size means a facility that's inaccessible for most kids unless they have cars or parental chauffeurs. And the fact that the youth center provides things that "individual schools cannot afford or have sufficient interest to sustain" shows that we can only conceive of youth as passive subjects of an adult institution; if one agency cannot do its job, another must step in to take its place.[10]

To go on:

Young people in the teen years have a great deal of energy and vitality which is often seen as disruptive and undesirable to "Nice Communities." Frequently institutions and businesses shun persons in this age bracket.

And rather than deal with this as a fundamental injustice, we build places to legitimize it. By defining places where teens are welcome, after all, we can immediately infer that there are other places where they are not.

And the program closes with:

However, some urban areas suffering from 'semi-comatose quietness' can use a healthy dose of teenage noise and bustle. Such a center should be designed to encourage and project this energy and activity.

This is an incredibly naive statement. Putting a teen center into any "semi-comatose" neighborhood is a guaranteed political grenade, as it was for Curtisville's neighbor, Port City:

A youth center housed in [Port City's] Stasson Memorial Building would draw crime, drugs and troublemakers, some neighbors said at a meeting Thursday night. Others, including many of the dozens of teenagers at the meeting, said the center would be a safe place for young people to study, get counseling, run a snack bar, perform on stage, and just hang out.

But some neighbors said they fear that the center would be a hangout for those with other activities in mind. One of them, Claude Drehl, said it would be a "magnet for gang activity.

The young people here are nice looking. I don't think the youth center was intended for them," Drehl said. "I think it was intended to cluster in one spot a bunch of troublemakers."

Others questioned whether a center anywhere would be good for the community. "There is no institution man has made that will ever replace a mother and a father who love their children," Stasson building neighbor Dorothy Claybourn said. "I simply feel it will not work."

—Port City *Patriot*, March 10, 1995

Putting any large institution into a neighborhood is a threat to that neighborhood, which is the biggest hindrance to any ideas of mixed-use planning: when someone proposes neighborhood shopping or neighborhood restaurants, the image we have is of Safeway or Kmart or McDonald's because that is how we Modernists shop and dine out. Nobody wants one of those enormous car magnets in their neighborhood, and rightly so. Teen centers are the same—why should an artificial concentration of one population be inflicted on any neighborhood? The more fundamental fact is that we no longer consider the possibility of shopping or dining or teen recreation on any but this megalomaniac institutional scale. Just look at the list of spaces in this proposed teen center:

> Auditorium (6000 square feet)
> Entrance (1500 square feet)
> Game room (2300 square feet)
> Gallery (1100 square feet)
> Music (2400 square feet)
> Radio station (1500 square feet)
> Video/cable studio (1500 square feet)
> Photography lab (1100 square feet)
> Computers (600 square feet)
> Arts (3600 square feet)
> Crafts (4700 square feet)
> Reading/library (1000 square feet)
> Lecture hall (1000 square feet)
> Meeting rooms (1100 square feet)
> Various offices for clubs, etc.
> Total Gross Area—43,512 square feet.

Forty-three thousand square feet. An acre, plus an unspoken half-acre for the parking that would be required. A teenage acre under adult supervision, segregated from the rest of the community by both space and time. An acre that would serve all of the social, recreational and creative needs of ten to fifteen percent of the community, and leave the rest of the town for us.

CHAPTER TWENTY-FIVE

November 18th, Where Joy was Found

It took me three months to see what I'd been looking at.

By that time, mid-November, I'd measured the entire Curtisville High School campus, producing a floor plan and site plan and dozens of photographs. I'd given a questionnaire—designed months earlier in Milwaukee—to all eight hundred students, and interviewed about forty students and a dozen teachers. I had a small compost heap of paper from which little heat was produced: some vague categories, gleanings of uncertain value.

By mid-November, I'd sat in on over thirty of Curtisville High's thirty-eight classrooms. Some of them seemed to work and most didn't, but I couldn't have explained why, or even what I meant when I thought that a class was "working." I'd visited many of Curtisville's neighborhoods, the soulless downtown strip and the fancy named subdivisions, farmhouses along the old grid roads, mobile homes and shacks hidden on the far side of the freeway. More notes, more photographs, more recognition of happiness and unhappiness and confusion about why.

I was ultimately able to salvage some pieces from those first three months of work. But on November 18, 1994, I discovered the point.

The 18th was a Thursday, and I was headed for the evening performance of original skits by Curtisville High's Advanced Theater Workshop class. There was nothing special about this trip for me—I'd gone to football games, volleyball games, cross-country meets, school dances, and the Homecoming parade before this. All part of the job, more data to collect.

Just as I took off my jacket and picked an aisle seat in the Multi-Purpose room, Irene and Mara spotted me from the backstage door and ran out to me. "Herb! We need you to sneeze! Can you sneeze??"

"What??"

"We need you to sneeze! Ryan is going to be like this dinosaur . . ."

"Like from Jurassic Park . . ."

"Right, and he's going to be looking out into the audience for a victim, and when you sneeze, he'll run over and grab you."

I said, "Uhh . . . sure, okay. I can do that. Should I struggle?"

"Just a little, maybe. He'll probably drag you around or something. So, can you sneeze?" I did so. "This'll be great!" they laughed. Then they were gone, racing back through the stageside door. I have to admit that I was pleased—one of my unspoken goals for the year was to gain acceptance by the kids, to finally be popular in high school.

But once the lights went down and the curtain opened, I forgot all about Ryan and the sneezing and the dinosaur. I forgot that I was supposed to be there for research, and didn't touch my notebook. I forgot that I knew all of their names, forgot that they weren't professional actors—I forgot that they were actors at all. The twenty-five of them had written, blocked out, costumed, lighted, and performed over twenty skits, and they brought me to that place where I had no consciousness of myself, my surroundings, my purpose. I was absorbed, anticipating, laughing, astonished.

They had no elaborate costumes or stagesets—Andrew Lloyd Webber could easily spend the equivalent of the school's annual theater budget every thirty seconds. Ryan's dinosaur costume was a green t-shirt, a pair of green tights, and a big tied-on stuffed tail, but I know that only from memory. When he was on the stage or diving through the audience (he selected a different victim), he was as much a velociraptor as the ones Spielberg created, with his tiny front paws and leering grin. The two hundred of us in the audience sat on our blue fiberglass seats on the plywood roll-down bleachers and got a theater experience that would have cost a forty-dollar ticket in San Francisco. We had two and a half hours of joy.

I had built my study on three simple questions: How do teenagers use spaces? How do they apply meanings and values to any particular place? How do conflicts about those places arise between teens and adults and between particular subsets of teens, and how are those conflicts resolved? After a year, I think I know some of those answers, and the idea of joy is at the heart of all of them.

That sounds simple, perhaps naive. But I came to Curtisville in July, and became more and more depressed the more I learned. Here I was, in this growing community of new homes and businesses; in a school with a multi-million dollar budget, mostly staffed with competent, concerned people. Both the kids and the adults were telling me that something was missing, and I could tell that something was missing, but I couldn't tell what it was. I was more and more confused about the lack of satisfaction and intensity and desire that I saw. I couldn't put my finger on the problem.

And then, in the middle of November, I came to the short performances of the Advanced Theater Workshop. These kids did demanding work under difficult and tense conditions with a live audience, and they were absolutely great. And the difference was joy. The love for what they were doing was so clear, all over their faces and through their motions, it just burned off the stage. And joy was what I'd seen in those handful of classes that "worked." Joy was what I'd heard in the laughing, teasing conversations on the Quad and at the Arco station. Joy was the fuel that moved skateboards and horses and pickup trucks. And joy was what was missing from most of Curtisville, and from most of its high school as well. I just didn't have the word before.

Few of us do; it's an embarrassing word. We don't even know quite what joy means anymore. It's not the same as happiness, nor pleasure. Joy seems anachronistic and old-fashioned—a blessed state no longer attainable, reduced to a girl's first name along with hope and grace. But joy still lives, even though the word is almost lost to us.

ᘒ

Yet we have all experienced times when, instead of being buffeted by anonymous forces, we do feel in control of our actions, masters of our own fate. On the rare occasions that it happens, we feel a sense of exhilaration, a deep sense of enjoyment that is long cherished and that becomes a landmark in memory for what life should be like. . . . The best moments usually occur when a person's body or mind is stretched to its limits in a voluntary effort to accomplish something difficult and worthwhile.[1]

The author of this passage, Mihaly Csikszentmihalyi, is a psychologist at the University of Chicago. He has spent thirty years looking at a condition he calls *flow*, "the state in which people are so involved in an activity that nothing else seems to matter; the experience itself is so enjoyable that people will do it even at great cost, for the sheer sake of doing it."

And after a lifetime of study, he lays out a handful of common qualities of the flow experience. The first and most central is that we need to be challenged, to struggle, in order to lose ourselves to the intensity of flow; joy seems to come from doing things that are just a little bit beyond us, so that we must concentrate or crash immediately. That immediacy is the second key: flow activities have moment-to-moment feedback that we feel immediately rather than receive later in an evaluation. We can see things happen at our command; we can feel when we're sharp and when we're off. And flow activities are always ends in themselves rather than things undertaken in order to get to something else. They might be useful actions, but if they are it is only a happy coincidence. We might be proud of our achievements, but the pride is only after the fact. The joy lies exactly in the moment of the doing.

Curtisville's teenagers told me about joy and flow without using the words. Kirk spent all of his down-time—between classes, standing in line at the student store—playing Hacky Sack. He was devoted to keeping the little woven ball in the air. "Hacking is great. Sometimes you can get a rush if you've got a sweet hack going." Mara was the student lighting engineer for theater productions. "It's not fun, but it's very rewarding. Running around tearing my hair out, and having a million things to oversee and a million things to do, it's a great chaotic thing." She also owned a horse. "I can ride him with a piece of string in his mouth and nothing else. He can feel my legs and my weight and my balance, and we get out there on trail or on a road and we run, and we can run and run and run, and I move this way and move that way and it's . . . he talks to me and I talk to him. It's like a beautiful dance." Tom told me about Magic, an extraordinarily complex card game: "It's never the same, no game is ever the same."

The aftermath of that joy, regardless of its form, is a more complex person: a self which is more competent, more daring, able to consider more and manage more, a self which is dissatisfied with less. They knew that they could keep the ball in the air at will, that they had mastered the rules, that the horse would obey and that the theater would be correctly lit; because of that mastery, they could push harder, try new ideas, improvise. Csikszentmihalyi would approve. "After each episode of flow a person becomes more of a unique individual, less predictable, possessed of rarer skills."[2]

The words may sound awkward in our modern ears, but we all can recognize "flow" or joy when we see it. When a person has lost self-consciousness and entered into complete concentration on a fraction of the world around, joy is among us.

After that November night, after the word "JOY" practically hovered at the back of the stage in hundred-watt bulbs, my own work came alive. I looked all over campus for joy, all over *town* for joy, and once in a while I found it. What surprised me is that in the places where I saw it, I also saw learning, patience, attention, lots of effort, beautiful and exciting environments, high achievement—all of the things that we try to get at from all of the wrong directions. All of our attention on codes and standards and measured achievement, even on our new 1990s words "excellence" or "quality"—that's all wrong. It has no chance of success at all, because without joy, there is no reason to pursue anything. *With* joy, the outside standards are meaningless; when we do what we love to do, we keep after it, we always want to know more and do more and keep going. There is no such thing as good enough.

One pre-joy piece of my work that survived that night was the first questionnaire. I had asked the kids where they went to be with a group of friends, where they went to be alone, and where they went to be with one particular friend. The locations they listed weren't surprising, though they did vary by age and by sex and by hometown. What was surprising was why they chose those spots. Their reasons were the elements of joy, although the categories emerged from their answers long before I understood what they meant.

There were a number of chosen places in which people talked about doing things for simple *physical gratification*. Teenagers seem to be a sensory bunch: acoustically ("kicking loud ass beats"), thermally ("lots of sun, some shade on hot days"), and especially through motion and contact ("it also has a tree swing that is fun to swing on"). When I watched kids standing around in the Quad at school or sitting at the Arco at lunch, they were rarely still. They moved constantly, always rocking and turning and leaning and bumping up against columns and curbs with their heels. The spots where they gathered in the woods were easy to identify, marked not just by the crushed-down grass and accumulated litter but also by the fact that every nearby tree limb within reach had all of the bark peeled off and the wood rubbed shiny by years of inquisitive hands. We talk about teenagers as being energetic and "hyper," but much of that is an enlivened tactile sense always searching for contact with something.

There is a "right now"-ness about the teenagers I spent time with, an *immediacy and focus to their actions* that enlivens their gatherings and adds depth and complexity to their lives. One student wrote of riding her horse with friends, to have "the precious challenge of holding an intelligent conversation and still concentrate on controlling the horse." This immediacy is part of what makes them so susceptible to boredom in their fifty-minute classes. These kids get a lot packed into their five-minute school breaks—they eat, drink, make out, socialize, redo their hair and make-up, and incidentally exchange the last period's books for the next period's books and make their way across campus to the next room. They lose themselves to some extent, melt their self-consciousness through their absorption in what is at hand. If classrooms were as spirited as hallways, school could be a wonderful place.

They talked about *a sense of abandon* in their recreation: skateboarding, surfing, riding horses, playing soccer, driving on the beach.[3] The people who talked about this just loved to move in a way that couldn't be predictable, to try to control the inherently uncontrollable. "We go dancing . . . we can relax and let loose;" "I have a giant trampoline;" "Sometimes I enjoy just being out in the water with no one else surfing, so I can get all the good waves."

Skateboarding and surfing are prime examples of an attempt to be in tune with shifting circumstances, but some "real sports" also carry the same sense of wildness. Kids who played soccer, volleyball, or basketball often described the seductiveness of motion, because these are sports in which anything can happen at any moment and they might have to take a shot or make a pass or defend the goal when they're almost upside down and in the process of falling. Hunting, hikes in the woods, dancing to exhaustion, Hacky Sack, or "just being goofy" are all sprung from the desire for play and exploration, of searching for unknown experiences and letting go of their reserve; so, unfortunately, are drinking and drugs.

Kids talked about two *places of escape*—places of nature (the forest, a lookout at the ocean, a fort in the woods) or "my room." These kids talked a lot about wanting to get away—from their parents and siblings, from school and school problems, from even their friends. "I go to my room, because my friends aren't there," they said, or "Nobody bothers me when I'm at the creek." They were immersed all day in family and school and work and homework, being pushed and pulled from the outside, often unable to generate the kind of involvement in the present that leads to joy; the opportunity to turn the lock on the door and be alone was crucial. They talked very frequently on the questionnaire about going someplace because it was "quiet," but they weren't talking about auditory quiet—they were talking about stillness and calm, about a counterpoint to the constant motion of their days. "I climb a mountainside and watch the sun set, to think over things that happen to me."

The security that came from knowing that they were alone and would stay that way often seemed to lead to a real *questioning of the self*, an introspection that took many forms: writing poems, painting, reading, doing ceramics, playing or listening to music, or just sitting and thinking: "It is quiet and peaceful and I can think;" "My horse can hear all my problems but he can't tell anyone or start rumors;" "The beach is a place to let frustrations out and relax;" "I can clear my mind and get exercise at the same time."

A great number of people said that they went to some place or another simply "*to be with* him/her," but others were more explicit. They said that they liked a place because "her family makes me feel loved" or because "we can talk out our problems and help each other." Even going to the Union Plaza because "we can make fun of hippies" or to the mall to "make fun of oriental gangs" is really based on strengthening the definition of "us," albeit at the expense of somebody else. Conversation that builds relationships is a skill, and gathering places are central to the ability to exercise that skill.

People-watching and potential human contact is still a great sport, and going where the people are is still a big draw; in its simplest formulation, "We see a lot of our old friends and get to talk with them. And we meet girls." There were some specific places where this occurred, all of them several miles from Curtisville: Seaside Mall in southern Port City ("We can shop, go to a movie, and most importantly, check out guys together"), the Friday and Saturday night cruise in downtown Port City ("Somewhere to go and see lots of people"), and the central plaza of Union ("There is always something to do"). But the possibilities of social life animated teenage gatherings from school hallways to impromptu walks through town. They were all mobile experiences, modern promenades, mingling on the grand scale. Because the manifest reason for being on the cruise or in the mall or at the plaza was to move, there was less risk in starting a conversation; if it didn't work out, kids could say with full justification, "Well, gotta go. Bye." But it was very often the case that the kids came to these places with one set of friends, hung around with a different person or group while they were there, and left with still someone else. They were there to be social.

Curtisville's kids enjoyed being kids for the most part, but they resented being treated like kids. They got treated like kids (that is to say, like irresponsible potential criminals who need to be constantly monitored and directed and protected) all day long. Being able to do things in which they exercised *control*, whether that entailed spending some money, working on their truck, driving somewhere of their own choosing, having sex, or just being able to decorate their own rooms without permission, was deeply satisfying. The choices that fell in this category weren't all hedonistic, either; people took great satisfaction in jobs and volunteer positions that offered both responsibility and independence. But to have a lock on their bedroom door was equally satisfying—just to be able to say that they had a chunk of space over which they made the rules, into which no one could come without their permission. "When somebody wants something they knock & I respect that & if I want to be alone I can say 'I want to be alone' and I have that privacy."

The saddest category of chosen places carried comments like "There's nowhere else;" "It's convenient" (or "easy" or "safe"); "I'm allowed to go there;" and "What else is there?" There was a strong sense of resignation among a number of kids in their place choices, more strongly expressed among younger respondents because they didn't drive and often had tighter rules about where and when they could be out. These places of last resort were especially frustrating for them because they usually weren't under the kids' control, even though they were being used for things such as escape or belonging for which control is clearly desired.

Leaving aside these last places that were taken because nothing else was left, the categories of flow emerged over and over when I read those 674 questionnaires: physical sensation, immediacy and focus, a sense of abandon, an escape from hectic pressures, the opportunity for serious thought, a connectedness to chosen friends and the spark of possible new acquaintances, and the satisfaction of control. These may not seem like an especially "teenage" set of reasons for choosing places. When I talked to Curtisville's teachers about *their* most important places, they described different sorts of places, but used the same kinds of words. When History teacher Patricia Maher talked about her apartment, she said, "I have total control over everything that goes on in there, it's consistent, it's comfortable. Everything in it is just the way I want it to be. I don't have to do anything or be anything for anybody at any time." Stacy Morton in Special Education said that her new home was "my spot, totally my spot, my own decorating." Business teacher Helen Kidder thought of her church, calling it "a place to belong." Dan Jacobs, in English: "At home, I built an office. I built it. It's a little box, but it's mine. It is my box. And it was designed to support what I do and how I do it." John Morris, History: "In the summer we get together at my parents' home and hang out by the pool and have big dinners and such. When we make it down to Southern California it's an event. My sister will come up from San Diego, my sisters will come from Santa Barbara, my brother will come from Santa Barbara, my brothers will come up from my folks' place. The months leading up to it, there's this anticipation in me, you know, this excitement: 'Right on, I'm going to see the family, I'm going to see the family.' " Will Forrest, Physics and Chemistry: "I have an apple tree and cherry tree and about fifty roses, I have a rose garden and flower garden and things like that. And I love to putter and do things with my hands and anything that's mechanical or electrical, I'll take it apart to see how it works. My shop opens into the back yard as well as through the garage."

All of these unique spaces named by the students and their teachers were facts of geography or architecture; they could be logged into a database, drawn on a map. But the places weren't just locations or addresses, not just a connected set of architectural pieces or the volume of air contained within them. Every place worth mentioning included the story they told about a location, the emotional relationship they created with it, the self-image that it helped them build. They loved places that made them feel better about themselves, the places that helped tell stories in which they were secure, capable, attractive. They loathed the places that made them feel like failures; places that make it clear that no one cared, places that demanded what they could not give. And they were torn by painful and precarious places that carried conflicting stories of love and abuse, of responsibilities without choice, of loyalty without desire. These narrative acts of imagination are the sole difference between a "space" and a "place."[4] We plan and build spaces, but we always and only inhabit places.

Whenever they could, Curtisville's teenagers and adults seemed to choose places that they had control over, that reflected their own hand. Places that let them feel confident, loved, secure. Places that were home to the acts that brought them joy.

November 18th was the defining day for my year at Curtisville mainly because it appeared so suddenly within an ocean of days like October 27th.

The high school Quad was drizzly and windy; instead of being home to dozens of moving conversations, it was simply four olive-painted concrete block walls surrounding wet pavement. On days like this, the campus seemed barren and uncentered, wandering, unable to find its way.

During third period, I sat in on Mr. Peterson's The Individual in Society class, an example of which you've already seen. On October 27th, the assigned topic had been ways to deal with a conflict between a student and a teacher, and the class had become an opportunity to vent.

"I hate it when Mr. Springs stands like right next to the door and waits for the clock to tick, and as soon as it does, he'll mark you tardy if you're not in your seat. And he's all, like, 'Class starts at the tick.' What are we gonna miss in the first minute of class?"

"Miss Shaw is just completely rude."

"Mr. Jacobs uses all these words that nobody knows, and he thinks he's, like, better than you are."

Comments like these are not out of the ordinary. A coffee machine in most offices has heard worse about the boss. But the conversation was interesting enough to pull Eddie out of the surfing magazine he was reading. He said, "Mr. Niesen is all serious about our notebooks that we turn in, and when we do an assignment, we have to put our name in the top corner, and then the course name goes under that and then the number goes under that and then the date goes under that, and if any of that stuff is in the wrong order, he takes points off for it. I mean, what does it matter if the date goes on top of the homework number or something if we got the homework right?"

Kirk followed quickly. "Yeah! And three tardies loses a whole grade. If I'm getting a C in English, why should being late three times make it into a D?"

Mr. Peterson broke the growing swell of complaints. "There's lots of requirements that you're going to run into that seem unimportant or picky. Like filling out a job application; if you put things in the wrong place, you might not get hired." Then he smiled, and said, "But sometimes it does seem silly. Let me give you an example. In our neighborhood, there are a couple of empty lots, and somebody wanted to build apartment buildings there. And they would have been out of place, they would have been a lot bigger than the houses, really different than the houses that were there. So we all went to this board hearing where they were going to take public input about these apartment buildings. And we talked about it for an hour and a half, about twenty people came to give their opinion on why it was a bad idea to build these apartments there. And at the end of an hour and a half, the board said, 'Well, they've filled out all the right forms and what they're doing is legal, so we're going to approve the permit.' And we all said, 'Wait a minute! You wanted our input, and we all said we didn't want these in our neighborhood.' And the guy said, 'We're required to take public input, but everything they want to do is legal, so we have to give them the permit.' And I said, 'So we just wasted two hours at this meeting, then. Why did we even come here if you already knew what the answer was? Why didn't you just tell us at the beginning that the permit was approved, and we could have all just gone home?'"

Mr. Peterson hesitated, looking for the moral to the story. He finally said, "So there are a lot of requirements that seem kind of silly, and that's just a part of life." And the conversation turned back to rude, unfair teachers. But Mr. Peterson's message stuck with me, and became the counter-focus to my evening of joy. He had made evident what I had already seen: that much of school was geared toward making kids quietly compliant with rules that don't make sense, in preparation for an adulthood full of rules that don't make sense.

The high school's department chairs gathered early in the spring to discuss alternative schoolday schedules. During the previous year, the school had experimented with "block scheduling," in which every other school day had three double-length periods instead of the six fifty-minute periods that were common. Tom Cooper, the math chair, said, "On the long days, I got to try some new creative things, and they went pretty well. I think the kids got a lot out of it. But we were only able to get one curriculum day in per class day, even though it was twice as long. So every time we had the block period, we lost a day to the curriculum. So now when they go to take the Golden State or the SATs and they don't score as well as kids from other schools, then they're gonna wonder what happened."

Allow me to translate for those not up to speed on educational language. The California Department of Education issues suggested curricula for all high school subjects, which offer both an outline of topics that should be covered within a course and a timetable in which to cover them. The idea of the double-length class day was not to jam two regular class periods back-to-back but to examine a single topic in greater depth. This, of course, meant that fewer topics would be covered during the year. Tom feared that the kids would be penalized when it came time to take the standardized tests that mean so much for college admissions (and for school prestige and local real estate values) by not having covered the full range of topics that the tests, linked to the state curricula, would assess.

Our nation is increasingly dominated by very large institutions, from federal and state agencies that control local education and city planning and even playground safety to national chain businesses that displace local products and craftsmanship. Distant and enormous, these institutions have the legal status of human beings combined with resources and power previously reserved for kings. Their lives are separate from the people they employ and from the people they serve. They will survive regardless of the existence of any of their constituents, from customer to CEO.

Such institutions—the California Department of Education, Kmart, the Environmental Protection Agency, McDonald's—exercise control over thousands of specific locations and touch the lives of millions of Americans, guided by a belief in standardization. This desire for standardization seems to have at least two conceptual parents: the first is the mobility of people and capital, and the second is a presumption of mistrust (whether of those people defined as "others" or of human nature in general). Inflexible rules and standards are born of a desire to play by the same rules everywhere, which presumes that the people and businesses who are most mobile are those who must be most specifically catered to rather than those who are most firmly rooted in local traditions and beliefs. These rules and standards are born of an associated anonymity and lack of agreement, an absence of shared beliefs so profound that a definitive position must be established and enforced. To say that a hamburger patty will always be 3.25 inches across and weigh 1.6 ounces is to believe that your franchisee will make an inferior product without that guideline (and to believe that an inconsistent product is by definition an inferior product, to believe that we as consumers want replicable experiences regardless of our physical location). To provide a massive standard curriculum for U.S. History courses is to believe that Al Lawton at Curtisville High School will offer a diminished classroom education without it.

America was heralded as a nation ruled by law and not by man, designed as a corrective to the abusive monarchs and corrupt courts left behind in Europe. Our founders consciously moved from the world of human judgment and entered the world of laws in order to avoid the worst possible abuses of power. But as laws become finer grained and avoid ever-lesser abuses, we also trim off the possibility of exploration and achievement beyond the standards. When one specific act is all that is allowed, we lose the capacity for remarkable invention as well as the ability to chisel and cheat. We lose connection to things that are locally relevant and important. We avoid our responsibility for recognizing and judging good from bad in the close-at-hand world. We surrender the challenges that can lead to joy.

Even worse, we lose the ability to think critically, the ability to value what we know from evidence to be true. Read Tom Cooper's statement again: "On the long days, I got to try some new creative things, and they went pretty well. I think the kids got a lot out of it. But we were only able to get one curriculum day in per class day, even though it was twice as long. So every time we had the block period, we lost a day to the curriculum. So now when they go to take the Golden State or the SATs and they don't score as well as kids from other schools, then they're gonna wonder what happened." Within the space of twenty seconds, he said that the extended periods were successful in his room *and* that they shouldn't be tried again.

There is a telling moment in a public relations package prepared by the California Department of Education to help us understand why we should have standardized testing of all high school students.[5] On a transparency entitled, "Quotes from Business Leaders—What Successful Students Will Need to Know and Be Able to To [sic] to Be Successful" are the following quotes:

> Students need to be able to work in an environment where the problem presented is not a problem that's in a book. It's a problem that drops out of the sky, and you don't know what techniques will be needed to solve it. You have to try new things and perhaps invent something totally new.—Stanley J. Benkoski, Vice President, Wagner Associates, Sunnyvale

> We have calculators and the technology to crunch out the numbers. . . . We need people who are thinkers, who will solve problems and look for creative solutions. . . . We need to instill in young people a willingness to try creative problem-

solving.—Gloria Hoo, Marketing Manager, Tech Museum of Innovation, San Jose

Students will need to know how to think and how to apply what they learn in their classrooms.—Gordon Henshaw, President, Diamond Systems Inc., Gardenia

Students need to clearly understand what they will be expected to know and to do when they reach the market-place. Employers need to be able to articulate their expectations in a common language that can be applied across the state. That's why the performance levels or standards developed for reporting state assessment results are so important. They provide a definitive description that can be understood by parents, students, teachers and employers alike of what students need to learn to be able to do.—Jere Jacobs, Pacific Telesis Group, San Francisco

On a single transparency, drawn from a single seminar, are two strikingly different positions. On one hand, education is hailed as an ability for "creative problem-solving," to deal with "a problem that drops out of the sky," "to apply what they learn," "to try new things and perhaps invent something totally new." On the other hand, we want "a common language" for our expectations, a state assessment that will "provide a definitive description . . . of what students need to learn to be able to do." Didn't anybody notice some discrepancy when this discussion went on, or when they assembled the PR materials? And can it be any surprise who held which position? The creative problem-solvers were two entrepreneurs and a curator of a shrine to innovation. The proponent of standards for assessment worked for the phone company.

When things become institutionalized, the rational systems and their rules get more and more clear, and the real emotional goals—that imagined and desired future—get harder and harder to find. We seem to be bent on making our human encounters reliable and accountable and consistent. We are not standard people, but we believe very strongly in standardized processes.

※

Mara and Louisa sat in the library with the rest of their Spanish class, working on an assignment—sort of. Mara, who was leaps ahead of her class as always, took the opportunity of a quiet moment to write in her journal instead. Louisa, equally unchallenged, uncapped a pen and wrote sideways in the margin of Mara's journal, "I'm bored!"

Bertrand Russell defined boredom as doing one thing while you really wish you were doing something else.[6] When I asked Curtisville's kids about the emotions in their lives, boredom and routine were at the top of the list. When I lived with each of my volunteers for their designated three days, they typically spent a lot of time planning some big event for Friday night or Saturday, something that was going to relieve their boredom: a dance, a beach party, driving the cruise, making an out-of-town surfing trip. But the drawback was that the rest of the week was even more boring, because all they could do was pre-live that wonderful event, waiting for that one big thing that might not even come.

We have hundreds of words to describe our emotions, but they seem to reduce to two things as shown in Figure 11: whether we think something is stimulating or not stimulating, and whether we think it's good or bad.[7] And so all of the words that we use to describe emotions are really clustered into four groups, with the differences within the groups being one of degree rather than of kind. In the "not-stimulating/bad" group, we've got words that teenagers use a lot—*boring, routine, everyday, the grind*. There are the emotions arising from circumstances that are negative but which aren't very engaging. They tell us unattractive things about ourselves, but things that aren't very central to us, not known or cared about intimately. The "stimulating/bad" group includes words like *stress, anger, fear, worry*: situations that are negative, but which are more self-immersed, more immediate. In the "stimulating/good" cluster of words we find *happy, pleasant, elated*: circumstances that are both immediate and positive. The final category, "not-stimulating/good," includes words like *calm, reposed, relaxed*: positive, but less intense.

Places and emotions are inseparable. We constantly ask questions about our surroundings, questions that with time become completely internalized and automatic. "What does this mean for me? If I am here, then what kind of person am I? What is my likely future here? What kind of actions are appropriate for me and for

↑certain behaviors are acceptable in certain environments
from large public space — to

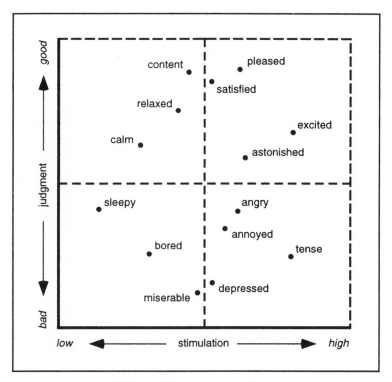

Fig. 11. Matrix of emotions.

others?"[8] We live in our places through our imaginations, and it is this imagined story that leads directly to the world of the emotions. Our emotions refer to what we think is likely to happen in the future—anger is about seeing a desired future with something in the way, boredom is about seeing an alternative that's kept out of reach, grief is about a life to be faced without the departed one—just as our stories about places are related to our future selves.[9] But our modern institutions, our system of education, our urban planning, our assemblage of laws and codes, have little room for our imaginations. They can offer only a series of objective questions to be solved, known, maximized, remembered, tested.

For most of us, most of the time, the institutions that surround us only make a moderate impression on our consciousness. We are hardly aware of CalTrans when we drive on the freeway, or of the corporate headquarters in Arkansas when we walk into a Wal-Mart.

Living room / vs / bedroom.

They are as peripheral to our lives as we are to theirs, emerging visibly only at times of major change—store openings and closings, layoffs, mudslides that carry away roads.

Teenagers live in much more proximate contact with institutions, because kids don't have the resources that allow adults to cushion the blow. Every place they use is owned by someone else. They cannot build places. They cannot purchase places. They typically cannot modify places. They can only inhabit places, which means to be subject to someone else's rules. They feel the curfew, they feel the closing time at the beach or the no-loitering laws at the convenience store, they feel the capriciousness of the bells that tell them when and where to move through their days at school. If rules are the logical extension of mistrust, then rules about teenage behavior are doubly so, because most adults are certain that kids don't share our assumptions. We fear and dislike teenagers as we do any foreigners.[10]

As diverse as Curtisville's teenagers are, they share one central fact, a fact they also share with teenagers in Maine and Wisconsin and Missouri. Teenagers are defined through our civic, legal and educational institutions as a class—minors—and that class status intrudes on almost everything they try to do. School, jobs, home, sex, curfew, parks, driving, recreation, and almost all other facets of teenage life are impacted through the legal status of "minor." To class someone as a minor is to charge them with incompetence, with volatility, with the inability to manage their own affairs.

Whenever kids try to find some joy within this bleak landscape, they almost always find that there's a rule against what they try to do. An extraordinary amount of the planning in city government isn't planning at all, but simply a default to the even more distant rule systems of insurance carriers and lawyers. The city I lived in (Union, six miles south of Curtisville) was a member of an insurance pool which refused to offer coverage for skateboarding. Not only could the city not build an often-requested skate park, they couldn't even officially tolerate skating on sidewalks and in parks. The city's skateboarding ordinance prohibited skateboarding on sidewalks only as they were specifically listed, pursuant to City Council action. But every time a skate spot got popular, the Council passed a resolution adding that spot to the official list of forbidden skateboard areas.

Kids also run up against the rational insistence upon singular definitions for all things, even when that demand runs counter to the experiential world of use. A slab of asphalt with yellow stripes may be "a parking lot" between 8 A.M. and 6 P.M., but outside that window of time it's a bicycle racetrack, a meeting hall, a skate park, and more. We define all of those activities—and more importantly, all of those meanings, all of those potential places to belong—as illegitimate when we insist on the unitary definition of the place as a parking lot, and we lose out on a lot of potential richness in our public life. Another Union City Council resolution stated that public facilities must only be used for their posted purposes, in response to complaints about roller hockey games at the local tennis courts. Roller hockey, the "youth sport," was reduced in status in favor of tennis, the "adult sport." But the roller hockey players were just doing what humans have done for millennia, defining their needs and finding an environment to suit. A tennis court could hardly be better designed for roller hockey: it's a flat, solid pavement with no traffic, surrounded by fences to stop errant shots. Rather than applaud their ingenuity, we define teenagers off the tennis courts.

We use school to introduce these kids into the divisive ways of thinking that our culture depends upon for both its operation and its sustaining beliefs. We introduce the sequential and divided curriculum, the sharp grade divisions, the sharp temporal divisions, the sharp division between one student's success and that of another, the sharp division between student and teacher, the "right" time and the "wrong" time for each activity. We divide the whole and complete world into amazingly small bits, and we do it so thoroughly and so systematically that it becomes the entire galaxy for these kids; it's the only system they see. They learn to ask questions within the framework, because questions that lie outside it can't be asked; institutional language is a language of division, a language that sets analytical units in relationship to one another rather than synthesizing the world as it appears. What these kids are being taught throughout their schooling and in their communities is the division of object and subject, the rational split that lies at the heart of western thought. We tell them that all problems and all solutions lie somewhere "out there" in the correct manipulation of external things, and that objective factual knowledge is the basis for their future lives.

We seem as a culture to be doing everything we can to make the world less spontaneous and more uniform, to move away from personal responsibility and personal moral positions and toward simple adherence to standards that may not make sense in any particular case. We place our trust in a state-specified curriculum rather than in the judgment of a ten-year veteran teacher who sees his classroom working well. We nullify the rewards given for learning with penalty points for infractions that clearly didn't hinder that learning. We put up signs that tell children not to run when they play.

We can devise a lot of reasons for doing things the way we've done them. They all seem to make sense, because we're so thoroughly used to them. But our reliance on rules and standards represents a fundamental way of experiencing the world, a lifestyle that is based on a presumption of mistrust combined with a worship of precision, uniformity, efficiency, and economic gain.

A lifestyle with little room for joy.

Philosopher Eugene Borowitz, in trying to understand nineteenth and mid-twentieth century European thought, may shed some light on the questions that face us fifty years later:

> Marcel defines a *problem* as an unknown that one approaches in objective fashion. It is outside the thinker, so he can reach out to it dispassionately and from a distance. Objective thought is appropriate to problems, and much of great interest is gained when objectivity is used in its appropriate context. The questions: What is ice? What causes cancer? How high can you build a building? are true problems. And men are grateful that by being studied in an unemotional way, solutions for them may be found.

> Such issues should be called problems whether the difficulties they present are solvable or not. Suppose it were not possible, as far as men could tell, to discover a cure for cancer. That does not affect the status of the question or the right way of studying it. A problem, in Marcel's existential interpretation, is a difficulty that may properly be related to in an objective, impersonal, uninvolved way.

Modern man goes astray in thinking that every issue is a problem and that every question should be dealt with in an objective way. Marcel, however, argues that there are some riddles that fall into another category, one he terms "mystery." A mystery is a question in which, once it is posed, the investigator finds himself personally involved. He cannot separate his self from his difficulty. . . . problems may be solved, declares Marcel, but with a mystery no solution is ever possible. Man cannot resolve the self to a set of rational ideas, or the enigmas in which the self finds itself to a logical pattern. One can but stand before a mystery and acknowledge it.[11]

When trying to learn what a group of people seem to find valuable, it helps to look at what they do and what they make. Every act of creation or consumption is a statement of what the maker thinks is good. The decision may be limited by all sorts of contextual rules, but within those limits, people generally do the best that they can do, and that tells you a lot about their conception of "best." Human behavior and artifacts are articulate in ways that language often is not. They become, when read together, a cultural story, a landscape of collective dreams.

A word in current vogue among academics who look at this sort of interpretation is "narrative." To narrate is to give an account or tell the story, and this is not—can never be—simply a recounting of cold facts. Narration is a creative act: choosing what to include and exclude, what to emphasize and how to order it all. Narration both reveals and creates the meanings behind the simple events. In this way, the narrative includes the cultural frame within which one tells stories. For example, when telling the story of a homeless person, one narrator might talk about laziness, poor choices, and personal irresponsibility. All of these are choices about which parts of the story to relate, and are tied into a larger overarching narrative made up of things like sin, individualism, and free will. Another narrator might tell the same story in terms of chance events, harsh employers, and abusive parents. This is another set of choices about what parts of the story are important, and are tied to a competing narrative made up of things like power, fate, and limits to freedom.

When we speak of places as stories, it is important to remember that there are these larger stories at the cultural level as well as the dozens or hundreds of individual stories created by each person who encounters a place. These cultural narratives are the master stories into which the particular and personal stories fit, the bigger "why" behind the smaller ones.

I spent my year learning many ways to read Curtisville and its places. The school, the neighborhoods, the cars, the homes, the places of recreation, all of them only make sense within personal and cultural stories without which they are merely things, without which in fact they never would have been made. I found two strong and competing narratives at work—call them perhaps teenage Existentialism and institutional Modernism—that framed the smaller personal stories and readings.[12] They were the same two opposed narratives that Borowitz identified fifty years earlier: the framing of the world as "problem" or as "mystery."

A late twentieth century American town and its high school might seem like an odd location from which to discuss two philosophical movements with roots in nineteenth century Germany and Scandinavia. But the most basic conflicts between teenagers and adults—in schools, at home, and in the community—are, at their core, conflicts between an Existential and a Modern way of understanding and living in the world.

There are, by most accounts, several key ideas in Modern thought. One is the idea of "progress," by which is usually meant material and technological progress. When we talk about the standard of living, what we mean is purchasing power, quality and durability of goods, the ability to have more and bigger things. Progress is seen as being inevitable, in fact, given the ingenuity of human thought in creating materials and processes of ever-greater intricacy and cleverness.

This progress is typically measured in mass terms rather than individual; progress is defined by aggregate measurement. The Gross National Product and the Dow-Jones Industrial Average are the same sorts of measurement as statewide testing of student competence, a summation of inputs which hides individual differences within them. The state of the individual is, in the Modern analysis, mostly irrelevant; what is not only important but in fact unstoppable is the general trend, which by its very continuation is defined as positive, an upward curve.

Whether looking at the aggregate or the individual case, though, assessment of progress is defined as quantitative and material rather than as essential and emotional. The automobile, for example, is often heralded as a device which opens new horizons for us; we forget that it substitutes one way of experiencing the world for another, that we spend less time with a deep knowledge of the local in exchange for more time with a broad knowledge of many places. The car allows us to get to work and chores and play effortlessly, and helps us create streetscapes with no life. Soren Kierkegaard lived fifty years before the car, a hundred years before television and a hundred and fifty years before the Internet, but predicted them all: "In our age where passionate commitment is strikingly lacking, our human relationships gain in scope what they lose in intensity—we talk about more things and we are acquainted with more people, but we know them less well."[13]

Within Modernism, the duty of the individual is to find a role within which he or she can serve the needs of society and thus further the progress which has been and will continue to be made. The process of human development is seen as preparation for set roles: parent, employee, citizen. We encourage specialization, and respect the legitimate authority of those who occupy the roles "above us" in the hierarchy. The nature of the individual is secondary to the nature of the role, and there is no room within the system for those who choose none of the established roles.

Modernism, in the words of geographer Edward Soja, is basically a set of "hegemonic programmes for social progress."[14] As befits the conciseness of the definition, each of his words is vitally important to our understanding. "Hegemonic" refers to the overarching nature of the narrative, the fact that a common conception drives every manifestation. "Programmes" are rational and applied frameworks that can be transported to different circumstances with little or no modification: a set of interlocking rules, evaluative standards and rewards aimed at a "good" outcome. "Social" is the scale at which Modernism works, resulting in a focus on the general tendency rather than the individual circumstances which comprise it.[15] "Progress" lies at the heart of the Modernist belief world, the idea that there is a common ideal toward which we should all strive, and which is in fact approachable.[16] Even little "for," tucked in the middle of the definition, is important to our understanding of Modernism, implying that there is a known (or at least knowable) cause-and-effect relationship between our programs and the desired progress.

If every word in that definition were replaced by its antonym, the resulting phrase could stand as a definition of Existentialism.[17] For the existentialist, the hegemonic program is not nearly as important as the unique (and uniquely meaningful) personal act. Social progress is not a goal, but rather a by-product of fulfilled, joyful people. And the definite linkage of acts to their outcomes is not nearly as certain as the Modernists believe. We create ourselves through our actions, but both the actions and the selves are constrained by larger historical and institutional circumstances beyond our control.[18] The rationalist knows about the world through thought and logic, through reduction to basic causes and the search for objective and generalizable laws; the existentialist knows the world—his own world, her own world—through intuition and feeling, accepting the unique and ambiguous event in its entirety and searching for a tentative and temporary resolution.

Philosophical historian William Barrett offers a summary definition of existentialism:

> There is no prefabricated human nature that freezes human possibilities into a preordained mold; on the contrary, man exists first and makes himself what he is out of the conditions into which he is thrown. "Existence precedes essence," as the formula puts it. . . . man is the one animal who not only can, but must ask himself what his life means. We are all philosophers in this sense whenever we reach a point in life where total reflection upon ourselves is called for. Most of the time we try to avoid such occasions for total reflection by temporary expedients: we plug leaks in the ship without bothering to ask where it is heading. But if the problem is fundamental, expedients do not serve and we are faced with such questions as: What am I ultimately interested in? What is the point of it all? What meaning does my life have?[19]

Existential thought arose in response to the Industrial Revolution, that moment of Modernism in which the speed of change was thrown into hyperdrive and the definition of progress became hardened and uniform. It is no accident that Karl Marx (more sociologist than economist, after all) developed the concept of *alienation* in response to the worker's ever-diminished position within the growing mechanical and economic systems. Existentialism is the call to the individual in mass society; not the heroic cartoon individual leading the charge toward progressive social change, but all of us who are by nature unsure and tentative and still must act.

Existentialism is the natural position of the teenager surrounded by the all-encompassing machines of school, work, community, and the larger economic world. The basic job of adolescence (to use the Modernist term for people who search for themselves, which could be a lifelong act but which institutions attempt to manage and limit through shunting people into ever-more-constrained roles) is to come to grips with one's own meaning in the world. In Marcel's terms, teenagers are vitally interested in the mystery of being, in the questions that have no answers but which demand imperfect and active responses.

Where can joy be found in all this? Joy comes from that action that makes us feel as though we are, perhaps, finding our selves in the world. Joy is in action, and action is the response to mystery. We have made the leap of faith, however small. We have said, "Yes, this is my place, this is what I ought to do," and can embrace the world with some momentary certainty, some assurance: not knowing whether we are "right," but believing that we are taking a good path. Places of joy will be those places in which we make those actions.

Our objective world is made up of physical entities and their properties—existence, quantity, boundaries, dimensions, mass, density, and duration. We can describe these objects and their relationships in unambiguous terms. We can answer questions about these things, questions which will mostly begin with What or How or Who or When or Where, through objectivity and reason.

But the world as we live it is constituted by what things mean; how we make sense of them; and how and why they have importance to us. Questions about meaning are generally *Why* questions, and can't be answered except directly from the self who is experiencing and trying to make meaning of the world. All of the factual questions are answerable, in time, and we have reduced most of our professions to solving "problems." But underlying all factual questions is the nagging *Why?*, the mystery that we must answer without complete knowledge.

One of the most engaging things about the teenagers of Curtisville High, and the one that got their teachers and parents most exasperated, was that they constantly asked, "Why?" When they got homework, they'd say, "Why are we doing this?" When they watched people in other social groups, they'd say, "Why would anybody do that?" whether "that" was driving the cruise or putting decorative rocks around a driveway or dyeing their hair green.

After half the year, I came to apply one simple gauge to assess teaching quality: poor teachers hated the why questions. I was about to follow Kirk for a week, and I asked his math teacher Rob Niesen about him. "Kirk's a very smart kid, but he's a screwball," Rob answered. "He's not a rebel, but he questions things. If I tell him that class starts at the click, he'll say, 'Class hasn't started yet, what does it matter?' Or if I say you can't eat in class, he'll say, 'Why not?' He's smart, he's intelligent, he picks up on things quickly, but there's no sense of why behind it. He'll say, 'Why do we have to do this or that?'" This clearly galled Rob, who added as though Kirk were present with us, "If I tell you to do something, do it!"

Most teenagers do become more like most adults over time, but hardly because of some hard-wired genetic map. Anthropologist John Ogbu says quite plainly, "Whatever else education may be, from the standpoint of society (parents, teachers and pupils) it is a preparation of children for adult life as adults in their society conceive it."[20] Adults see teenagers as potential adults, which is to say potential converts to the Modernist narrative. The school takes on the role of mission in the primitive juvenile world, to bring the undeveloped youth into line with the adult path.[21]

"Adult path," of course, is far too easy a phrase. There are many adult paths, and our institutions pursue only the most mainstream and middle class. The adult world as presented by the California

Department of Education is not the adult world of the surf nomad or the professional musician or the serious intellectual. The adult world envisioned by the Curtisville community planning board does not include unsupervised hangouts or neighborhood stores or walking to work. The adult world they speak of is the world of the bureaucratic nine-to-fiver, the worker who both in fact and in attitude treats work and community as something outside the self, problems to be addressed and then left behind at the end of the day. This should come as no surprise given that our institutions are run by exactly those people, who believe their narrative to be not only legitimate but singularly true. The tools chosen by these missionaries are state frameworks and curriculum guides and zoning plans, and success is gauged by performance assessments and standards "that reflect the needs of a competitive world-class economy."

In the face of the middle-class mission, I seemed to find four basic teenage responses, cultures of actions and beliefs that—after

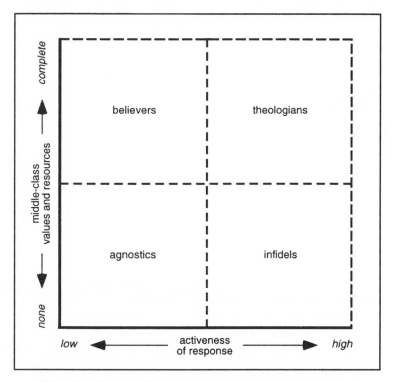

Fig. 12. Matrix of teenage response to institutions.

several attempts at appropriate naming—I finally called the *infidels*, the *agnostics*, the *believers* and the *theologians*.[22] The infidels do not accept the story of the dominant culture, and feel within it a personal threat to be actively opposed. They challenge the system openly, get busted, and feel further persecuted and more alienated than ever before. In the great majority of cases of teenage "misbehavior" I witnessed, I found that what looks from the outside like sullenness or delinquency or disruptiveness or apathy are in fact reasonable acts in the face of obstacles that seem larger, more systemic, and more pervasive that we can see from our side of the shore.[23]

Tami is a perfect example of an infidel, a kid who doesn't believe what she's told and can't keep quiet about her opposition:

> Teachers stand up there and they preach about acceptance and tolerance and that other good baloney, and then as soon as I say something that I personally believe in, they go, they just start doing this: "Welll . . .", you know, like that. And I said, "the only reason why the Union"—we were studying the Civil War—"the only reason why the South lost is because the North had more money and if they didn't free the slaves, we would still have slavery in the United States." And it's true, I've read this, trust me, I've read a lot up on it. Mr. Haney, my history teacher, just kinda sputtered for a couple of minutes, and then he goes, "Well," tried telling me about dadadadada. Or I would talk [in Government class] about political prisoners in the United States and human rights abuses in the United States or the government making cases against citizens that support "unpopular" causes. And she's like, "Well, I don't know what you're referring to" or "I don't think they would do something like that." And they, like, they would stand up there and preach tolerance, but as soon as I walk into the class, you know, they don't . . . I don't know, it's just sometimes I get the feeling that teachers are playing favorites. I'm trying to just . . . I have to make it until June, I hope.

By comparison, the agnostics also dismiss the story of the dominant culture, but they feel it to be irrelevant, safely ignored. They come to school and do little, but don't openly challenge the authorities because they recognize that they are out-powered. They put up with what they see as the silliness of rules because they've learned to slide within and around them to do what they need.

When I did my interviews, Corrine and Juan taught me about agnostics. I had asked about favorite and least favorite places:

"Corrine, what was your least favorite place?"

"I think the school. 'Cause it seems like we spend a lot of time here that doesn't need to be spent here."

"What about you, Juan, do you like school?"

"Yeah."

"What do you like about it?"

"Socializing. Being around friends. I can already tell, like, when you get out of school it's going to be boring. Just right now I can tell, like when I don't go to school, like on weekends and stuff, or whatever."

For the agnostics, the institution is a nuisance from which they might draw some interaction, but which offers little of personal usefulness.

The believers are the opposite side of the coin from the agnostics; the believers have accepted the story of the dominant culture, internalized it, made its goals their own.[24] Interestingly, school isn't especially interesting for these folks any more than it is for the agnostics—it exists as a means to an end. Aster, a senior who was clearly a high school success, told me:

> I don't like school because . . . I don't know, the way kids treat other kids, how negative they can be. How they treat their teachers and how they treat learning. They come here like they're being . . . well, they *are* being legally forced to do it but it's to their advantage, and they don't realize that, they just come and like, hang out and see who's going out with who, and everything. It just bugs that heck out of me sometimes. Or the teacher will say, "Okay, we're going to have homework tonight," and I think to myself, you know, "Oh, I've got more homework," but some kids are just like, "Oh, God, why do we have to do that stuff?" And I don't think to myself that, I just think, "Okay, it's just more stuff that I've gotta do tonight," but it's all benefiting me. I don't have

math this year, but I think I'd think, "Why do I have to do that?" when I had math, because I didn't like math. But other subjects, it's to my advantage, and I just think, "What are you going to do during college?"

For the believers, the present discomfort is subsumed to a higher promised future. Both the believers and the agnostics are found in great numbers in the high school and in subsequent adult institutions.

If the believers are the flip side of the agnostic, the theologians are the flip side of the heretic, and equally out of place in the school. For the theologians, the material gain of learning is secondary to its potential for immediate personal growth. Aster and Mara have equivalent grades, and have taken equivalent classes. But compare Aster's narrative of school, above, with Mara's:

I don't like that when I ask a teacher a question that's in-depth, they will just scan over it . . . "We'll get to it later," and it's never gotten to. I don't like that fact that I've never been given the chance to satiate my curiosity, that I've been squelched. That if I want to learn this, and we're actually going over it in class, it's just touching the surface. I want to go more in depth, and I'm generally considered a pest for that. I don't like that I'm not given respect from anybody, nobody's given respect for intelligence that they may or may not possess. The kids who are below average ranking, they get special treatment, special classes and everything to help them learn, which is wonderful, which is really necessary, but the rest of us who need to learn more aren't given that option. Because at this school we don't have advanced placement, we have no, no like, special courses. Last year, in my English 2 class, which was supposed to be advanced English, was general and basic mixed in, people learning how to use nouns. And that's great, they need to go and learn how to use a noun, but I already know how to use a noun, I want to go farther than that, I want to do more than that. They don't give me enough. I'm always hungrier, I'm just . . . I want more than this. I want more than just to read the book and answer the questions at the end of the chapter.

That's not learning, that's mimicry. I want to learn. That's simply . . . that this is supposed to be a place of learning and I have difficulty learning here. 'Cause they don't . . . they don't care to teach me. That's probably why it is, it doesn't fulfill my needs.

It is both puzzling and tragic that so many of Curtisville's teenagers were fighting at every opportunity for the more unique and complex self while all of Curtisville's institutions were seeking to make those selves more systematic, simple and compliant. The talk was about placing children first, but the acts that were visible throughout the landscape were acts that betrayed them.

If the job of education is "socialization" and enculturation, then it's no surprise that many kids who stand outside that culture resent it. They are told to get in line, stop talking, take fixed periods to do things, learn about things that may not be relevant to daily life or understandable future benefit, respect private property beyond the point of not stealing it or not damaging it, play carefully. The actions of the young, read through the narrative of Modernism, are defined as immaturity; when read through the Existential narrative of self-domain and self-creation, they can be seen as a half-aware critique of the world they're about to enter.

We most often see the differences between teenagers and adults as the result of incomplete development, and suppose that they will become more like us with time. Whether that explanation is based in physiology or in psychology, it is distinctly Modernist, based in theories of inevitable biological and social change, rooted in stories of scientific and sure knowledge, objective material success, "programmes for social progress." But many teenagers have a dissenting narrative, a competing system of beliefs. They are another culture, separate within our own as surely as if they had come here from overseas. That they do not immediately fit in should not surprise anyone.

Adolescence is neither a condition nor a stage nor a phase. Adolescence is the search for the self, trying both to find and to make the person that they are and will continue to be. Teenagers are caught in the heart of the moment in the existential dilemma, placed into a system not of their own choosing and having to make a set of conscious decisions about their response, their position within it. When I speak of adolescence, I am not talking about a set of inherent psycho-physiological patterns, the one-way genetic road down which "they" travel to become "us;" I am talking about the power-laden point of conflict between two sets of ideals, the intrusion of one way of living upon another. There *is* a generation gap, and it has little to do with age.[25] It has to do with power and status, with imposition and submission. It is a cultural divide, as distinct as black and white, as broad as the Rio Grande.

CHAPTER TWENTY-SIX

Collaborators

After my year of immersion, I spent much of the summer resisting the first steps of writing the year's work. I'd half-heartedly looked for a job to take the place of my fellowship, and hung around at Julian's with the Drama Geeks for several hours every afternoon and evening. But it was getting near the beginning of August, and I knew that a lot of kids were going to be heading off to college in another three or four weeks. If I wanted one last shot with them, I'd have to do it quickly.

My friend Laura and I had often talked in the past about handing out cameras and seeing what parts of Curtisville the kids would take pictures of if they had the chance. I called her. "Do you want to come up in a couple of weeks and help me run a workshop?" Laura is a professional urban designer, and her master's thesis at Berkeley was one of the few good documents in the field of teenagers and their communities.[1] It wasn't hard to convince her to drive the five hours up from Santa Rosa for the weekend.

Then I started the guest list, beginning with all of my volunteers. Benjamin would be on vacation with his parents, and Laurie in Mexico with her church group. Ethan was going back to Sierra County to visit relatives, and Duane was working. Irene was in Los Angeles, and Maggie had returned to Ireland. That left Kirk, Tami, Mara, Matthew, and Ivy. I'd gotten no response from Tami all year on anything else I'd asked her to do, so I wasn't going to bother her with this.

To augment that group, I thought of who else I knew well who hadn't been able to participate in the other things I'd cooked up. Becky was a part of the poker circle, and I was increasingly seeing her as something other than the ditzy cheerleader she portrayed. Carrie had introduced herself to me after the first night of my year-end performance; we had a good talk. She came back for the second night, and we talked again. Ryan had asked a meaningful question from the audience, and he and I had become closer right at the end of the school year. Julian was the ringleader, the poet and provocateur. Bev, the founder of Union's *All Youth Combined*, had led the attempts to create a teen-administered Union youth center; even though she didn't live in Curtisville, I knew she'd be an active and interested contributor, perhaps supplying the outsider's voice. She was leaving to start school at Reed College the following week.

After ensuring that all of my invitees could spend an entire Saturday at my apartment, I bought nine disposable cameras, labeled each one with the name of its respective recipient, and delivered them with the sheet of instructions shown in Figure 13.

Julian grabbed his camera and his instructions and went off to take half of his pictures ten minutes after I gave it to him. The others all finished their assignments within a couple of days, and I collected their cameras and had the photos developed.

On Friday, Laura arrived at my apartment at six, and we drove up to Curtisville so that I could show her the sights. "What a sad place," she said over and over. "Look at how wide these streets are."

We went back to my place and had dinner while she looked at the photos I'd mounted in clusters on newsprint sheets all over the living-room walls, one cluster per photo topic. Laura was pleased at the perceptiveness of the kids' photos—they seemed to have captured everything we'd hoped they might. Then we scripted out the next day's events and went to bed.

On Saturday morning, I drove up to Curtisville to pick up Julian, whom I'd asked to help me do last-minute assembly of food and papers. We went to work a little after nine, and the house was full of kids by ten. Some of them, like Mara, were accustomed to working hard before nine; others, like Ivy, were barely conscious before noon.

I asked everyone to introduce themselves and tell a little about how long they'd lived in Curtisville, and what part of town they

Howdy.

Here's your instructions. There are 15 shots in this camera, and 15 things below to take a photo of. Check each one off as you do it, but the order doesn't matter. Also, if you're shooting one and you don't think you got a good picture, don't worry about it — just go on to another one.

For each one, go to the place that comes to your mind — not what you think "most people" would think of, or what you think I want you to answer. You get to define each one of these places and then photograph it.

The only rules are:
        your photos MUST BE OUTDOORS!
        your house MAY NOT appear in any photo.

Ready??

Okay, take a photograph of the following places within Curtisville:

___the center
___the edge of town
___the entrance to town
___an eddy (a place to pause)
___a part of Curtisville you don't know very well
___a place where you would live if you could choose anywhere in Curtisville
___a social place
___a lonely place
___an exciting place
___a place where you like to walk
___a beautiful place
___an ugly place
___a boring place
___a painful or stressful place
___a calm, peaceful place

Figure 13. Workshop photograhy instructions.

lived in. Most of them struggled to find their houses on the USGS topographic map of Curtisville that I kept pinned over my desk, but they were all able to describe their neighborhoods to everyone else's satisfaction. Becky, who lived about as far into the woods as it was possible to go and still be in Curtisville, said, "Some people want to live way out in the country, and that's fine, and that's what my dad wanted. But I hated it, because it took me hours to get into town, and once I got there, it was time to turn around and come home."

After we all knew everyone and their neighborhoods, I asked them all to go around the room and to write a comment underneath every photo they'd taken; once that was done, to take a colored pencil and to make comments underneath any picture at all. Both of these jobs together took the better part of a loud and conversational hour, after which we sat and talked about which set of photos best captured their assigned themes. They'd had the easiest time finding the edge and entrance to town (though they weren't too happy with what they'd found), and had a harder time agreeing on what was at the center (or whether there was one at all). Ivy described Curtisville as a "convenience town," full of "places to go and no places to be," a video store at its geographic and metaphoric heart.

We broke for lunch and spent more time looking at the photos. Several kids took the opportunity to teach Laura about Curtisville and what opportunities there were for teenagers, and the food went pretty fast. There was a long discussion over lunch about places to walk, and how kids felt conspicuous if they walked down Main Street, and that the 10 P.M. curfew was just another sign that you weren't expected to be outside in Curtisville at any time. Mara—one of the most constantly active and busy and joyous kids I'd ever met—said she occasionally gave in to her temptation to sleep all day simply because it was something to do, it filled the hours.

At about one o'clock, we all re-gathered in the living room, and I got people settled in to go through their afternoon assignments. We began with an exercise that both Laura and I had been taught by Clare Cooper Marcus, an inspiring teacher of our own at Berkeley. After some giggles and last-minute joking, I got everyone to close their eyes, and began to lead them through a visualization of their ideal community, using the same sorts of questions I'd asked them to photograph in Curtisville. Where was the entrance to town, and what was it like? Where was the center of town, and what was in it? Where was the edge of town, and how would they know it was the edge? And where was their home in all of this?

After fifteen minutes of imagination, I brought them all back to my living room and gave everyone a sheet of notebook paper and a few crayons. Over the next fifteen minutes or so, they all drew the town they'd just experienced.

At the end of drawing period, we taped the results up over the piano, and everyone talked about the towns they'd just seen. In every case, the town was more or less radial, with an identifiable and solid-edged center composed of a village green wrapped with businesses, all surrounded by housing. The businesses that were labeled and in the center were public places: restaurants, live theaters, nightclubs, a museum, game rooms.

The outskirts of town were right up against the surrounding forests or fields or ocean, so that leaving the town (at a handful of distinctly marked points) meant entering nature or agriculture, and leaving the countryside meant entering a dense collection of buildings. Most people identified their own homes as being on the outskirts of town, near that boundary but within easy walk of the downtown core. Essentially, they'd taken an idealized Union as their model, a small mercantile town set in a beautiful landscape and not allowed to go beyond firmly set limits.

At this point, about three o'clock, I asked them to do the hardest thing of all: to integrate what they'd learned from each others' photos, from their own ideal towns and from the discussions, and to make a set of rules about the physical characteristics of a good community. Kirk had to leave for work, so the remaining eight broke up into pairs and went to work while Laura and I roamed the apartment and helped them when they seemed to be stuck.

Becky and Matthew worked on their definition of good social places. The list they created was:

- easily accessible to everyone
- lots of events, something to do, people always there
- good looks, physical appearance of care
- diversity of things to do
- people-watching, lots of visible movement
- no heavy traffic
- everything faces in (a sign of respect, a focus and concentration of energy)
- fun and affordable
- comfortable
- entertaining

Julian and Ivy wrote about eddies and rest stops:

- lots of places to stop and lean
- buildings close together and close to the street
- there should be places to stop within the motion (wide paths and alcoves) as well as places to stop where everyone else is stopped (like cafes)

- the calm center ("eye of the hurricane") in the dense ring of downtown is a large-scale version of the eddy, while a bench on the sidewalk in front of a store is the small-scale version

Bev and Mara examined the edges and entrance to town:

- the edge is where the buildings stop, the end of commercialism
- an obvious line and contrast between the man-made and natural
- the entrance is somehow announced—by a sign, scenery change, different by where you're coming from, not so much as where you're going.
- it develops a sense of community, gives the town identity and character
- it grabs people's interest, a good first impression
- it makes people know and feel they're in Curtisville
- people will enjoy the officiality of *being* in Curtisville, makes them want to stay in Curtisville and shop, hang out, be around

Ryan and Carrie dealt with the center of town:

- a centerpiece for conversation (statue, gazebo, fountain)
- green and growing things (back to nature, primal instincts)
- shops, cafes, maybe a club, public density
- benches, places to stand, places to pause
- not a heavy traffic area
- accessible to all within walking distance
- no hard angles, only round
- nothing too tall or obtrusive or fancy
- people together in public are the most important attribute here

These are lists made by eleventh and twelfth grade students, people with no formal training in architecture and urban planning, people who lived in an awkward environment and recognized its awkwardness and also recognized some attributes that made other places better. The lists they devised are familiar to me; they are the theoretical basis of thinking that is at the heart of progressive city planning today. The kids didn't have access to the learning or the theory; they also didn't know that some of America's most desirable neighborhoods—from Georgetown in Washington, D.C. to Downer Avenue in Milwaukee to Elmwood and Rockridge in Oakland and the Castro in San Francisco to summer resort towns throughout the eastern half of the country—are built along the guidelines they'd just created. They just knew their circumstances and their needs. Same result.

By five, the lists of rules had been made and presented, and everyone was worn out. I thanked them all for their hard work and intelligence, they pulled my surprise birthday present out of the shower where they'd hidden it, and the party was on. Significantly, my gift—planned several days in advance—was a scavenger hunt through the streets and Plaza of my adopted home town, Union; each clue led to another landmark that was familiar to all of us because we shared in our love of the town. Even before the knowledge we made manifest in our workshop, they had already devised a plan that would take us out in public, bringing our celebration to the rest of the community.

ès

Eight months later, I was having a couple of beers with Al Lawton and Matt Moreno. Al was the senior social sciences teacher at Curtisville High, and Matt had been his student teacher two years ago. The three of us shared a love of liberal politics, a commitment to real education and a laughing disdain of public school bureaucracy. Al had asked me a few times to come in and do a day's class on social research methods in his Sociology course at Curtisville, but the date hadn't been set; he was having a hard time thinking about a good researchable question for their semester project. I suggested something spatial. "One of the things that I did a lot was to go to the mall, and count the numbers of kids that went past me to see whether girls were in larger or smaller groups than boys or groups that were mixed-sex."

Al looked dubious. "Yeah, but I don't think these kids would be curious about that. You guys and I know about asking social questions, we think that's fun—but how can I get these kids to even think of something social that they'd be curious about?"

"I just think you've got to start with something local, something they already know, and get them to pursue that."

"Like what?" Matt said. He was a substitute teacher at the time, but he was about to apply for a new opening in History at Curtisville, and was thinking about projects of his own.

"I don't know . . . Well, here's one that I had fun with, and I think it worked pretty well. At the end of last summer, I got these nine kids who'd already been involved with my project . . ."

"You mean you'd already been working with them and developed a personal relationship?" Al asked.

"Yeah."

"Well," he said, laughing, as though I'd instantly disqualified it from classroom consideration.

"So anyway, I invited them all over to my house one Saturday . . ."

"Well," he laughed again, as though that explained everything already.

"It gets better," Matt added. I'd told him and his wife about the workshop over dinner a couple of months earlier.

"So, I'd already given each of them a disposable camera the week before and asked them to take some pictures—like, I asked everyone to take a picture of the center of town, and to take a picture of the edge of town, and a part of town they didn't know anything about." I laughed, suddenly remembering. "I spent a ton of money on all this . . ."

"What's a ton?" Al demanded.

"A couple of hundred bucks."

"Wow!" he said, nodding, as though that explained everything. Matt was nodding, too; I think I'd left out the money part when I told him.

"And I collected their pictures a couple of days early and got them all mounted on butcher paper, so that I had nine photos of the center of town all together, and nine pictures of where they wanted to live all on another sheet . . ."

More nodding.

"And when they came over that morning, all these sheets were on the wall waiting for them. And we started by asking everybody to just look around at all of the pictures, and to make comments under everybody's picture. Like, "I've been there, it sucks!" or "That's a cool place" or whatever . . ."

Nodding.

"And then we talked about which ones were easiest to make comments on, and which ones came to mind quickly, and which ones we all seemed to agree on. And then I fed them lunch."

Nodding.

"And then after lunch, I did a guided fantasy—you know, a sort of low-level hypnosis, taking them on a trip of their favorite place . . ."

"How did you make it generic enough?" Al asked.

"I just took them to a place, I called it their ideal town, and I'd ask them what they saw when they looked around, and what they heard, what they smelled . . . And then after taking them all around their town, I brought them back, you know, ten nine eight seven and all, and then I had them draw what they'd seen. I gave everyone paper and crayons and told them they had ten minutes—I gave them fifteen."

Matt and Al kept nodding.

"Then we pinned all these drawings to the wall, and everyone explained what they saw. Then I asked them to take this perfect place and combine it with what we'd done that morning . . ."

"You mean you dashed their hopes and brought them back to Curtisville?" Al laughed.

"No, no, we took the things that they'd seen in their ideal place and the things that we'd talked about in terms of what makes someplace the center of town, and what makes a place exciting, and I asked them to make a set of rules about what a center of town should be, or what an edge of town should be."

"And they could do that?"

"Oh, yeah."

More nodding.

"And then they presented that in groups of two. And then it was five o'clock and everybody was tired, so that was it. And then we had my birthday party from five until about eleven-thirty."

They just kept nodding more vigorously throughout the whole story. Everything I said gave validation to what they felt every day in the classroom, because I was able to break every rule of American schooling to get my work done. I didn't have a curriculum guideline package, or a public use permit, or a CPR card. I didn't have a food preparation license, or an on-site committee, or a drug and tobacco policy. I'm not certified by the State of California to do anything beyond drive a car and vote. But I had some extraordinary advantages that allowed learning to go on: I had a tiny group, chosen for their relationship with me and with each other and for their prior knowledge of what I was trying to do, not for their age or grade level. I gave them a party and fed them all day. They were invited because they knew I respected and loved them. We believed each other and wanted to hear what each other had seen, where we'd been, what we'd learned. Every person there was important to our progress.

We met in my home, with my lifestyle and personality all around. We had seven hours to work, which meant that we had lots of time for the unexpected and unscripted. We were working toward a concrete outcome. We focused on the specific and the local. We took one project and worked on it until we were finished.

We collaborated. Nothing was done for long in private, but in twos and threes. We incorporated social and educational ways of being all day rather than keeping them strictly separate. We ate and laughed and I smacked Julian on the head once in the middle of the afternoon because he wouldn't keep quiet, and he led the celebration when I was marched through Union wearing feathers and balloons to humiliate me for my birthday.

I'd prepared for a week, in several different ways, and so had they. I'd brought in a friend for the weekend, a professional planner who'd also studied teenagers' environments, and it took both of us to guide and channel the discussions. But we were talking about something that we were all clearly captivated by, and none of us were afraid to talk about it.

Finally, most importantly, they were teaching me, and we all knew it.

CHAPTER TWENTY-SEVEN

Rereading Curtisville

Of the books I have read in which an outsider comes into a new culture to learn and report back, there is a strong similarity to their final chapters. James Spradley wrote about the alcoholic tramps of Seattle, and concluded:

> Institutional renewal must go on until we have a society based not on the unity of similarity, but on the acceptance of difference. Beyond our nation, living in other cultures, is a world of strangers. Recognizing the dignity of urban nomads is a small but important step to creating a world of strangers who are friends.[1]

William Foote Whyte wrote about the young Italian men of the Cornerville neighborhood in highly Irish Boston, and concluded:

> Can any program be effective if all the top positions of formal authority are held by people who are aliens to Cornerville? What is the effect upon the individual when he has to subordinate himself to people that he recognizes are different from his own?[2]

Herbert Gans went to another Italian "slum" in Boston, and concluded:

> Although there are an increasing number of knowledgeable planners and caretakers, public funds still are spent largely

for protecting the larger society from the self-destructive and antisocial behavior of the lower class, rather than for the elimination of the causes that create this behavior. . . . The planners and caretakers themselves have acquiesced in this evasion by misplaced confidence in existing programs.[3]

I could echo these statements. Curtisville is filled with teenagers who seem neither to understand nor to enjoy their community, and administered by people who seem neither to understand nor enjoy public interaction. To believe that these kids will grow out of their dissatisfaction and become the next batch of adults who buy property there is to disregard the differences between groups of teenagers, and also to disregard the ways in which their ideas could make Curtisville more satisfying for other residents as well.

ઠ્ર

I have been cautioned, and I cautiously agree, that I have not met the teenagers or the landscapes of Fargo or Moab or Thunder Bay, much less those of Detroit or Montreal or Los Angeles. These are only stories about the kids and landscapes of Curtisville, California.

But then again . . . even though Kirk and Julian and Tami and Mara live here in unique and specific ways, the conditions that exist in Curtisville aren't unique. Curtisville is not the only community in our nation which has accepted single-use zoning or minimum lot sizes. Curtisville is not the only community with a high school at the furthest edge of town, nor the only community which draws its students from an enormous countryside and its curriculum from the state capitol. Curtisville is not the only site in the world for the ranch house and the cul-de-sac neighborhood. The hidden program behind Curtisville and its school and its homes is carried in the minds of millions and millions of Americans, which is why Curtisville and its school look so much like so many other places. The physical environment is only the mental environment written out in longhand; every building, every foot of pavement in Curtisville has a program behind it, whether expressed or not. Every artifact is a statement of belief.

It would be both foolish and counterproductive to offer a handful of suggestions for Curtisville's layout and planning that would supposedly alleviate most of its problems. That it would be foolish I can explain by the accretive nature of landscape production, the fact that wholesale changes in an existing landscape are so rare as to be truly historical circumstances. Any change, no matter how useful, is set within an enormous landscape that already asserts its own power.

That it would be counterproductive I can explain by the holistic nature of the narrative that has guided the creation of what exists around us. To make changes within that framework would be to accept that narrative, to surrender to the terms that have already captured us. What we need is not new rules but a new story. In the words of Frank Smith:

> I have a serious suggestion to make. We should stop worrying about the problems of education, declare it a disaster, and let teachers and students get on with their lives. The trouble with the endless concern over "problems" in education is that many well-meaning but often misguided and sometimes meddlesome people believe that solutions must exist. They waste their own and other people's time and energy trying to find and implement these solutions. Typically, they try harder to do more of something that is already being done (although what is being done is probably one of the problems).[4]

Or, in the words of Douglas Biklen:

> We probably should abandon all hope of reforming institutions from within. To assume that one can instigate reform from within is to assume that closed institutions exist primarily to serve inmates and that dehumanization is an aberrant condition in an otherwise acceptable system. . . . institutions emphasize other, less charitable ends. With this knowledge we should frame our reforms. . . . I suggest, therefore, that any proposal for transforming institutions be accompanied by a detailed plan to evacuate these settings altogether.[5]

Instead of offering a few sketched town plans, a series of incremental changes to Curtisville that would be neither welcome nor effective in the face of strong beliefs, I'd like to reexamine the hidden programs of Curtisville.[6] To state outright the creed of faith that has driven these specific forms of town, school and home. To examine the directness in which those beliefs have been made concrete. And then to imagine a community that holds an alternate set of beliefs, a community in which a new program leads to a new landscape.

We can begin with an overview of Curtisville as it exists today, the place that is growing so rapidly, filled with teenagers who at best treat it as an interchangeable commodity, who at worst dislike it intensely. A basic list of the physical characteristics that give Curtisville its character includes:

- mega-institutions provide churches, recreation, schools, and businesses
- property is strictly zoned by land use
- nearly 100 businesses are on Main Street, only three elsewhere
- land parcels are large, and there are great distances between both residential and commercial buildings
- enormous spaces—from lawns to broad streets to parking lots—are unused most of the time
- housing increasingly sprawls into the surrounding forests and ranches
- new housing developments are gated, fenced or walled
- dozens of cul-de-sac streets feed into eight main arterial streets
- shopping is done in small, segmented car trips from one parking lot to another
- schools are held apart from the community
- specialized facilities are concentrated on school grounds
- education is conceived as theater, students as audience
- there are few public parks, no shared paths, no town hall
- nature exists mainly as a viewed object above the buildings
- there are no social gathering places in neighborhoods
- there is one bar, no theater, no nightclub
- most restaurants have drive-through service

We can compare that list against the goals that Curtisville's kids developed at their workshop:

- easily accessible to everyone
- lots of events, something to do, people always there
- good looks, physical appearance of care
- diversity of things to do
- people-watching, lots of visible movement
- no heavy traffic
- everything faces in
- fun and affordable
- comfortable
- lots of places to stop and lean
- buildings close together and close to the street
- an obvious line and contrast between the man-made and natural
- a centerpiece for conversation (statue, gazebo, fountain)
- green and growing things
- shops, cafes, maybe a club, public density
- benches, places to stand, places to pause
- accessible to all within walking distance
- no hard angles, only round
- nothing too tall or obtrusive or fancy
- people together in public are the most important attribute here

But remember that these are merely descriptive catalogs of a pair of artifacts; one material, one imagined. More important is the set of beliefs that guided each respective set of people to create what they did. In each case, they are not beliefs that can be chosen off a list, picking some but not others; they are deeply intertwined, one reinforcing the other in an internally consistent system. We can argue endlessly about whether or not these are "good" beliefs, and the debate will gain us nothing. Beliefs arise not in answer to problems but to mysteries.

What we can do, though, is to explore the outcomes of a set of beliefs and see whether or not we like them. Modernist assumptions have led directly to a physical environment, and a different set of assumptions would lead to a different environment. So let us take the set of beliefs that have formed Curtisville and compose a reasonable alternative set—equally consistent within themselves—that we might call Existential ideas.

Modernist idea #1: Kids and adults should be separate.
Existential idea #1: Kids and adults should be integrated, with teenagers welcome in the adult world.

I learned from Curtisville's kids that most of them who were passionate about some body of knowledge (and good at performing the skills that went with it) took up the study because they were drawn to it by someone that they respected and loved. But by ghettoizing teenagers into colonies during the working hours of the day, we remove them from the resources that could teach them. We prevent them from involvement in the processes by which the world works, and from the people who could be their guides. We limit their working lives to classrooms for passive receipt of facts and to hallways for peer contact, neither of which is as effective for their personal growth as adult mentorship in the context of real work.

Not only do we hinder teenagers through segregation, we remove ourselves from their uncomfortable but valuable question: "Why?" Any serious learner of a new system will challenge it with ideas that may lead to innovation and rethinking. The business community is increasingly awake to the possibilities for growth and improvement offered by consultants who offer an outsider's view of established practices. If we take on teenaged participants as honest apprentices in our organizations, we will be inundated with "Why?," and our institutions will be continually reborn.

Modernist idea #2: Children are the passive receivers of education and services.
Existential idea #2: Real learning involves an active search for experience and knowledge.

I saw some classrooms that worked at Curtisville High School, where students were eager to learn, where they were pushing their instructors for more. Kids behaved, in a very few classrooms, like they behaved all the time in sports and play and dance and music and private reading and computer use. But for the most part, the forms of our modern education have driven that enthusiasm from the room, replaced by the orderly ennui of thirty kids dragged along at a common pace.

Cultural critic Ivan Illich argues that:

Most learning happens casually, and even most intentional learning is not the result of programmed instruction. Normal children learn their first language casually, although faster if their parents pay attention to them. Most people who learn a second language well do so as a result of odd circumstances and not of sequential teaching. They go to live with their grandparents, they travel, or they fall in love with a foreigner. Fluency in reading is also more often than not a result of such extracurricular activities. Most people who read widely, and with pleasure, merely believe that they learned to do so in school; when challenged, they easily discard this illusion.[7]

This is exactly the process described by Mihaly Csikszentmihalyi when he describes the concept of flow in learning:

Many people give up on learning after they leave school because thirteen or twenty years of extrinsically motivated learning is still a source of unpleasant memories. Their attention has been manipulated long enough from the out-side, by textbooks and teachers, and they have counted graduation as the first day of freedom. . . . Ideally, the end of extrinsically applied education should be the start of an education that is motivated intrinsically. At that point the goal of studying is no longer to make the grade, earn a diploma, and find a good job. Rather, it is to understand what is happening around one, to develop a personally meaningful sense of what one's experience is all about.[8]

Real learning takes place when desire meets challenge. When people take on a serious task with a serious outcome, they develop capabilities in response to the demands of the task.[9] By striving, they learn.

Modernist idea #3:   We live in a national and global economy, and mobility is inevitable.

Existential idea #3:   The local is of deep and lasting importance.

The philosopher Alfred North Whitehead offered almost seventy years ago his own plan for local education:

> To have constructed the map of a small district, to have considered its roads, its contours, its geology, its climate, its relation to other districts, the effects on the status of its inhabitants, will teach more history and geography than any knowledge of Perkin Warbeck or of Behren's Straits.[10]

More recently, poet Gary Snyder tells us:

> I am consumed with the thought that virtually every society on earth needs to step back (in mind) and consider once more who they are, what their deepest loyalties are, what life is for. Of all the memberships we identify ourselves by (racial, ethnic, sexual, national, class, age, religious, occupational), the one that is most forgotten, and that has the greatest potential for healing, is place. We must learn to know, love, and join our place even more than we love our own ideas. People who can agree that they share a commitment to the landscape/cityscape—even if they are otherwise locked in struggle with each other—have at least one deep thing to share. . . . Creeks, apples, raccoons, neighbors, suburbs, factories are the building blocks of life. They all take place in some watershed. The sandhill cranes still fly over them every year.[11]

We work and love and breathe only in the material world, alive to the stuff around us. Armed terrorists might worry us, but our neighbors affect our happiness much more intensely. The Nature Channel shows us exotic animals, but the cedar waxwing in the backyard tells us it's fall. The latest headline is less relevant than the rain on our windows.

But we can only learn so much if we are constantly making preparations to leave. Not only have we no time, we have no desire to make connections that we will only break apart. We lose the capacity to sustain any relationships, to look for joy and endure hardship. All choices become provisional and temporary. We become emotional nomads, always ready to move along.

Modernist idea #4:   Conflicts are decided in favor of those who have the resources to prevail.

Existential idea #4:   Conflicts are decided in favor of the person or group with fewer resources to buffer any ill effects.

Modernism has a simply stated rule for conflict resolution: might makes right. Clare Cooper Marcus and Wendy Sarkissian have offered a simply stated but compelling alternative:

What happens when basic needs have been reasonably accommodated and conflicts still develop? Should a limited budget be stretched to include a preschool play area or visitor parking, a communal laundry or an extra dwelling? We believe that such conflicts usually can, and should, be resolved in favor of residents who are most at risk environmentally. Thus the needs of a child who may spend most of her waking hours within a housing complex should take precedence over the needs of an occasional visitor. The needs of parents or disabled or elderly people trapped at home most of the day should take precedence over the needs of the employed commuter.[12]

The kids I knew were remarkably generous as long as they knew they could also get what they needed. They encouraged me to go ahead of them in line at the Arco; they shared enormous parts of their lives and asked only for my openness in return. They balked only when doing someone else's will meant that they could not do what they wanted at all: when, by limiting themselves to six students in the store, they could not have lunch in time; when, in order to follow the lesson plan, they had to have their own questions go unanswered.

Why are we not as generous to teenagers in return? Why, when adults already have the economic and material resources kids lack, do we insist on making all of the rules to our advantage as well? It requires bravery to believe that we will not be significantly harmed by helping others. It requires generosity to accept mild inconvenience so that another person will not suffer a crippling hindrance. It requires humility to know that we grow by helping others. These are the declarations of chivalry.

Modernist idea #5:   Economies of scale are sensible in all areas of life.

Existential idea #5:   Small and many are beautiful.

One of the triumphs of industrialism is the ability to bring enormous mechanical systems (and recently, with computers, knowledge systems) together in order to manufacture objects with less and less labor input, and thus to reduce their cost. The underlying assumption is that consuming more things is good—we call this a "higher standard of living." In order to consume more things, individual things must cost less. But when this economic calculus is the only one we consult in our decision making, we move inexorably toward the large institution that has the capital to invest in labor-saving systems.

Economist E. F. Schumacher reminds us that labor can be seen as more than a commodity or a duty: labor can be our gift to the community, and a practice that leads to skill and confidence and growth.[13] When we—as workers or as employers—define work without those noble qualities, we voluntarily reduce ourselves to variables in the economists' equations. In pursuing economic efficiency above all other goals, we sacrifice the diversity of local businesses and institutions to the single entity which can produce or sell or educate or entertain the most inexpensively.

This sacrifice of smallness has economic terms—profits flow out of the community, local investment is driven by distant motives—but it has more important terms. Fewer and larger organizations allow less diversity of goals and methods, less diversity of interaction and management.[14] People with different beliefs struggle to claim or define their own places, because places come to look and feel much the same. Our store and school managements are replaced by people who have no passion for what they do and make, and we are all diminished for not being introduced to those absent passions.

Social life acts on these same principles of small scale as well. Youth centers may be scaled for hundreds of kids, but hangouts are claimed by much smaller groups, because conversations don't happen among hundreds. Learning doesn't naturally occur in pods of twenty-five; it happens for individuals, for small clusters. We need to remember that we are not industrial units to be processed at least cost, that efficiency is not always our highest calling.

Modernist idea #6:   People are, most centrally, consumers.
Existential idea #6:   People are, most centrally, citizens.

As purchasers, as voters, as home buyers, we are inundated with meaningless choices that not only mask but create deeper similarities. Our demand for the lowest prices and the greatest number of options in every consumer choice leads us also to decisions about the landscape. If we insist on being able to choose from between thirty-six brands of deodorant and nineteen styles of link sausage in the same store, then we have also chosen one kind of store. If we insist on having low-priced tacos and hamburgers and fried chicken and pizza and submarine sandwiches all immediately available, then we have also selected one kind of merchant who will give it to us, and one kind of streetscape to put all of those similar merchants on. We receive amazing diversity at the smallest scale of consumer products, in exchange for an intense reduction of choice at the largest level of our communities.

If we spent our critical energies on shaping and sustaining the character of our public and shared lives instead of on whether to buy the shampoo/conditioner that adds body or the one that fights oiliness, our communities would become the work of our own hands rather than a landscape owned and managed by enormous institutions that keep us pacified with bogus choices and cents-off coupons.

Modernist idea #7:   Objective, consistent, and encompassing rules and codes are the basis for interaction.

Existential idea #7:   Negotiated agreements are both achievable and desirable.

As institutions get larger, Schumacher predicted that their regulations would become more and more rigid and encompassing. This is exactly what has happened over the past fifty years, according to attorney Philip K. Howard in his book *The Death of Common Sense*:

> We seem to have achieved the worst of both worlds: a system of regulation that goes too far while it also does too little. This paradox is explained by the absence of the one indispensable ingredient of any successful human endeavor: use of judgment. In the decades since World War II, we have constructed a system of regulatory law that basically outlaws common sense. Modern law, in an effort to be "self-executing," has shut out our humanity.

He also argues that there is a way out:

> The fears that keep us quivering in law's shadows are, in fact, the rudiments of a strong society. Constant exposure to uncertainty and disagreement is critical to everything we value, like responsibility, individualism, and community. . . . One basic change in approach will get us going: We should stop looking to law to provide the final answer. Law should articulate goals, award subsidies, allocate presumptions, and provide mechanisms for solving disagreements, but law should almost never provide the final answer. Life is too complex. Our public goals are too complex. . . . When accomplishment or understanding is important, we have no choice: Law can't think, and so law must be entrusted to humans and they must take responsibility for their interpretation of it.[15]

When we surrender the creation of school curricula to national publishers and state agencies, or the creation of our neighborhoods to traffic engineers and lending guidelines, we abdicate our social responsibilities, and negate our abilities to be kind or responsive or understanding. We become less human.

| **Modernist idea #8:** | Social classes and their neighborhoods should be separate. |
| **Existential idea #8:** | Social classes should claim their own spaces, but should also come into regular contact with each other as citizens and equals. |

Political science professor Evan McKenzie talks about walled and increasingly self-governed communities:

> I call it secession by the successful. When we think about citizenship in our communities, we think of some concept of rights and responsibilities. But common interest developments encourage secessionist mentalities. They give people a variety of incentives for not seeing themselves as belonging to their city or county, since they belong to associations that provide services such as recreation centers, swimming pools, and parks. Meanwhile, those cities and counties shrivel from neglect.[16]

This secession and abandonment can do nothing but foster resentment among have-nots, who can read the meaning behind the fences and decorative gates and culs-de-sac that protect (from whom, after all?) the relatively well-to-do. Better to encourage small-scale contact on our sidewalks and business areas that will allow us to see one another as people, with concerns and lives that are not entirely alien to our own.

| **Modernist idea #9:** | Business, services, and residences should be separate. |
| **Existential idea #9:** | Zoning should be primarily by scale of development rather than by type. |

A neighborhood of 1500-square-foot houses would be overwhelmed both visually and in traffic with the addition of a Kmart or a teen center or a high school or a major restaurant. But older cities everywhere hold examples of corner groceries and taverns and bookstores that not only blend into the neighborhoods but offer casual and welcome opportunities for public life. There is a place for large institutions, from factories to supermarkets to baseball stadiums, places that cater to huge crowds drawn from broad regions. Let them cluster together to share large roads and large parking areas, but don't class the hairdresser or the accountant or the florist in with that category. Their small shops will disappear in the shadows of the giants, and our neighborhoods will be poorer without their presence.

Modernist idea #10:   Countryside is a necessary refuge from undesirable city living.

Existential idea #10:   Countryside and city life both contribute to a complex, satisfying landscape.

The desire to "get away from it all" has resulted in our increasingly common pattern of petite ranchettes spreading further and further into the countryside.[17] The housing pattern of dispersed half-acre lots, with its associated increases in car travel and demand for utilities, constitutes an enormously resource-expensive way to build a city. It also makes a trip to real wilderness a more time- and resource-consuming venture for the majority of us. This is not just a big-city phenomenon: Curtisville's residents are spread as far as the ocean and the rivers and the timber companies will allow.

The citizens of Oregon recognized in the early 1970s that the sprawling patterns of development they saw in Los Angeles and the East and South Bay regions near San Francisco were starting to occur in Portland and Eugene and Salem and their smaller towns as well, and they did something about it. They instituted a state planning code that incorporated strict (and small) development boundaries around their communities.[18] This has resulted in a replication of an earlier pattern of living spaces in which most workers and managers lived in town, and farmers and ranchers lived out of town where the resource they needed—land in large parcels—was available. It has also spurred intelligent public debate about what makes good cities, because most Oregonians recognize that they do indeed live in town. Curtisville's residents denied that they lived in a considerable city, and that denial took the form of minimum lot sizes, vast spaces between buildings, and the mostly symbolic possession of nature via the lawn and the hedge and the view of the trees uphill.

Modernist idea #11: High densities of people are unsafe and unhealthy.

Existential idea #11: Concentration of people can encourage social connection and public safety.

The confusion between density and crowding is behind most of the sprawl we see in our communities, behind the desire to get away from all of those people. Some of the most desirable neighborhoods in our country are very dense, but are not seen as being crowded; people are able to go about their lives without undue hindrance from others. Curtisville's residents, on the other hand, increasingly believe that their community is crowded. This should not be a surprise: all of the town's travel is constrained into automobiles, onto a few busy streets, headed to a few enormous institutions, at a few hours of the day. Numerical density does not lead inevitably to perceived crowding, but an area unequipped for social life does.

Jane Jacobs talks about the security benefits of busy sidewalks and close-knit neighborhoods:

> The first thing to understand is that the public peace—the sidewalk and street peace—of cities is not kept primarily by the police, necessary as the police are. It is kept primarily by an intricate, almost unconscious, network of voluntary controls and standards among the people themselves, and enforced by the people themselves.[19]

In communities where the physical environment lends itself to public living, the sight of other people milling about does not send the residents scurrying for cover or calling the real estate agents. It is taken as a sign that something interesting and lively is going on, an invitation to watch or participate.

Modernist idea #12: Home and land ownership is the key to community.

Existential idea #12:   Easy social contact is the key to community.

The sanctity of the house and family is of little comfort if the surrounding neighborhoods—and the neighbors—are threatening. Sociologist Ray Oldenburg has studied the history and demise of what he calls "third places," or in the partial list that forms the subtitle to his book, "cafes, coffee shops, community centers, beauty parlors, general stores, bars, hangouts, and how they get you through the day." He identifies several important social functions of these places: they encourage political and cultural dialogue; they lead to other forms of community association and interaction; they act as agencies of social control in which the regulars police their own and others' behavior to common norms; they allow an escape from workplace and home routines but still maintain limits on acceptable actions; and they act as stations of surveillance in the public spaces around them.[20]

In much the same way, planning critic Jane Jacobs described several uses of that most humble of hangouts, the sidewalk. Sidewalks provide social contact, public safety, and a playground that assimilates children into adult social patterns.[21] By forcing children off the streets and into institutionally provided recreation, by taking hangouts away from neighborhoods, we have destroyed the social cohesion and civility of our communities and made strangers of one another.

Modernist idea #13:   Places should closely fit their specialized functions.

Existential idea #13:   Environments should be easily converted to new and multiple uses.

Landscape historian Paul Groth has described a major shift in the basic conception of our buildings and roads between the nineteenth and twentieth centuries.[22] The earlier era saw what he calls the "isonomic" landscape, in which elements were small and interchangeable and relatively uniform. It was the age of the grid street plan, the row house, the downtown of connected small rectangular stores behind continuous block-long facades. The surface uniformity of these checkerboard landscapes hid a great diversity of ever-changing uses; a garage became a five-and-dime became a furniture showroom became two storefronts with furniture behind one and surfboards behind the other.

By contrast, Groth labels the post-Civil War industrial period—and even more our own age—a time of the "monomic" landscape, characterized by specialization of buildings to fit their functions, by integrating the building with the processes that go on inside it, by an increased segregation of transportation modes and social functions. It is the age of airports and limited-access freeways, of gas stations and gymnasiums, places which suit their activities perfectly but which are hard to convert or claim for other uses.

The Modern landscape pattern contributes to the difficulty of the young and the old in using their cities without cars, given that the only connections through town are on major arterial roads. It contributes to the great separation of commercial buildings, located as they are in seas of separately owned, single-purpose paving. It lends itself toward a rigidity in use that doesn't allow for easy modification or multiple purpose. It encourages the institutionalization of our communities.

Architect Christopher Alexander has been one of the strongest advocates for multiplying the roles that places carry. He wrote:

> The difference between prose and poetry is not that different languages are used, but that the same language is used, differently. In an ordinary English sentence, each word has one meaning, and the sentence too, has one simple meaning. In a poem, the meaning is far more dense. Each word carries several meanings; and the sentence as a whole carries an enormous density of interlocking meanings, which together illuminate the whole. . . . it is also possible to put [architectural] patterns together in such a way that many many patterns overlap in the same physical space: the building is very dense; it has many meanings captured in a small space; and through this density, it becomes profound.[23]

If these Existential articles of faith, these thirteen theses, were held widely by the residents of a particular place, there would be some material outcomes that would be nearly inevitable. For starters, if more people held themselves within the city, the land outside the city would be continuous, wide-ranging, and in fact more accessible for more people in less driving time (not to mention for people without cars). Many of our environmental problems—loss of habitat and species diversity, fossil fuel depletion, greenhouse gas concentration—would be enormously eased.

School would be brought back into town. Or more properly, many small schools based around work and practice would be dispersed throughout the public areas of the community, bringing teenagers into constant and close contact with adults who could show them not only skills and attitudes but also compelling visions of whole adult lives. These local schools would include places for performance, places to explore skills in a public setting, places in which useful products made in school were actually used—the kinds of places where each individual would bear a responsibility to themselves, to their fellow participants and to their larger community. These specialized facilities would, of course, no longer be the particular domain of teenagers, just as the experience of public life and the expectation of public duty would no longer be.

The community would be filled with places for informal public life as well, innumerable gathering spots as small as taverns and as large as parks. These would be located not on a handful of available sites with no regard to the needs of the surrounding community, but banded together sensibly to increase their social gravity: some in larger civic cores, some in smaller neighborhood clusters. A park with no other social spaces around it will be little used, not because of its inconvenience but because it is a revealing admission of need to go there. A park, even a poorly equipped park, at the edge of a busy sidewalk with bars and coffee shops and movies and bookstores and passers-by, will be a busy park because it can be used in a more natural and relaxed fashion.[24] You wouldn't have to "go to the park," because the park would be where you already were.

This gravity of public activity means that there would not be a uniform sprinkling of social-commercial amenities throughout the town, but rather more and less concentrated areas of public life. Any family or individual could choose how closely they wish to participate in this public life by choosing how close they live to one of the centers.

The resulting neighborhoods would almost certainly have distinctive appearances and different populations, but they would be connected to one another at many edges. The security-walled development and the exclusive cul-de-sac would be terrifically inconvenient in a smaller, more pedestrian town where commercial and social possibilities might lie in several directions.

Within these condensed and intertwined communities, buildings would look fairly similar in overall mass within specific neighborhoods, because the land would almost certainly be zoned by building size rather than by building function. A small restaurant or a small store would be no threat to the sanctity of homes around it. Quite the contrary—the increased activity would bring more surveillance to the street, more eyes to observe potential misbehavior. It would allow adults to walk for small chores or pleasure trips, and thus bolster street life even further. And it would vastly multiply children's and teenagers' exposure to and understanding of ways of earning a living, and offer them easier possibility of working odd jobs themselves as a first entry into the economic world.

Commercial buildings and landscapes would be fairly modest and somewhat generic in their basic layout, so as to be usable for the greatest number of potential tenants. The nature of business is to grow and decline, to have periods of success and periods of failure. A small and roughly rectangular space can house almost any function, from residence to small retail shop to independent school to professional office. A uniquely specialized building like a chain supermarket or a car-based restaurant is difficult to amend to any other purpose—how many businesses or institutions need a dual tractor-trailer dock, forty thousand square feet of floor space, and three hundred parking stalls? How many kinds of businesses need a drive-through window?

The increased number and decreased scale of businesses, just like the increased number and decreased scale of schools, would serve to reduce the institutionality and coldness of public life. No longer would the concept of grocery shopping be limited to a hectic car trip to a mega-market for a week's worth of food. No longer would dining out be restricted to a paper bag balanced on the center console of the car. No longer would cashiers need name badges on their aprons to simulate familiarity, nor would decision makers reside hundreds of miles away and make personnel cuts via the fax machine. No longer would Curtisville's teenagers have to leave town for other nearby communities whenever they wanted to be citizens.

ॐ

Beliefs have the power to change artifacts, but artifacts hold their own strength: their material conditions shape and guide the actions of their holders, lending their forces of repetition and convenience and utility to help form our thoughts about what is right and good. If our imagined Existential landscape were to be plunked down from the sky tomorrow to replace the Curtisville that exists now, it would probably serve to change a lot of Modern beliefs through the experience of new patterns of living that have different satisfactions.

But landscapes are built in snippets, and changes in established places and beliefs are incremental and slow. Most projections indicate that the fifteen thousand who live in Curtisville now will become thirty thousand in the next twenty years, and it is seductive and common to think that the community is at some unique branching point for its future. There *is* time—barely—to make Curtisville into something more than a water-provision district, more than a series of individual lots each of which has captured its tiny slice of tidy and defensible nature. There is time to make Main Street a place where people walk voluntarily and run into one another by joyful accident. There is time to prevent the forests above town from being eaten away in half-acre bites, one secluded house at a time.

It won't happen, though. The community planning volunteers and Service District board members share the beliefs about privacy and class and property ownership and car travel that have led to Curtisville's present condition. They will not make their town into a diverse, social city; their beliefs preclude it. Curtisville exists in the form that it does for a reason: it matches the expectations of comfortable community held by a great number of people.

Urban planning analysts have argued for decades about whether consumer demand has driven our common forms of suburban development, or whether the economic logic of land development has resulted in a handful of patterns that limit consumer housing and community choices. This chicken-and-egg real estate analysis misses one vastly important point, however: not everyone who lives in Curtisville has chosen to live there.

Curtisville's children and teenagers had no say in where they lived. They were not consulted about housing or community choices before their families arrived. Their residency was an accident of birth, or of divorce, or of parental job opportunity. The rational choices that their parents made about lower housing costs and convenient access to Highway 420 and views of the hillside forests were made in response to a set of conditions that included car ownership and permanent employment and limited free time and fixed social roles and capital to invest in a home. None of these conditions are shared by their teenaged children; it can be no surprise that those kids, in the course of their own thoughtful deliberations, chose other places. When they wanted public life—which they wanted a lot of—they drove or rode the bus to Union or Port City and then walked the town or the mall. When they wanted nature, they drove or bicycled to Oyster Beach or out into the forest. When they wanted solitude, they locked themselves in their rooms. Curtisville itself, that land mass of a dozen square miles outside their homes, offered them nothing.

And yet, in this midst of this barren landscape, joy burst up through the dry ground in unexpected places. It appeared in classrooms where rules were broken or bent, where the messy act of learning took precedence over tidy frameworks. It visited sporting fields, both official and impromptu, on which people strove to do something they hadn't been able to do before. It lived in older friends' garages, masquerading as the disassembled front end of a pickup, and it inhabited both the mosh pit and the stage. Joy found those places where the leveling pavement of Modernism had left a small crack, and forced its way through. That so many of those cracks were adjacent to teenagers is no coincidence; they had not yet fully succumbed to the ways of thinking and acting that would mark their final transition from "adolescence" to "adulthood."

With any luck, they never will.

Notes

Preface

1. Not only have all peoples' names been changed through this book, but so have all of the names of businesses and governmental agencies, cities and counties. Also, the facts of cartography and geographical relationships have been mildly amended. The issues and ethics of privacy are interesting. In every case but one, the kids I interviewed and followed *wanted* me to use their real names, wanted to present themselves to the world as real people. The name changes have been done more to protect the privacy of adults who were not the focus of the stories—parents, teachers, school administrators—than those who supposedly "need" protection due to their status as minors.

Chapter 1

1. An extended discussion of the knowledge of reason versus the knowledge of immersion can be found in Michael Polanyi's *Knowing and Being: Essays of Michael Polanyi*, ed. Marjorie Grene (Chicago: University of Chicago Press, 1969).

2. The geographer J. Nicholas Entrikin, in his book *The Betweenness of Place: Towards a Geography of Modernity* (Baltimore: Johns Hopkins University Press, 1991), describes "narrative" as "seeing things together," a synthetic rather than analytic way of knowing that is at the heart of "place." It is this synthetic scholarship that I pursue, because it is people's synthetic experiences that interest me.

3. Ruthellen Josselson, "A Narrative Introduction," in *The Narrative Study of Lives*, ed. Ruthellen Josselson and Amia Lieblich (Newbury Park, CA: Sage, 1993).

317

4. Laurel Richardson, "Writing: A Method of Inquiry," in *Handbook of Qualitative Research*, ed. Norman K. Denzin and Yvonna S. Lincoln (Thousand Oaks, CA: Sage, 1994).

5. Jean-Paul Sartre, "A Plea for Intellectuals," in *Between Existentialism and Marxism*, trans. John Matthews (New York: Pantheon, 1974).

6. David Bartholomae and Anthony Petrosky, *Ways of Reading: An Anthology for Writers* (3rd ed.) (Boston: Bedford, 1993).

7. An extended discussion of these beliefs about ethnographic writing can be found in my 1998 article, "Kinder Ethnographic Writing," *Qualitative Inquiry* 4:2, 249–264.

Chapter 2

1. Almost every geographer, it seems, who has done landscape analysis has also put forth a primer on how to read a landscape. Perhaps the best known, and a good starting point, is Pierce Lewis' "Axioms for Reading the Landscape: Some Guides to the American Scene" in *The Interpretation of Ordinary Landscapes*, ed. Donald Meinig (New York: Oxford University Press, 1979). Among the alternatives that have guided me is Denis Cosgrove's "Geography is Everywhere: Culture and Symbolism in Human Landscapes," in *Horizons in Human Geography*, ed. Derek Gregory and Rex Walford (London: Macmillan, 1983), 118–135, which deals extensively with different cultures inhabiting the same landscape at once and the different artifacts they place. Edward Relph's "Seeing, Thinking and Describing Landscapes" in *Environmental Perception and Behavior*, University of Chicago Department of Geography Research Paper No. 209, ed. Thomas F. Saarinen, David Seamon and James L. Sell (Chicago: University of Chicago Press, 1984), 209–23, offers a passionate plea for seeing before thinking, for the value of description above theory. As much as any article can, Henry Glassie's "Studying Material Culture Today" in *Living in a Material World: Canadian and American Approaches to Material Culture*, Social and Economic Paper No. 19, ed. Gerald L. Poicus, (St. John's: Institute of Social and Economic Research, Memorial University of Newfoundland, 1991), has led me to a consistent way of thinking about things as clues both to the culture that made them and to the individuals who consume and use them. Together, these four articles would be my required reading in a deeper discussion of landscape interpretation.

2. Mall research locates at a fascinating intersection between sociology, urban planning, consumer psychology and real-estate economics.

Among the most interesting are Jerry Jacobs' social examination, *The Mall: An Attempted Escape from Everyday Life* (Prospect Heights, IL: Wavelength Press, 1984); John R. White and Kevin D. Gray's design and real-estate manual, *Shopping Centers and Other Retail Properties* (New York: John Wiley and Sons, 1996); and William Severini Kowinski's social history and travelogue, *The Malling of America* (New York: William Morrow, 1985). Kowinski's chapter 12, "The Invention of the Mall: *Eureka* in Edina, Minnesota" (115–124) offers an engaging look at architect Victor Gruen's ingenious development of the Southland Mall in 1956, and the race by Gruen and competing developer Edward DeBartolo to capitalize on the new building type.

Chapter 5

1. Roger Callois, *Man, Play and Games* (New York: Free Press of Glencoe, 1961), talks specifically about the mechanical amplification of vertigo, as in amusement park rides. Driving is only one of many such vertigo games that Curtisville's kids took part in—others included dancing to exhaustion, surfing, cliff diving, the mosh pit, or just tumbling on the beach or running through the woods. MTV, recognizing the popularity of these "wild" sports among its young audience, has created an athletic series called the "Extreme Games" which is a collection of vertiginous sporting events.

2. Grant McCracken, in his article "Culture and Consumption: A Theoretical Account of the Structure and Movement of the Cultural Meaning of Consumer Goods," *Journal of Consumer Research* 13 (June 1986): 71–84, delivers an intelligent discussion of the symbolic properties of brand name products and the ways that fashion and advertising conjoin cultural meaning with physical consumer objects.

3. This fact is noted by comedian George Carlin in his monologue about people who pick their noses in their cars, as though they were invisible. We do to some extent believe that we are wholly isolated in our cars, even at stop signs and traffic lights with cars parked next to us. The physical and auditory removal is a powerful signal that we are in private, even though we may only be surrounded by safety glass.

4. Russell W. Belk, "Possessions and the Extended Self," *Journal of Consumer Research* 15 (September 1988): 139–68, has coined the important term "the extended self" to talk about significant possessions, and claims that we invest them with our identity through processes of use, knowledge, mastery, creation, or modification, and the power to give away or sell.

5. Theodore Goldberg's 1969 study of cruising, "The Automobile: A Social Institution for Adolescents," *Environment and Behavior* 1, no. 2

(December 1969): 157–85, dealt with the externality of the car—its path, speed, number and locations of stops, encounters with other cruisers—but not at all with the social life within the car. Although harder to see, this is above all the reason for cruising. For a good view inside the car, see Thomas French, *South of Heaven: A Year in the Life of an American High School at the End of the Twentieth Century* (New York: Doubleday, 1993), 221–229.

Chapter 8

1. "bowl:" enough marijuana to fill the bowl of a pipe, typically shared among a small group.

Chapter 9

1. Mark Francis captures this perfectly when he talks of participatory landscapes. He cites S. H. Lennard and J. L. Lennard, *Public Life in Urban Places* (Southamptom: Gondolier Press, 1984); quoted in Mark Francis, "Control as a Dimension of Public-Space Quality," in *Public Places and Spaces*, ed. I. Altman and E. Zube (New York: Plenum, 1989), 147–72, as they say:

> A public space . . . is at once both stage and theater, for in public the spectators may at any moment choose to become actors themselves. Successful public places accentuate the dramatic qualities of personal and family life. They make visible certain tragic, comic, and tender aspects of relationships among friends, neighbors, relatives, or lovers. (148)

2. The best exposition of the physical forms of public interaction is still William H. Whyte's *The Social Life of Small Urban Spaces* (Washington D.C.: Conservation Foundation, 1980).

3. Philosopher James Ogilvy, in *Living Without a Goal*, (New York: Bantam Doubleday Dell, 1995), gives a telling comment on our changing concept of moviegoing in his discussion of Howard Hughes' last days:

> Decades before the invention of the VCR, Hughes was a pioneer in the practice of watching movies as an audience of one. He withdrew into his prototype electronic grotto to sit alone and watch old movies long before the time of videotapes. What is now so easy for millions to do he accomplished by having his own projector. Stacks of bulky thirty-five-millimeter film cans

cluttered his room. When people discovered at the time of his death that he had indulged himself in orgies of old movies, they regarded this unheard-of practice as a clear sign of madness. *What? Watch a movie alone? You watch movies in movie theaters. You watch television alone.* Today we cannot cast the stone of madness so quickly without risking our own glass houses now that most households have a videocassette recorder. Many now know the pleasures that Hughes indulged. His "madness" has been democratized by the advent of the VCR. (99)

Chapter 11

1. Michel Foucault, in "Of Other Spaces: Utopias and Heterotopias," refers to something like this negative space and time when he discusses "heterotopias:"

There also exist, and this is probably true for all cultures and all civilizations, real and effective spaces which are outlined in the very institution of society, but which constitute a sort of counterarrangement, of effectively realized utopia, in which all the real arrangements, all the other real arrangements that can be found within society, are at one and the same time represented, challenged, and overturned: a sort of place that lies outside all places and yet is actually localizable. (422)

2. Childress, "No Loitering: Some Ideas on Small Town Teenage Hangouts," *Small Town* 24, no. 2 (September/October 1993): 20–24.

Chapter 12

1. This dialogue comes from U.S. Department of Defense, *Exploring Careers: The ASVAB Workbook*, (Washington D.C.: Government Printing Office, 1994), pp. 4-2 and 4-3.

2. It is a common mistake to see school as a conflict between students and teachers. The conflict is built into the institutionality of the system itself, as Douglas Biklen notes in the "Politics of Institutions," in *An Alternative Textbook in Special Education: People, Schools and Other Institutions*, ed. B. Blatt, D. Biklen, and R. Bogdan (Denver: Love Publishing, 1977) regarding the asylum:

Unless we examine the broader issues of deviance and social control, for example, people may conclude that the conditions described can be altered or eradicated by making several changes in personnel, physical structure, and funding. . . .

Institutions are products primarily of society, not of individuals, and the effects of institutionalization can best be understood as originating from social rather than individual forces. (35)

Chapter 13

1. The first use of this phrase is by Alison King, "From Sage on the Stage to Guide on the Side," *College Teaching* 41, no. 1 (Winter 1993), 30–35.

Chapter 15

1. In Mihaly Csikszentmihalyi's book, *Flow: The Psychology of Optimal Experience* (New York: HarperPerennial, 1991), 74, he draws a diagram that compares the challenges provided by an activity to the skills that the individual brings to the activity. The state of flow, or complete absorption, is at or near the balanced line where skills and demands are roughly equal.

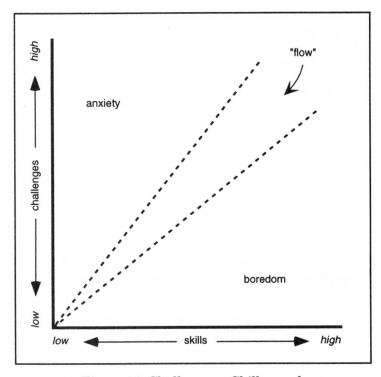

Figure 14. Challenges x Skills graph

But eighteen years before the writing of *Flow*, and in an entirely different discipline, the same graph and concepts appeared.

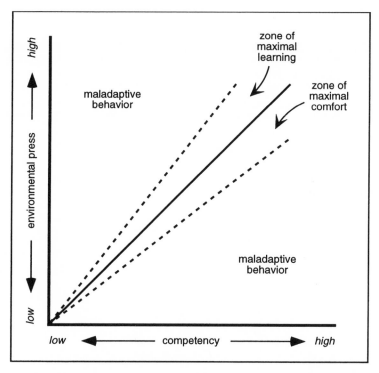

Figure 15. Environmental Press x Competency graph

According to M. Powell Lawton and Lucille Nahemow, in "Ecology and the Aging Process," in *Psychology of Adult Development and Aging*, ed. C. Eisdorfer and M. P. Lawton (Hyattsville, MD: American Psychological Association, 1973); quoted in M. Powell Lawton, *Environment and Aging* (Albany, NY: Center for the Study of Aging, 1986), 12, environments which place slightly higher demands than the individual is competent to manage fall within a range they describe as the "zone of maximum performance potential" or "maximum learning;" environments just below the level of competence are called the "zone of maximum comfort." Environments that are too far away from this balance —whether highly stressful or utterly boring—are often characterized by what Lawton and Nahemow refer to as "maladaptive behavior." The parallels with school are clear.

Chapter 16

1. I felt guilty about this need for escape for quite a while, berating my commitment and skills. Then I discovered Douglas Biklen's account of doing ethnography in a state school for the developmentally disabled, "Politics of Institutions," and read:

> One observer at the Southern State School wrote in his field notes, after only a few hours of observation, "I feel like I've spent the longest five hours of my life." . . . In the evening, after leaving the premises, the observer noted, "I almost felt as though I was escaping illegally. I can honestly say that I have never felt what the word 'freedom' meant until those moments when I drove off the grounds." (31)

Chapter 17

1. There has been a fair amount of research on childhood and teenage mobility when compared to a number of different outcome measurements. Anne B. Hendershott found, in "Residential Mobility, Social Support and Adolescent Self-Concept," *Adolescence* 24, no. 93 (Spring 1989): 217–32, that frequent moving was tied to low feelings of mastery over the environment, and the more recent the previous move, the greater the frequency of depression; both of these negative outcomes could be lessened by social support from family. Sally Shumaker and Gerald Conti's review of the history of mobility research, "Understanding Mobility in America," in *Home Environments*, ed. I. Altman and C. Werner (New York: Prager, 1985) 237–53, seems to demonstrate that involuntary moves are more stressful than voluntary, a finding not directly learned from kids but directly applicable to their circumstances. They wisely indicate, though, that the decision to move the household is highly complex, and that it may indeed be a positive circumstance.

2. This diagram, and the phrase B-L-G, came from Tom Hubka's course in *American Vernacular Architecture* at the University of Wisconsin—Milwaukee.

3. Most of the work that's been done in the realm of shared-wall spaces concerns apartments. In fact, that's probably a useful way to think about the teenager's room—it's a studio apartment that holds many of the functions of living, in ways that adults can spread throughout the house. See in particular Jill Stoner, "The Party Wall as the Architecture of Sharing," in *New Households, New Housing*, ed. Karen Franck and Sherry Ahrentzen (New York: Van Nostrand Rinehold, 1989), 127–40.

4. Amos Rapoport, *House Form and Culture*, (Englewood Cliffs, NJ: Prentice Hall), 1969.

5. Jane Jacobs, *The Death and Life of Great American Cities*, (New York: Vintage), 1961.

Chapter 19

1. Terence Lee, "Urban Neighborhood as a Socio-Spatial Schema," *Human Relations* 21 (1968): 241–68.

2. This point is raised by Mike Davis in *City of Quartz* (London: Verso, 1990), as well as by Philip Langdon in "A Good Place to Live," *The Atlantic Monthly*, March 1988, 269–88.

3. A number of women have written on the effects of suburban planning and isolated neighborhoods on single mothers, the poor, and the elderly, keeping them from full participation in community life: see especially Jacqueline Leavitt and Mary Beth Welch, "Older Women and the Suburbs: A Literature Review," *Women's Studies Quarterly* 1 and 2 (1989): 35–47; Linda McDowell, "Women, Gender and the Organisation of Space," in *Horizons in Geography*, ed. Derek Gregory and Rex Walford (Totowa, NJ: Barnes & Noble, 1989), 136–52; and Marsha Ritzdorf, "Women and the City: Land Use and Zoning Issues," *Urban Resources* 3, no. 2 (Winter 1986): 23–27. Jeanne Kay demonstrates, in "Landscapes of Women and Men: Rethinking the Regional Historical Geography of the United States and Canada," *Journal of Historical Geography* 17, no. 4 (1991): 435–52, that academic discussions are notable for their absence of women and their unstated belief that male history equals history.

The emergence of feminism and women's studies has slowly brought about an awareness of women's needs and roles in their neighborhoods, and the understanding that neighborhoods designed to be attractive to male heads of household may not be suited to women. There is, unfortunately, only a tiny corresponding body of youth studies that has advocated for the understanding of teenagers in their communities. Most likely, this is because adulthood brings with it a more lasting set of biases that will affect people for their entire lives, and activists and academics turn their attention to these causes. Simply put, women's advocates remain women, ethnic-group advocates remain ethnic minorities, disabled advocates remain disabled, but youth advocates grow up.

4. Jane Jacobs, *Great American Cities*, 119.

5. This is supported by the work of Louise Chawla, "Childhood Place Attachments," in *Place Attachment*, ed. I. Altman and S. Low (New York: Plenum, 1992), 67.

Chapter 23

1. Jonathan Kozol, *Savage Inequalities*, (New York: Crown Publishers, 1991).

2. Murray Silverstein and Max Jacobson, "Restructuring the Hidden Program: Toward an Architecture of Social Change," in *Programming the Built Environment*, ed. W. Preiser (New York: Van Nostrand, 1985), 150.

3. Trevor J. Barnes and James S. Duncan write about our metaphorical ways of knowing in "Introduction," in *Writing Worlds: Discourse, Text and Metaphor in the Representation of Landscape*, ed. Trevor J. Barnes and James S. Duncan, (London: Routledge, 1990), 1–17. They argue that metaphors allow us to:

> . . . see the world in a different way; a way that could not be imagined before the metaphor was used. . . . metaphors are implicated in the very fabric of society and social processes; if they are to work they must resonate against an existing set of social and cultural representations (11–12).

4. Architecture is, of course, as limited by codes as is our behavior. Clare Cooper Marcus and Wendy Sarkissian give the example in *Housing as if People Mattered* (Berkeley: University of California Press, 1986), of an enormous and carefully researched study of children's play areas in Britain which resulted in a rigorous set of standards for play areas nationwide. These standards led to underused or unused playgrounds in many individual applications. "Once standards are quantified, they may be applied in a rubber stamp fashion. Where standards relate to psychological and social matters, this encourages a blindness to real human needs." (18)

5. Derek Drummond, "The Impact of Mergers and Megalomania on the Urban Environment," paper presented at the 26th Annual Conference of the Environmental Design Research Association, Boston, MA, 1995.

6. James and Carolyn Robertson noted almost twenty years ago in *The Small Towns Book* (Garden City, NY: Anchor Books, 1978), the movement of decisionmaking from local to county to state governments:

> Increasingly, the daily business in the warrens of state government translates into directives and mandates that are a burden on local officials and render these officials helpless to deal with mounting demands for reform from hard-pressed citizens. In

effect, the state government, through the administration of its own and federal programs, has usurped the right of local jurisdictions to govern themselves. (197)

7. California Department of Education, *Reporting the 1994 State Assessment* (Sacramento: California Department of Education, 1994).

8. Of course, as Hugh Klein notes in "Adolescence, Youth and Young Adulthood: Rethinking Current Conceptualizations of Life Stage," *Youth and Society* 21, no. 4 (June 1990), 446–71: the very definitions of childhood, adolescence, and education are based around the needs of the organized industrial economy:

> The system of education thus took on an extra added level of importance; for now it not only helped prepare some children for the newly created complex jobs, but also sheltered them from undergoing the cruelties of child labor and/or indentured apprenticeship. (453)

Earlier conceptions of childhood were in turn linked to the economic realities of skilled independent crafts and agriculture.

9. Geographer Roger Lee notes in his article "The Future of the Region: Regional Geography as Education for Transformation," in *Geographical Futures*, ed. Roger Lee (Sheffield: The Geographical Association, 1985), 77–91, that the idea of specific place is central to specific social action, and that an education of generalities is an education that leads to subservience. He concludes:

> As for the future of regional geography: that, as should be predictable by now, depends upon how we act to make it. If we accept an education directed at technical control, it is largely irrelevant; if however,we seek an education defined by transformation, it is crucial. (90)

Chapter 24

1. The very idea that recreation is something to be provided rather than found is relatively new. Social historian Sanford Gaster, in "Urban Children's Access To Their Neighborhoods: Changes Over Three Generations," *Environment and Behavior* 23, no. 1 (January 1991): 70–85, explored the ways in which children in one New York neighborhood have been systematically cut off from opportunities for unsupervised neighborhood play and exploration in favor of a handful of professionally administered play environments. Norwegian historian Albert

Eide Parr, in "The Child in the City: Urbanity and the Urban Scene," *Landscape* 16, no. 3 (1967): 3–5, has written a compelling account— barely believable to modern readers—of the ways in which he, *as a five-year-old*, was allowed and even encouraged to travel by himself throughout his hometown of 75,000 residents.

2. Because of the anonymity of the community and region, citations to local newspaper and newsletter articles are not offered here.

3. Galen Cranz, *The Politics of Park Design* (Cambridge, MA: MIT Press, 1989).

4. All language from the playground signs is copyrighted 1986 by Quality Industries, Inc.

5. Roy Rosenzweig, "Middle-Class Parks and Working-Class Play: The Struggle Over Recreational Space in Worcester, Massachusetts, 1870–1910," *Radical History Review* 21 (1980): 31–46.

6. Paul Groth, "Vernacular Parks," in *Denatured Visions: Landscape and Culture in the Twentieth Century*, ed. Stuart Wrede and William Howard Adams (New York: Museum of Modern Art, 1991), 136.

7. Laura Hall, "Teenagers in Suburbia: A Case Study in Rohnert Park, California" (Masters thesis, University of California at Berkeley, 1990), 19.

8. For more on the environmental characteristics that allow good hangouts to arise, see Ray Oldenburg's *The Great Good Place* (New York: Paragon, 1989), 20–42, and my own article, "No Loitering."

9. It would be absurd, and thus useful, to imagine an architectural program for the design of a Chinatown or a servant's quarters or a sweatshop; these somewhat offensive stereotypes are no different than a teen center in that they are a conception by a powerful group of the needs of a less powerful group. This conception will always be—can *only* be—made in the image and the language of the masters. See Kay Anderson's "The Idea of Chinatown: The Power of Place and Institutional Practice in the Making of a Racial Category," *Annals of the Association of American Geographers* 77, no. 4 (1987): 580–98, a study of the social invention, by British settlers of Vancouver, of the concept of "Chinatown."

10. The danger of complete reliance upon institutions for social recreation can be shown through the work of John Woodward and his colleagues on the loneliness of rural teenagers: John C. Woodward and Barbara D. Frank, "Rural Adolescent Coping Strategies," *Adolescence* 32, no. 91 (Fall 1988): 559–565; and John C. Woodward and Violet Kalyan-Masih, "Loneliness, Coping Strategies and Cognitive Styles of the Gifted Rural Adolescent," *Adolescence* 35, no. 100 (Winter 1990):

977–88. Together, these articles show that when teenagers are held apart from adult society but only provided a handful of approved social outlets, it becomes more likely that individual kids will not be reached. There is little redundancy in recreation in a small town because the residents simply can't afford to provide very many options. As long as the conception of recreation is of something that must in fact be provided rather than discovered or invented within the community at large, teenage loneliness and alienation will continue to be a problem.

Chapter 25

1. Mihaly Csikszentmihalyi, *Flow*, 3.

2. Mihaly Csikszentmihalyi, *Flow*, 41.

3. The French sociologist Roger Callois, in his book *Man, Play, and Games*, 14–26, has written about an entire class of games he calls *ilnix* games, taken from the Greek word for whirlpool. The entire point of such games is to surrender control while at the same time attempting to reassert it, to make meaningful actions within unpredictable circumstances.

4. Herb Childress, "Place, Image and Narrative: A New Approach to Place Attachment," in *Proceedings of the 24th Annual Conference of the Environmental Design Research Association held in San Antonio, March 20–24, 1994*, ed. A. Seidel (Oklahoma City: Environmental Design Research Association, 1995), 55–61.

5. California Department of Education, *Reporting the 1994 State Assessment*.

6. Paraphrased from the sentence, "One of the essentials of boredom consists in the contrast between present circumstances and some other more agreeable circumstances which force themselves irresistibly upon the imagination." Bertrand Russell, *The Conquest of Happiness* (New York: Liveright, 1930), 56–57.

7. The diagram is amended from the work of Russell (American Psychological Association, 1980) as cited in Michael Argyle, *The Psychology of Happiness* (London and New York: Methuen & Co., 1987), 127. Reprinted by permission of James Russell and the American Psychological Association.

8. For a discussion of the self-in-place as the answers to a series of "pronominal questions," see Theodore Sarbin's article, "Place Identity as a Component of Self: An Addendum," *Journal of Environmental Psychology* 3 (1983): 337–42.

9. The nature of emotions as future-referent is pointed out most strongly in Jean-Paul Sartre's *The Emotions: Outline of a Theory*, trans. Bernard Frechtman (Secaucus, NJ: Citadel Press, 1976).

10. Mike Males, *The Scapegoat Generation: America's War on Adolescents* (Monroe, ME: Common Courage Press, 1996).

11. Eugene Borowitz, *A Layman's Guide to Religious Existentialism* (Philadelphia: Westminster Press, 1965), 106–8.

12. There are enough readings on both Modernism and Existentialism to keep an entire generation of graduate students busy (and confused). So I will offer the citations that have been my primary guides to these two competing narratives.

For Modernism, the book above all others for the past ten years has been Marshall Berman's *All That Is Solid Melts into Air: The Experience of Modernity* (New York: Simon & Schuster, 1982). An interesting extension of Berman's work is found in the debate between Berman and Perry Anderson: Perry Anderson, "Modernity and Revolution," *New Left Review* 144 (March/April 1984): 96–113 and Marshall Berman, "The Signs in the Street: A Response to Perry Anderson," *New Left Review* 144 (March/April 1984): 114–123. Another more architecturally specific work is Manfredo Tafuri's *Architecture and Utopia* (Cambridge, MA: MIT Press, 1976). In my search for Modernism, I have also been guided by many thinkers who refer to themselves as Postmodern, since they help to define Modernism as the intellectual tradition that they are acting both within and against. They include Frederic Jameson's "Postmodernism, or the Cultural Logic of Late Capitalism," *New Left Review* 146 (1984): 53–92; David Harvey's *The Condition of Postmodernity* (London: Blackwell, 1990); Edward Soja's *Postmodern Geographies* (London: Verso, 1989); Sharon Zukin's *Landscapes of Power* (Berkeley: University of California Press, 1991); Mike Davis' *City of Quartz* (London: Verso, 1990); J. Nicholas Entrikin's *Betweenness of Place*; and Peter Berger's and Thomas Luckerman's *The Social Construction of Reality* (Garden City, NY: Anchor Books, 1967).

With regard to Existentialism, I have found Marjorie Grene's *Introduction to Existentialism* (Chicago: University of Chicago Press, 1959) an easy and helpful path into a difficult set of ideas. I have also relied upon Edward Tiryakin's *Sociologism and Existentialism* (Englewood Cliffs, NJ: Prentice-Hall, 1962); William Barrett's "Introduction" to "Phenomenology and Existentialism," in William Barrett and Henry D. Aiken, eds., *Philosophy in the Twentieth Century: An Anthology*, volume 3 (New York: Random House, 1962), 125–170; Sartre's *The Emotions* and "Plea for Intellectuals"; Richard Rorty's "Philosophers, Novelists, and Intercultural Comparisons: Heidegger, Kundera, and Dickens," in *Culture and Modernity: East-West Philo-*

sophic Perspectives, ed. Eliot Deutsch (Honolulu: University of Hawaii Press, 1991), 3–20; and to go back to origins, many of the essays in Joseph J. Kockelmans' *Phenomenology: The Philosophy of Edmund Husserl and Its Interpretation* (Garden City, NY: Anchor Books, 1967) and Soren Kierkegaard's *Fear and Trembling* and *The Sickness Unto Death*, combined edition, both trans. Walter Lowrie (Princeton: Princeton University Press, 1941; Anchor Books, 1954).

13. Soren Kierkegaard, *Fear and Trembling*.

14. Edward Soja, *Postmodern Geographies*.

15. Anthropologist Clifford Geertz emphasizes this in *Local Knowledge: Further Essays in Interpretive Anthropology* (New York: Basic Books, 1983) when he says that at the level of cultural analysis, "it is dramatis personae, not actors, that in the proper sense really exist" (62). However in the Existential scene of the local and specific, the actor is more important than the role, and can (in fact, must) redefine the role within those larger cultural limits.

16. These defined ways of assisting progress, along with the definitions of progress themselves, are typically not local but are imported from larger institutions whose power extends into every community where their outposts are found. Geographer David Ley, in his chapter "Modernism, Post-modernism and the Struggle for Place," in *The Power of Place*, ed. James S. Duncan and John Agnew (London: Unwin & Hyman, 1989), 44–65, has engaged in a thoughtful discussion of the ways in which Modernism is anti-local and anti-vernacular, and how Modern administrators often deal with local knowledge as the target of re-education. Ley notes that "the ontology of a mass democracy overlooked the existence and the needs of individuals and minorities."

17. For an interesting and revealing list of Modern/Existential antonyms, see Gunnar Ollsson's "Social Science and Human Action or On Hitting Your Head Against the Ceiling of Language," in *Philosophy in Geography*, ed. S. Gale and G. Ollsson (Dordrecht, Holland: D. Reidel Publishing Co., 1979), 293.

18. There is an important linkage here with a current sociological theory known as Structuration, in which every individual is seen as both creator and surfer of larger political structures, neither free agent nor entirely powerless. As James Duncan says in "Individual Action and Political Power: A Structuration Perspective," in *The Future of Geography*, ed. R. J. Johnston (London: Methuen, 1985), 174–89:

> Structure is not merely context of background, it is a mode of action, a property of social interaction. . . . Structures then are processes, and as such are continually being modified as the action which constitutes them changes. (178)

19. William Barrett, "Introduction," 143.

20. John Ogbu, *Minority Education and Caste* (New York: Academic Press, 1978), 18.

21. Craig Haney and Philip Zimbardo use a more common metaphor in their article, "It's Tough to Tell a High School from a Prison," *Psychology Today*, June 1975, 26; their comparison has some architectural merit but misses school's largest cultural features: the programs of the school are taken for granted as a social good, and the inmates are seen as fortunate to be allowed access to those programs (at the same time that their attendance is in fact compulsory). The mission is more dependent on the hegemony of a supposedly shared and superior ideology, and is less outwardly forceful. It *seems* benign, and in that appearance lies its strength.

22. I came to this categorization independently of the work of psychologist James E. Marcia in his study "Development and Validation of Ego-Identity Status," *Journal of Personality and Social Psychology* 3, no. 5 (1966): 551–58. Marcia found:

> Four modes of reacting to the late adolescent identity crisis. . . . An *identity-achievement subject* has experienced a crisis period and is committed to an occupation and ideology. He has seriously considered several occupational choices and has made a decision on his own terms, even though his ultimate choice may be a variation of parental wishes. . . . The *identity-diffusion* subject may or may not have experienced a crisis period; his hallmark is a lack of commitment. He has neither decided upon an occupation nor is much concerned about it. . . . He is either uninterested in ideological matters or takes a smorgasbord approach in which one outlook seems as good to him as another and he is not averse to sampling from all. . . . The *moratorium* subject is in the crisis period with commitments rather vague; he is distinguished from the identity-diffusion subject by the appearance of an active struggle to make commitments. Issues often described as adolescent preoccupy him. . . . A *foreclosure* subject is distinguished by not having experienced a crisis, yet expressing commitment. It is difficult to tell where his parents' goals for him leave off and where his begin. He is becoming what others have prepared or intended him to become as a child. (551–552, emphasis mine.)

Obvious parallels exist between my divisions and Marcia's, but his emphasis on adolescence as psychological crisis and resolution leads him to different conclusions than a cultural approach that emphasizes identity as a component of a group membership and group response to power that likely lasts far beyond the chronological period of adolescence. A study more in that vein would be Paul E. Willis' examination of class and education in industrial England, Learning to Labour: How Working Class Kids Get Working Class Jobs (Aldershot, England: Gower Publishing Co., 1981).

23. Patricia Clemens and James Rust have found in their study "Factors in Adolescent Rebellious Feelings," *Adolescence* 14, no. 53 (Spring 1979): 159–73, that the degree of adolescent rebellion is significantly linked to the educational level of the parents; this corroborates much previous research showing that teenagers hold the same basic values as their parents. In other words, the vertical level of the graph is based on family class more intensely than on some individual traits. For an extended consideration of this same point in another country, see Paul Willis' *Learning to Labour* for a book-length treatment of English education and the children of the working class.

24. Douglas Biklen, in "The Politics of Institutions," 29–84, deals with the role of the believer in one specific institution: the state mental hospital. His discussion is pertinent in Curtisville High School as well:

> Inmates have been captured and incarcerated in much the same way that a country is conquered and colonized. Administrators and staff define the rewards (usually cigarettes, small amounts of change, points, extra privileges), as well as the acceptable ways of achieving those rewards. They are the colonizers. Inmates have only two possible responses. They can reject the system and languish in drab, locked day rooms and isolation cells, or they can play the game of seeking out the rewards, and thus perpetuate a system that is deigned to keep them satisfied but that manipulates them and uses them as pawns. (77)

25. This is borne out by research already cited by Clemens and Rust, "Adolescent Rebellious Feelings," and also by an overview of research provided by John C. Coleman, "The Nature of Adolescence," in *Youth Policy in the 1990s: The Way Forward*, ed. John C. Coleman and Chris Warren-Adamson (London: Routledge, 1992), 8–27. Both articles again show overwhelming overlap in parental and teenage beliefs and attitudes. The generation gap is not age based, but rather derived from tension over institutionally assigned roles and status.

Chapter 26

   1. Laura Hall, "Teenagers in Suburbia."

Chapter 27

   1. James Spradley, *You Owe Yourself a Drunk: An Ethnography of Urban Nomads* (Boston: Little, Brown & Company, 1970), 262.

   2. William Foote Whyte, *Street Corner Society* (Chicago: University of Chicago Press, 1943), 276.

   3. Herbert J. Gans, *The Urban Villagers: Group and Class in the Life of Italian-Americans* (New York: Free Press, 1962), 278.

   4. Frank Smith, "Let's Declare Education a Disaster and Get On With Our Lives," *Phi Delta Kappan*, April 1995, 585.

   5. Douglas Biklen, "Politics of Institutions," 83.

   6. Architectural historian Spiro Kostof, in *America by Design* (New York: Oxford University Press, 1987), wrote, "It is the designer's fate to be endowed with epiphanies of vision imprisoned within extremely narrow horizons of action."(5)

   7. Ivan Illich, *Deschooling Society* (New York: Harper & Row, 1970), 18.

   8. Mihaly Csikszentmihalyi, *Flow*, 141–42.

   9. Herb Childress, "Seventeen Reasons Why Football Is Better than High School," *Phi Delta Kappan*, April 1998, 616–619.

   10. Alfred North Whitehead, *The Aims of Education* (New York: Macmillan, 1929; reprint, New York: Mentor, 1964), 22.

   11. Gary Snyder, "Currents," *Utne Reader*, May/June 1995, 44.

   12. Clare Cooper Marcus and Wendy Sarkissian, *Housing as if People Mattered*, 20.

   13. E. F. Schumacher, *Small is Beautiful: Economics as if People Mattered* (New York: Harper & Row, 1973). Also note Michael Brill's argument, in "Transformation, Nostalgia, and Illusion in Public Life and Public Place," in *Public Places and Spaces*, ed. I. Altman and E. Zube (New York: Plenum, 1989), 7–29, that "government uses the same 'economic calculus' to make decisions as does business—cost justification, benefit-cost analysis, return-on-investment—all the paraphernalia of an organization that emphasizes economic more than social goals." (24)

14. Brill also notes these ideas when he says that small-scale public life "has eroded because economic principles of organization have, largely, replaced social ones." To expand:

> Each social relation is unique, personal, irreplaceable; each economic relation is a commodity: impersonal, impartially selected and interchangeable with all others, separating us from other people [and leading to] Alienation. And every time we go to the supermarket to save a dollar, rather than to our corner grocer, we reinforce economic principles at the expense of social ones. (Ibid., 13)

15. Philip K. Howard, *The Death of Common Sense* (New York: Random House, 1994), 11, 178, 186.

16. Evan McKenzie, *Privatopia* (New Haven: Yale University Press, 1994); quoted in Tim Vanderpool, "Secession of the Successful," *Utne Reader*, November/December 1995, 32.

17. As Lynn Richards notes in her study of a new Australian suburb, *Nobody's Home: Dreams and Realities in a New Suburb* (Melbourne: Oxford University Press, 1990):

> In people's accounts, country almost always means greenery and space. That makes it easy to attain—you just go far out. (30)

18. An excellent history and overview of Oregon's urban growth boundaries can be found online at the Oregon Department of Land Conservation and Development web site at www.lcd.state.or.us.

19. Jane Jacobs, *Great American Cities*, 31, 32.

20. Ray Oldenburg, *Great Good Place*, 66–85.

21. Jane Jacobs, *Great American Cities*, 74–88.

22. Paul Groth. These ideas are taken from a semester's worth of notes in Paul's Berkeley course, ED 169A, "Cultural Landscapes of the United States, 1690–1900." Another noted Berkeley architecture faculty member, Christopher Alexander, wrote about the same material in 1965 in his essay, "The City Is Not a Tree," *Architectural Forum*, April/May 1965, 106–36. Alexander notes:

> Play itself, the play that children practice, goes on somewhere different everyday. One day it may be indoors, another day in a friendly gas station, another day down by the river, another day in a derelict building, another day on a construction site

which has been abandoned for the weekend. Each of these play activities, and the objects it requires, forms a system. It is not true that these systems exist in isolation, cut off from the other systems in the city. The different systems overlap one another, and they overlap many other systems besides. The units, the physical places recognized as play places, must do the same. (123)

23. Christopher Alexander, Sara Ishikawa, Murray Silverstein, Max Jacobson, Ingrid Fiksdahl-King, and Slomo Angel, eds., *A Pattern Language* (New York: Oxford University Press, 1977), p. xli.

24. William H. Whyte, in *Small Urban Spaces,* notes the many ways that ease of use can be enhanced or hindered in city parks and plazas; the amount or quality of play or picnic equipment is not at the center of any of the discussion.

Bibliography

Alexander, Christopher. "The City Is Not a Tree." *Architectural Forum*, April/May 1965, 106–36.

Alexander, Christopher, Sara Ishikawa, Murray Silverstein, Max Jacobson, Ingrid Fiksdahl-King, and Shlomo Angel. *A Pattern Language*. New York: Oxford University Press, 1977.

Anderson, Kay. "The Idea of Chinatown: The Power of Place and Institutional Practice in the Making of a Racial Category." *Annals of the Association of American Geographers* 77, no. 4 (1987): 580–98.

Anderson, Perry. "Modernity and Revolution." *New Left Review* 144 (March/April 1984): 96–113.

Argyle, Michael. *The Psychology of Happiness*. London and New York: Methuen & Co., 1987.

Barnes, Trevor J. and James S. Duncan. "Introduction." In *Writing Worlds: Discourse, Text and Metaphor in the Representation of Landscape*, ed. Trevor J. Barnes and James S. Duncan, 1–17. London: Routledge, 1990.

Barrett, William. "Introduction" to "Phenomenology and Existentialism." In ed. William Barrett and Henry D. Aiken, 125–70. Vol. 3, *Philosophy in the Twentieth Century: An Anthology*. New York: Random House, 1962.

Bartholomae, David, and Anthony Petrosky. *Ways of Reading: An Anthology for Writers* (3rd ed.). Boston: Bedford, 1993.

Belk, Russell W. "Possessions and the Extended Self." *Journal of Consumer Research* 15 (September 1988): 139–68.

Berger, Peter, and Thomas Luckerman. *The Social Construction of Reality*. Garden City, NY: Anchor Books, 1967.

Berman, Marshall. *All That Is Solid Melts into Air: The Experience of Modernity*. New York: Simon & Schuster, 1982.

———. "The Signs in the Street: A Response to Perry Anderson." *New Left Review* 144 (March/April 1984): 114–123.

Biklen, Douglas. "The Politics of Institutions." In *An Alternative Textbook in Special Education: People, Schools and Other Institutions*, ed. B. Blatt, D. Biklen, and R. Bogdan, 29–84. Denver: Love Publishing, 1977.

Borowitz, Eugene B. *A Layman's Guide to Religious Existentialism*. Philadelphia: Westminster Press, 1965.

Brill, Michael. "Transformation, Nostalgia, and Illusion in Public Life and Public Place." In *Public Places and Spaces*, ed. I. Altman and E. Zube, 7–29. New York: Plenum, 1989.

California Department of Education, *Reporting the 1994 State Assessment*. Sacramento: California Department of Education, 1994.

Callois, Roger. *Man, Play and Games*. New York: Free Press of Glencoe, 1961.

Chawla, Louise. "Childhood Place Attachments." In *Place Attachment*, ed. I. Altman and S. Low, 63–86. New York: Plenum, 1992.

Childress, Herb. "Kinder Ethnographic Writing." *Qualitative Inquiry* 4, no. 2 (1998): 249–64.

———. "No Loitering: Some Ideas on Small-Town Teenage Hangouts." *Small Town* 24, no. 2 (September/October 1993): 20–24.

———. "Place, Image and Narrative: A New Approach to Place Attachment." in *Banking on Design? Proceedings of the 24th Annual Conference of the Environmental Design Research Association held in San Antonio, March 16–20, 1994*, ed. A. Seidel. Oklahoma City: Environmental Design Research Association, 1995, 55–62.

———. "Seventeen Reasons Why Football Is Better than High School." *Phi Delta Kappan*, April 1998: 616–619.

Clemens, Patricia W. and James O. Rust. "Factors in Adolescent Rebellious Feelings." *Adolescence* 14, no. 53 (Spring 1979): 159–73.

Coleman, John C. "The Nature of Adolescence." In *Youth Policy in the 1990s: The Way Forward*, ed. John C. Coleman and Chris Warren-Adamson, 8–27. London: Routledge, 1992.

Cooper Marcus, Clare and Wendy Sarkissian. *Housing as if People Mattered*. Berkeley: University of California Press, 1986.

Cosgrove, Denis. "Geography is Everywhere: Culture and Symbolism in Human Landscapes." In *Horizons in Human Geography*, ed. Derek Gregory and Rex Walford, 118–35. London: Macmillan, 1983.

Cranz, Galen. *The Politics of Park Design*. Cambridge, MA: MIT Press, 1989.

Csikszentmihalyi, Mihaly. *Flow: The Psychology of Optimal Experience*. New York: HarperPerennial, 1991.

Davis, Mike. *City of Quartz*. London: Verso, 1990.

Drummond, Derek. "The Impact of Mergers and Megalomania on the Urban Environment." Paper presented at the 26th Annual Conference of the Environmental Design Research Association, Boston, MA, March 1–5, 1994.

Duncan, James S. "Individual Action and Political Power: A Structuration Perspective." In *The Future of Geography*, ed. R. J. Johnston, 174–89. London: Methuen, 1985.

Entrikin, J. Nicholas. *The Betweenness of Place: Towards a Geography of Modernity*. Baltimore: Johns Hopkins University Press, 1991.

Foucault, Michel. "Of Other Spaces: Utopias and Heterotopias." *Photocopy, origin unknown,* 420–26.

French, Thomas. *South of Heaven: A Year in the Life of an American High School at the End of the Twentieth Century*. New York: Doubleday, 1993.

Gans, Herbert J. *The Urban Villagers: Group and Class in the Life of Italian-Americans*. New York: Free Press, 1962.

Gaster, Sanford. "Urban Children's Access To Their Neighborhoods: Changes Over Three Generations." *Environment and Behavior* 23, no. 1 (January 1991): 70–85.

Geertz, Clifford. *Local Knowledge: Further Essays in Interpretive Anthropology*. New York: Basic Books, 1983.

Glassie, Henry. "Studying Material Culture Today." In *Living in a Material World: Canadian and American Approaches to Material Culture*. Social and Economic Papers No. 19, ed. Gerald L. Poicus. St. Johns: Institute of Social and Economic Research, Memorial University of Newfoundland, 1991.

Goldberg, Theodore. "The Automobile: A Social Institution for Adolescents." *Environment and Behavior* 1, no. 2 (December 1969): 157–85.

Grene, Marjorie. *Introduction to Existentialism*. Chicago: University of Chicago Press, 1959.

Groth, Paul. "Vernacular Parks." In *Denatured Visions: Landscape and Culture in the Twentieth Century*, ed. Stuart Wrede and William Howard Adams, 135–37. New York: Museum of Modern Art, 1991.

Hall, Laura. "Teenagers in Suburbia: A Case Study in Rohnert Park, California." Masters thesis, University of California at Berkeley, 1992.

Haney, Craig and Philip G. Zimbardo. "It's Tough to Tell a High School from a Prison." *Psychology Today*, June 1975, 26.

Harvey, David. *The Condition of Postmodernity*. London: Blackwell, 1990.

Hendershott, Anne B. "Residential Mobility, Social Support and Adolescent Self-Concept." *Adolescence* 24, no. 93 (Spring 1989): 217–32.

Howard, Philip K. *The Death of Common Sense*. New York: Random House, 1994.

Illich, Ivan. *Deschooling Society*. New York: Harper & Row, 1970.

Jacobs, Jane. *The Death and Life of Great American Cities*. New York: Vintage, 1961.

Jacobs, Jerry. *The Mall: An Attempted Escape from Everyday Life*. Prospect Heights, IL: Wavelength Press, 1984.

Jameson, Frederic. "Postmodernism, or the Cultural Logic of Late Capitalism." *New Left Review* 146 (1984): 53–92.

Josselson, Ruthellen. "A Narrative Introduction." *The Narrative Study of Lives*, ed. Ruthellen Josselson and Amia Lieblich. Newbury Park, CA: Sage, 1993.

Kay, Jeanne. "Landscapes of Women and Men: Rethinking the Regional Historical Geography of the United States and Canada." *Journal of Historical Geography* 17, no. 4 (1991): 435–52.

Kierkegaard, Soren. *Fear and Trembling* and *The Sickness Unto Death*. Combined edition. Translated by Walter Lowrie. Princeton: Princeton University Press, 1941; Anchor Books, 1954.

King, Alison. "From Sage on the Stage to Guide on the Side." *College Teaching* 41, no.1 (Winter 1993): 30–35.

Klein, Hugh. "Adolescence, Youth and Young Adulthood: Rethinking Current Conceptualizations of Life Stage." *Youth and Society* 21, no. 4 (June 1990): 446–71.

Kockelmans, Joseph J. *Phenomenology: The Philosophy of Edmund Husserl and Its Interpretation*. Garden City, NY: Anchor Books, 1967.

Kostof, Spiro. *America by Design*. New York: Oxford University Press, 1987.

Kowinski, William Severini. *The Malling of America*. New York: William Morrow, 1985.

Kozol, Jonathan. *Savage Inequalities*. New York: Crown Publishers, 1991.

Langdon, Philip. "A Good Place to Live." *The Atlantic Monthly*, March 1988, 269–88.

Lawton, M. Powell and Lucille Nahemow. "Ecology and the Aging Process." In *Psychology of Adult Development and Aging*, ed. C. Eisdorfer and M. P. Lawton. Hyattsville, MD: American Psychological Association, 1973. Quoted in M. Powell Lawton. *Environment and Aging*. Albany, NY: Center for the Study of Aging, 1986.

Leavitt, Jacqueline and Mary Beth Welch. "Older Women and the Suburbs: A Literature Review." *Women's Studies Quarterly* 1 & 2 (1989): 35–47.

Lee, Roger. "The Future of the Region: Regional Geography as Education for Transformation." In *Geographical Futures*, ed. Roger Lee, 77–91. Sheffield: The Geographical Association, 1985.

Lee, Terence. "Urban Neighborhood as a Socio-Spatial Schema." *Human Relations* 21 (1968): 241–68.

Lennard, S. H. and J. L. Lennard. *Public Life in Urban Places*. Southampton: Gondolier Press, 1984. Quoted in Mark Francis. "Control as a Dimension of Public-Space Quality." In *Public Places and Spaces*, ed. I. Altman and E. Zube, 147–72. New York: Plenum, 1989.

Lewis, Pierce. "Axioms for Reading the Landscape: Some Guides to the American Scene." In *The Interpretation of Ordinary Landscapes*, ed. Donald Meinig. New York: Oxford University Press, 1979.

Ley, David. "Modernism, Post-modernism and the Struggle for Place." In *The Power of Place*, ed. James S. Duncan and John Agnew, 44–65. London: Unwin & Hyman, 1989.

Males, Mike. *The Scapegoat Generation: America's War on Adolescents*. Monroe, ME: Common Courage Press, 1996.

Marcia, James E. "Development and Validation of Ego-Identity Status." *Journal of Personality and Social Psychology* 3, no. 5 (1966): 551–58.

McCracken, Grant. "Culture and Consumption: A Theoretical Account of the Structure and Movement of the Cultural Meaning of Consumer Goods." *Journal of Consumer Research* 13 (June 1986): 71–84.

McDowell, Linda. "Women, Gender and the Organisation of Space." In *Horizons in Geography*, ed. Derek Gregory and Rex Walford, 136–52. Totowa, NJ: Barnes & Noble, 1989.

McKenzie, Evan. *Privatopia*. New Haven: Yale University Press, 1994; Quoted in Tim Vanderpool. "Secession of the Successful." *Utne Reader*, November/December 1995, 32–33.

Ogbu, John. *Minority Education and Caste*. New York: Academic Press, 1978.

Ogilvy, James. *Living Without a Goal*. New York: Bantam Doubleday Dell, 1995.

Oldenburg, Ray. *The Great Good Place*. New York: Paragon, 1989.

Ollsson, Gunnar. "Social Science and Human Action or On Hitting Your Head Against the Ceiling of Language." In *Philosophy in Geography*, ed. S. Gale and G. Ollsson, 287–307. Dordrecht, Holland: D. Reidel Publishing Co., 1979.

Parr, Albert Eide. "The Child in the City: Urbanity and the Urban Scene." *Landscape* 16, no. 3 (1967): 3–5.

Polanyi, Michael. *Knowing and Being: Essays of Michael Polanyi*, ed. Marjorie Grene (Chicago: University of Chicago Press, 1969).

Rapoport, Amos. *House Form and Culture*. Englewood Cliffs, NJ: Prentice Hall, 1969.

Relph, Edward. "Seeing, Thinking and Describing Landscapes." In *Environmental Perception and Behavior*, University of Chicago Department of Geography Research Paper No. 209, ed. Thomas F. Saarinen, David Seamon and James L. Sell, 209–23. Chicago: University of Chicago Press, 1984.

Richards, Lynn. *Nobody's Home: Dreams and Realities in a New Suburb*. Melbourne: Oxford University Press, 1990.

Richardson, Laurel. "Writing: A Method of Inquiry." *Handbook of Qualitative Research*, ed. Norman K. Denzin and Yvonna S. Lincoln. Thousand Oaks, CA: Sage, 1994.

Ritzdorf, Marsha. "Women and the City: Land Use and Zoning Issues." *Urban Resources* 3, no. 2 (Winter 1986): 23–27.

Robertson, James and Carolyn Robertson. *The Small Towns Book*. Garden City, NY: Anchor Books, 1978.

Rorty, Richard. "Philosophers, Novelists, and Intercultural Comparisons: Heidegger, Kundera, and Dickens." In *Culture and Modernity: East-West Philosophic Perspectives*, ed. Eliot Deutsch, 3–20. Honolulu: University of Hawaii Press, 1991.

Rosenzweig, Roy. "Middle-Class Parks and Working-Class Play: The Struggle Over Recreational Space in Worcester, Massachusetts, 1870–1910." *Radical History Review* 21 (1980): 31–46.

Russell, Bertrand. *The Conquest of Happiness*. New York: Liveright, 1930.

Sarbin, Theodore. "Place Identity as a Component of Self: An Addendum." *Journal of Environmental Psychology* 3 (1983): 337–42.

Sartre, Jean-Paul. "A Plea for Intellectuals." Chap. in *Between Existentialism and Marxism*. Translated by John Matthews, 228–85, New York: Pantheon, 1974.

———. *The Emotions: Outline of a Theory*. Translated by Bernard Frechtman. Secaucus, NJ: Citadel, 1976.

Schumacher, E. F. *Small is Beautiful: Economics as if People Mattered*. New York: Harper & Row, 1973.

Shumaker, Sally A. and Gerald J. Conti. "Understanding Mobility in America." In *Home Environments*, ed. I. Altman and C. Werner, 237–53. New York: Prager, 1985.

Silverstein, Murray and Max Jacobson. "Restructuring the Hidden Program: Toward an Architecture of Social Change." In *Programming the Built Environment*, ed. W. Preiser, 149–64. New York: Van Nostrand, 1985.

Smith, Frank. "Let's Declare Education a Disaster and Get On With Our Lives." *Phi Delta Kappan*, April 1995, 584–90.

Snyder, Gary. "Currents." *Utne Reader*, May/June 1995, 44.

Soja, Edward. *Postmodern Geographies*. London: Verso, 1989.

Spradley, James. *You Owe Yourself a Drunk: An Ethnography of Urban Nomads*. Boston: Little, Brown & Company, 1970.

Stoner, Jill. "The Party Wall as the Architecture of Sharing." In *New Households, New Housing*, ed. Karen Franck and Sherry Ahrentzen, 127–40. New York: Van Nostrand Rinehold, 1989.

Tafuri, Manfredo. *Architecture and Utopia*. Cambridge, MA: MIT Press, 1976.

Tiryakin, Edward. *Sociologism and Existentialism*. Englewood Cliffs, NJ: Prentice-Hall, 1962.

U.S. Department of Defense. *Exploring Careers: The ASVAB Workbook*. Washington D.C.: Government Printing Office, 1994.

White, John R. and Kevin D. Gray. *Shopping Centers and Other Retail Properties*. New York: John Wiley and Sons, 1996.

Whitehead, Alfred North. *The Aims of Education*. New York: Macmillan, 1929; reprint, New York: Mentor, 1964.

Whyte, William Foote. *Street Corner Society*. Chicago: University of Chicago Press, 1943.

Whyte, William H. *The Social Life of Small Urban Spaces*. Washington D.C.: Conservation Foundation, 1980.

Willis, Paul E. *Learning to Labour: How Working Class Kids Get Working Class Jobs*. Aldershot, England: Gower Publishing Co., 1981.

Woodward, John C. and Barbara D. Frank. "Rural Adolescent Loneliness and Coping Strategies." *Adolescence* 32, no. 91 (Fall 1988): 559–65.

Woodward, John C. and Violet Kalyan-Masih. "Loneliness, Coping Strategies and Cognitive Styles of the Gifted Rural Adolescent." *Adolescence* 35, no. 100 (Winter 1990): 977–88.

Zukin, Sharon. *Landscapes of Power*. Berkeley: University of California Press, 1991.

Index

passive audience, 96–7, 126, 143, 213, 221–4, 300–1
teenagers
and cars. *See* cars
control over places, 157, 160–1, 207–8, 260, 262
cynicism, 119, 149
developmental focus, 278, 283–4, 315, 332–3n
gender roles, 36
goals for planning, 18, 25, 181–2, 289–93, 299
immediacy, 258, 261
introspection, 173–5, 259, 261
in love, 26, 32–4, 92, 142, 176, 196
physical gratification, 27, 108, 109, 258, 261
physical immersion, 60, 94, 105, 106, 142, 258–9, 261, 319n, 329n
places of escape, 137–9, 259, 261
questions about adulthood, xvii, 173
respect for private property, 133, 181–2, 189, 220
and responsibility, 36–41, 55–61, 130–1, 133, 138–40, 186–8, 190–1, 260
separation from adults, 121–2, 163–5, 197, 219–21, 248–51, 300, 312
social contact, 79, 260
suspicion of, 113, 147–8, 150, 249, 270
transition to adulthood, 46–7, 59, 72–3, 189, 209, 220–1
and work, 35–41
territory, 108, 149, 245
theologians, 279–80, 282–3
Timber County, 7–8, 229, 231
Tiryakin, Edward, 330n

Union, 8, 260, 270–1, 289, 291
late night street use, 75–7, 80
street dimensions, 11–4, 80
urban planning, 178–80
density, 12-4, 18, 309
feminist issues, 325n
high school location, 220
See also cars, and city planning; cul-de-sac; teenagers, goals for planning

Welch, Mary Beth, 325n
White, John R., 318–9n
Whitehead, Alfred North, 302
Whyte, William Foote, 295
Whyte, William H., 320n, 336n
Willis, Paul E., 333n
Woodward, John C., 328–9n

youth center, 107, 237–51
program, 246–51, 328n
See also hangouts, vs. youth programs

Zimbardo, Philip, 332n
zoning, 179, 296, 298, 307, 308–9, 313
Zukin, Sharon, 330n